Naval Eyewitnesses

The Experience of War at Sea 1939–1945

James Goulty

Pen & Sword

MARITIME

AN IMPRINT OF PEN & SWORD BOOKS LTD
YORKSHIRE – PHILADELPHIA

First published in Great Britain in 2022 by
PEN & SWORD MARITIME
an imprint of Pen & Sword Books Ltd
Yorkshire – Philadelphia

ISBN 978-1-39900-071-0

A CIP catalogue record for this book is available from the British Library.

Typeset by Concept, Huddersfield, West Yorkshire, HD4 5JL.
Printed and bound in England by CPI Group (UK) Ltd, Croydon CR0 4YY.

Pen & Sword Books Ltd incorporates the Imprints of Aviation, Atlas, Family
History, Fiction, Maritime, Military, Discovery, Politics, History, Archaeology,
Select, Wharncliffe Local History, Wharncliffe True Crime, Military Classics,
Wharncliffe Transport, Leo Cooper, The Praetorian Press, Remember When,
White Owl, Seaforth Publishing and Frontline Books.

For a complete list of Pen & Sword titles please contact
PEN & SWORD BOOKS LTD
47 Church Street, Barnsley, South Yorkshire, S70 2AS, England
E-mail: enquiries@pen-and-sword.co.uk
Website: www.pen-and-sword.co.uk
or
PEN & SWORD BOOKS
1950 Lawrence Rd, Havertown, PA 19083, USA
E-mail: uspen-and-sword@casematepublishers.com
Website: www.penandswordbooks.com

Contents

Preface

In 1939 the Royal Navy was one of the instruments that helped bind the British Empire together. It ensured that the then large British merchant fleet could freely manoeuvre across the world's oceans without interference, and protected the country. Those joining the Royal Navy were frequently made aware that they were effectively inheriting this proud tradition, so that any actions on their part that marred this image would not be tolerated. Consequently, as an institution the Navy was inherently conservative, but this sense of tradition tended to appeal to recruits, even in wartime, when the service was compelled to absorb large numbers of reservists and Hostilities Only (HO) personnel. Total strength was over 863,000 by mid-1944, including 72,000 members of the Women's Royal Naval Service (WRNS).[1] Certainly many of the men and women whose personal testimonies are drawn upon in this volume appear to have developed a deep attachment to the Senior Service, and to have been immensely proud of their war service. Similarly, the reader will find plenty of instances where officers and ratings enjoyed aspects of their service, despite the privations of wartime.

However, it is important to remember that the war at sea was just as brutal and stressful for its participants as the war on land or in the air. British naval casualties for the entire war were 1,525 ships of all types lost, equating to over 2 million tons of shipping, and over 50,000 personnel killed, many of them from the Royal Naval Reserve (RNR) and Royal Naval Volunteer Reserve (RNVR).[2] An example of the cruel nature of naval warfare was the loss of SS *Aguila* in August 1941. A small, slow-moving transport ship, she was sailing to Gibraltar when her convoy was assaulted by a number of U-boats, one of which torpedoed her. According to her skipper, who survived, it was 'like potting a sitting bird'. Twelve Wren cypher officers, ten Chief Wren special operators and a naval nursing sister were killed instantaneously. This led Vera Laughton Mathews (Director WRNS, 1939–1946) to describe the sinking as: 'One of the worst blows our Service suffered.'[3]

Likewise, 28,000 seafarers aboard British merchant ships were killed during the war, and thousands more died from wounds suffered during their service or in 'collisions and coastal shipwrecks resulting from the conditions of war'. Equally significant was the loss of 4,800 merchant ships, equating to 21.2 million tons.[4] Had the supply of food, raw materials and armaments from overseas been wholly severed, then it is unlikely that Britain would have been able to continue the war. Merchantmen were equally important during the amphibious operations embarked upon by the Allies, as the war gradually shifted towards the offensive. During Operation Husky, the Allied invasion of Sicily in July 1943, for example, around 500,000 tons of shipping was assembled. This included fourteen British hospital ships and five hospital carriers, plus merchantmen operating as troopships and those bringing in supplies and equipment and evacuating POWs.[5] Merchant shipping also had an important role in the build-up of Allied forces in Britain as a precursor to the opening of the Second Front in June 1944.

A number of sources have been consulted for this volume, notably naval histories, reference books, personal memoirs and the oral testimony of veterans. Full details of these can be found in the accompanying bibliography and chapter notes. Readers might similarly appreciate the sequence of events in the Timeline, which provides additional background for the personal experiences narrated in the text. As many wartime recruits discovered, the Navy was a distinctive organisation with its own language or slang, plus it was as prone to employing acronyms as did the army and the RAF, all of which contributed towards its corporate identity. Accordingly, the accompanying Glossary might also help readers.

Personal experiences clearly varied depending in which branch of the Navy an individual served. Chapter 1 deals with life aboard capital ships, such as battleships, and contrasts this with service aboard smaller vessels, including destroyers and minesweepers. As one of the veterans who joined before the war testified, there was a distinct difference between 'big ship men' and 'little ship men', and this carried over into the war. Naval aviation and aircraft carriers form the subject of the second chapter. The Fleet Air Arm had its own strong identity, making it almost a navy within a navy. As the chapter explains, it was deeply unfortunate that tensions between the Royal Navy and the RAF over the development and control of naval aviation blighted the inter-war period, and was only being resolved on the eve of war. For the crews of aircraft carriers their experience was also a special one, with intense comradeship. Another strand of the chapter considers the various types of small carriers, including escort carriers and MAC ships, whose contribution has perhaps been overshadowed in the public consciousness by that of the larger carriers, such as the famous HMS *Ark Royal*.

Aspects of underwater warfare, notably submariners, and the experiences of Charioteers (human torpedoes) are highlighted in Chapter 3. To complement this, attention is also given to anti-submarine warfare (ASW), and its essential role in winning the Battle of the Atlantic. Similarly, Chapter 4 discusses convoy work, with reference to both naval experiences and those of merchant seamen. Convoys were one means of countering the U-boat threat in the Atlantic, and required a high degree of skill and seamanship, both from the escorts and the merchantmen constantly trying to maintain station. Equally, in the Arctic and Mediterranean, convoys formed major naval operations in their own right. Chapter 5 concentrates on amphibious warfare, the means by which the Allies planned to invade Nazi-occupied territory in Europe and the Mediterranean, and which also proved important in the Far East, especially for the Royal Marines. As the chapter demonstrates, Operation Neptune, the naval component of D-Day, was predominantly a Royal Navy affair. Yet when the war started, the Navy lacked the men, craft and doctrine necessary to prosecute large-scale amphibious operations. This capability had to be built up during the war, and was heavily reliant on RNVR officers and HO personnel, many of whom manned landing craft and did not necessarily have any natural aptitude as sailors.

Discipline and morale feature in Chapter 6. Definitions of morale tend to cite esprit de corps as being central to it. Certainly this was important to the Navy, but morale was a more nuanced and complex issue than basic definitions imply. The chapter shows how important a variety of issues were to enabling men and women to cope with war, ranging from leave arrangements to access to food, regular mail deliveries, and access to alcohol, tobacco and sex. Inextricably linked with morale was discipline. The chapter conveys the sort of working environment that most officers and ratings operated under, albeit there could be differences depending on the type of ship in which an individual served. Another part of the chapter illustrates that much wartime naval life revolved around various shore establishments, especially for the majority of Wrens. Likewise, the importance of discipline to the Merchant Navy is also outlined, particularly with regard to young men who enlisted with a view to embarking on a career at sea.

Finally, Chapter 7 covers demobilisation, and shows that by late 1945 the Navy had to adjust to the unfolding post-war situation and become smaller, although it remained important. Attention is also drawn to the reflections of both wartime naval personnel and merchant seamen from a variety of backgrounds.

Today, owing to the passage of time, the numbers of Second World War veterans still alive to tell their stories is sadly dwindling. Consequently, it is increasingly important that we try to understand what that generation endured, and never forget the sacrifices made in the name of freedom. Hopefully, this book not only proves interesting and informative, but also forms a fitting tribute to those men and women who served during the war at sea during 1939–1945. In this regard I am especially grateful to the Imperial War Museum and Second World War Experience Centre for allowing me to use their collections which contain a rich vein of material on personal experiences from the war years. A range of other sources have also been consulted, including the Official Histories and personal memoirs, and readers will find that these are fully attributed in the relevant chapter notes and bibliography.

James H.R. Goulty
November 2022

Acknowledgements

Thanks to Pen & Sword Ltd for publishing this book. In this regard, I am particularly grateful to Rupert Harding for all his editorial support, which has been invaluable. Likewise, I am indebted to the copy editor Sarah Cook for reviewing the manuscript and captions and seeing that the book made it through the production stages.

The research and writing had to be conducted during the pandemic, and I am especially grateful to the Second World War Experience Centre for allowing me to access material electronically and for letting me quote material and use some of the photographs from their archive as illustrations. In this respect Anne Wickes and Amanda Herbert-Davies from SWWEC provided assistance, for which I'am extremely grateful. Similarly, Anthony Richards (Head of Documents and Sound) at the Imperial War Museum kindly allowed me to quote from their extensive collection of oral histories. Equally I am indebted to wartime RN veteran George Henderson, who agreed to be interviewed back in 2015 and had several conversations with me about his wartime experiences. He kindly also furnished me photographs and allowed me to borrow the log he compiled as a young seaman while serving aboard LST-8 covering the period from about February 1943 to September 1944. My sister-in-law Jess Trevett very kindly allowed me to consult a copy of the Service Record for George Albert Trevett (her late grandfather), plus let me use photographs of him during his wartime service with the Fleet Air Arm. David Smith (ex-RN, 1964–1988) similarly provided documents and photographs relating to the wartime naval service of his father: JX678420 Coder George Smith. I am also very grateful to David Smith for providing many of the photographs that appear in the book.

For the loan of several naval books, and for his conversations especially about battleships, I thank my friend Alastair Fraser, former librarian at the University of Durham, and a fount of knowledge on naval/military/aviation matters. Equally, for their words of wisdom and advice I'd like to thank: Lieutenant Commander David Carter and Lieutenant Commander Duncan Young, and thanks to Keith Newman for putting me in touch with them. Likewise, I am very grateful to Commander David Hobbs for offering me his opinion on the planned layout of this book, and alerting me to areas that needed more attention. Last but not least, thanks to all my family, especially my Mum and Poppy the Boxer, for their continued love and support, and helping me to keep going. Similarly, I am deeply grateful for the love of my brothers and their families and for all their encouragement on my ventures with Pen & Sword Ltd. I hope that my young nieces and nephew will grow up in a world that is less troubled by war, and that they and their generation will in time come to appreciate more about the wartime era which their great-grandparents' generation had to endure when they were young.

Glossary

AA – Anti-Aircraft

AB – Able Seaman

ADDL – Aerodrome Dummy Deck Landings

AFO – Admiralty Fleet Orders

AG/WOP – Air Gunner/Wireless Operator

AIO – Action Information Organisation

AMC – Armed Merchant Cruiser

Andrew – The Royal Navy

Asdic – Allied Submarine Detection Investigation Committee (British name for Sonar)

ASW – Anti-Submarine Warfare

ATS – Auxiliary Territorial Service

BAMS – British American Minesweepers

BEF – British Expeditionary Force

BPF – British Pacific Fleet

Bunting Tosser – A Signalman

BYMS – British Yard Minesweepers

CAM Ship – Catapult Armed Merchantman

CAP – Combat Air Patrol

COPP – Combined Operations Pilotage Parties

CPO – Chief Petty Officer

CTC – Combined Training Centre

CVE – American-manufactured Escort Carrier

CW – Commissioned Warrant Candidate

DBS – Distressed British Seaman/Subject

DD – Duplex Drive (Amphibious Tank)

DEMS – Defensively Equipped Merchant Ship

DSC – Distinguished Service Cross

DSEA – Davis Submerged Escape Apparatus

xiv Naval Eyewitnesses

DSM – Distinguished Service Medal
DSO – Distinguished Service Order
EFS – Elementary Flying School
EFTS – Elementary Flying Training School
ENSA – Entertainments National Service Association
ERA – Engine Room Artificer
FAA – Fleet Air Arm
FEPOW – Far East Prisoner of War
Fo'c'sle – forward part under deck in a ship, often the accommodation area
FOO – Forward Observation Officer (Army)
Gulpers – a large draft of proffered rum
HACS – High Angle Control System
HFDF – High Frequency Direction Finding
HO – Hostilities Only
Jimmy the One – First Lieutenant
Kamikaze – (Divine Wind) Japanese Suicide Aircraft
Killicks – Leading Seaman
LBK – Landing Barge Kitchen
LCA – Landing Craft Assault
LCA (HR) – Landing Craft Assault (Hedgerow)
LCF – Landing Craft Flak
LCG (L) – Landing Craft Gun (Large)
LCI (L) – Landing Craft Infantry (Large)
LCI (S) – Landing Craft Infantry (Small)
LCM – Landing Craft Mechanised
LCP (L) – Landing Craft Personnel (Large)
LCS (M) – Landing Craft Support (Medium)
LCT – Landing Craft Tank
LCT (R) – Landing Craft Tank (Rocket)
LSD – Landing Ship Dock
LSF – Landing Ship Fighter Direction
LSH – Landing Ship Headquarters
LSI – Landing Ship Infantry
LST – Landing Ship Tank
MAC ships – Merchant Aircraft Carriers
MAD – Magnetic Airborne Detector

MBE – Member of the British Empire
MFDF – Medium Frequency Direction Finding
MGB – Motor Gun Boat
Midshipman – an officer of the lowest rank
ML – Motor Launch
MMS – Motor Minesweeper
MN – Merchant Navy
MNBDO – Mobile Naval Base Defence Organisation
MTB – Motor Torpedo Boat
MV – Motor Vessel
NAAFI – Navy Army Air Force Institutes
NAS – Naval Air Squadron
NCO – Non-Commissioned Officer
NGFS – Naval Gunfire Support
OOD – Officer of the Day
OOW – Officer of the Watch
ON – Operation Neptune Naval Orders
OS – Ordinary Seaman
PO – Petty Officer
POW – Prisoner of War
PT – Physical Training
RA – Royal Artillery
RAF – Royal Air Force
RASC – Royal Army Service Corps
RCAF – Royal Canadian Air Force
RDF – Range and Direction Finding (Radar)
RM – Royal Marines
RN – Royal Navy
RNAS – Royal Naval Air Service
RNAS – Royal Naval Air Station
RNPS – Royal Naval Patrol Service
RNR – Royal Naval Reserve
RNVR – Royal Naval Volunteer Reserve
RPO – Regulating Petty Officer
SOASC – Senior Officer Assault Ships and Craft
SO Escort – Senior Officer of an Escorting Force

TAG – Telegraphist/Air Gunner

Ticklers – a hand-rolled cigarette.

TS – Transmitting Station

Ukkers or **Uckers** – Ludo

USN – United States Navy

VC – Victoria Cross

VD – Venereal Disease

VLR – Very Long Range (aircraft)

WAAF – Women's Auxiliary Air Force

Winger or **Wings** – a junior rating befriended and taken under the wing of an older sailor

Writer – Clerk

WRNS – Women's Royal Naval Service (Wrens)

W/T – Wireless Telegraphy

YMCA – Young Men's Christian Association

Timeline

Key dates in the War at Sea, *c.*1939–1945

1921
Nov–Feb . . . . . . 1922 Washington Naval Treaty: naval arms race is halted.

1930
22 April . . . . London Naval Treaty restricts warships further.

1936
15 Jan . . . . Japan leaves London Naval Conference.
25 March . . . . . . Britain, USA and France sign London Naval Treaty

1938
Sept . . . . Munich Crisis: Czechoslovakian Sudetenland handed to Nazi Germany.

1939
Spring . . . . Rest of Czechoslovakia occupied.
Summer . . . . Britain and France offer guarantees to Poland.
August . . . . U-boats and 'Pocket Battleships' deploy to Atlantic.
23/24 Aug . . . . . Nazi-Soviet Non-Aggression Pact.
31 Aug . . . . Royal Navy mobilises.
1 Sept . . . . Germany assaults Poland.
3 Sept . . . . British Prime Minister Neville Chamberlain forms a War Cabinet with Winston Churchill as First Lord of the Admiralty. Britain and France declare war against Germany. SS *Athenia* is torpedoed off the NW coast of Ireland by U-30 (112 dead, including 28 Americans).
7 Sept . . . . Convoy system is initiated.
14 Sept . . . . U-39 sunk by Royal Navy destroyers.
17 Sept . . . . Aircraft carrier HMS *Courageous* sunk by U-29 whilst on anti-submarine patrol.
26 Sept . . . . German flying boat shot down by Skuas from the aircraft carrier HMS *Ark Royal*.
14 Oct . . . . Battleship HMS *Royal Oak* sunk by U-47 at Scapa Flow.
13 Dec . . . . Battle of the River Plate.
17 Dec . . . . *Graf Spee* scuttled outside Montevideo Harbour.

1940

Feb . . . . Britain breaks German Enigma Code.

16 Feb . . . . Destroyer HMS *Cossack* captures German supply ship *Altmark* in Norwegian waters.

31 March . . . . . . *Atlantis*, first of the German armed merchant raiders, sets sail.

7 April . . . . Allied forces prepare to invade Norway.

9 April . . . . Germans invade Denmark and Norway.

10–13 April . . . . Battles of Narvik.

14 April . . . . British landings in Norway.

10 May . . . . . . Germany invades France and the Low Countries.
British forces seize Iceland.

16 May . . . . . . Mediterranean closed by Admiralty to normal merchant traffic.

26 May–4 June . . Operation Dynamo: Allied withdrawal from Dunkirk.

4–9 June . . . . . . Allied evacuation from Norway.

8 June . . . . Aircraft carrier HMS *Glorious* and her escorts sunk by German battlecruisers *Gneisenau* and *Scharnhorst*.

10 June . . . . Italy declares war on Britain.
Commencement of Italian air attacks against Malta.

22 June . . . . France signs armistice with Germany.

3–5 July . . . . Force H based at Gibraltar neutralises French naval forces at Mers-el-Kebir and other ports.

1 Aug . . . . Hitler issues Directive 17 regarding the invasion of Britain.

2 Aug . . . . Operation Hurry: First ferry flight of aircraft to Malta from the ageing aircraft carrier HMS *Argus*.

16–19 Aug . . . . . British personnel evacuated from Berbera, British Somaliland by the Royal Navy, following Italian invasion.

16 Aug . . . . U-51 sunk by an air-dropped depth charge: the first time such a feat was achieved.

17 Aug . . . . Hitler announces blockade of Britain.

27 Aug . . . . RAF Coastal Command establishes a convoy protection base in Iceland.

Sept . . . . Britain strengthens the Home Fleet and expects a German invasion.

3 Sept . . . . British-USA lend-lease: fifty old 'four stacker' destroyers given to Britain in return for use of British naval bases.

20–22 Sept . . . . . Convoy HX-72 loses twelve ships to U-boats.

23–26 Sept . . . . . French fleet in Dakar attacked by Royal Navy and Free French.

12 Oct . . . . Hitler postpones Operation Sealion, the invasion of Britain.

17–19 Oct . . . . . Convoy SC-7 loses twenty-one out of thirty ships.

19–20 Oct . . . . . Convoy HX-79 loses twelve out of forty-nine ships. Escort numbers for convoys start to be increased.

5 Nov . . . . AMC *Jervis Bay* defends thirty-two merchantmen of Convoy HX-84 from *Admiral Scheer*. *Jervis Bay* and five other merchant ships lost.

11–12 Nov . . . . . Operation Judgement: twenty-one Swordfish aircraft from HMS *Illustrious* strike the Italian fleet at Taranto.

18–19 Nov . . . . . Air-to-Surface Vessel (ASV) radar on an RAF Sunderland flying boat achieves first operational detection.

1941

2 Jan . . . . Liberty Ship programme announced (mass-produced, standardised merchant ships manufactured in the USA).

12 Feb . . . . Heavy cruiser *Hipper* sinks seven ships out of nineteen in Convoy SLS-64.

March . . . . First Liberator (VLR) aircraft enters RAF service. Flown by RAF Coastal Command, these played a significant role in helping to counter U-boats during the Battle of the Atlantic.

28 March . . . . . . Battle of Matapan.

6 April . . . . Royal Navy lands 6,000 troops in Greece.

22 April–5 May . Royal Navy evacuates British forces from Greece.

18 May . . . . *Bismarck* and *Prinz Eugen* sail for the Atlantic.

20 May . . . . Germans attack Crete.

24 May . . . . HMS *Hood* sunk by *Bismarck*.

27 May . . . . *Bismarck* sunk.

27 May–1 June . . Royal Navy conducts Allied withdrawal from Crete and suffers heavy casualties.

June . . . . HMS *Audacity* commissioned, the first escort carrier to be converted from a merchantman.

12 June . . . . Royal Navy lands Anglo-Indian force at Assab in Italian East Africa.

1 Nov . . . . First action involving a CAM ship.

14 Nov . . . . U-81 sinks HMS *Ark Royal* near Gibraltar.

25 Nov . . . . Battleship HMS *Barham* sunk in the Mediterranean by U-331.

7 Dec . . . . Imperial Japan attacks American naval base at Pearl Harbor.

10 Dec . . . . Force Z: HMS *Prince of Wales* and HMS *Repulse* sunk by Japanese naval aircraft flying from Indochina (modern-day Vietnam).

19 Dec . . . . Italian frogmen use 'human torpedoes' to damage battleships HMS *Queen Elizabeth* and HMS *Valiant* in Alexandria.

21 Dec . . . . HMS *Audacity* sunk by U-751 west of Portugal.

1942

Feb . . . . Admiral Somerville's Eastern Fleet starts to arrive in the Indian Ocean.

11–13 Feb . . . . . Operation Cerberus ('Channel Dash'): *Scharnhorst, Gneisenau* and *Prinz Eugen* return to Germany from Brest via the English Channel.

27 Feb . . . . Battle of the Java Sea.

9 March . . . . Albacore aircraft from HMS *Victorious* mount an unsuccessful strike against *Tirpitz* in open seas.

28 March . . . . . . Operation Chariot: Raid on St Nazaire.

2–8 April . . . . . . Japanese carrier-based aircraft attack Ceylon (modern-day Sri Lanka).

4–9 April . . . . . . HMS *Hermes*, HMS *Dorsetshire*, HMS *Cornwall* and HMS *Hollyhock* all sunk by Japanese naval aircraft.

30 April . . . . HMS *Edinburgh* attacked by U-456 and destroyers in the Barents Sea; scuttled two days later.

5 May . . . . Operation Ironclad: British invade Vichy-held Madagascar.

10 July . . . . First two ships of PQ17 arrive in Archangel. Twenty-three ships were lost after convoy ordered to scatter.

4 Aug . . . . U-73 sinks aircraft carrier HMS *Eagle* during Operation Pedestal, one of the famous Malta convoys.

19 Aug . . . . Operation Jubilee: Allied raid on Dieppe; Britain and Canada suffer heavy casualties.

6 Nov . . . . Vichy French surrender Madagascar.

8–11 Nov . . . . . . Operation Torch: Allied invasion of French North Africa.

15 Nov . . . . HMS *Avenger* (CVE) blows up near Gibraltar after being hit by a torpedo from U-155.

1943

16 March . . . . . . Forty-two U-boats attack Convoys SC-122 and HX-229.

28 April–6 May . Convoy ON-52 fights off fifty-one U-boats, sinking seven of them. Simultaneously, U-551 sinks seven ships in 24 hours west of Freetown.

30 April . . . . New Navy command established to coordinate convoy protection, especially use of aircraft carrier convoy escorts, long-range bomber support, and actions of Support Groups.

22 May . . . . Admiral Donitz temporarily suspends U-boat action against convoys.

9–10 July . . . . . . Operation Husky: Allied invasion of Sicily commences.

27 Aug . . . . HMS *Egret* sunk in Bay of Biscay by a German Hs293, an air-launched, rocket-propelled, anti-ship missile.

9 Sept . . . . Operation Avalanche: Allied landings at Salerno, Italy.

11 Sept . . . . Italian fleet surrenders in Malta.
Italian warship *Roma* sunk by German air-launched Fritz X glide-bombs.

21 Sept . . . . X-Craft (midget submarines) target *Tirpitz* in a Norwegian fjord.

4 Oct . . . . Admiral Cunningham becomes First Sea Lord.

21 Oct . . . . Death of Sir Dudley Pound (First Sea Lord, 1939–1943).

2 Dec . . . . Luftwaffe raid on Bari: blows up ammunition ships and sinks seventeen others.

11 Dec . . . . Admiralty announces two-day Atlantic battle with U-boats.

26 Dec . . . . Battle of the North Cape: the Royal Navy sinks *Scharnhorst*.

1944

22 Jan . . . . Operation Shingle: Allied landings at Anzio commence.

7 Feb . . . . First U-boat with 'Schnorkel' arrives in the Atlantic.

20 Feb . . . . Admiralty announces three U-boats sunk and several damaged by air attack in the Straits of Gibraltar.

3 April . . . . Aircraft from HMS *Furious* and HMS *Victorious* and four CVEs attack *Tirpitz* in Norwegian fjord causing damage. Another attack in July was hindered by a dense smoke screen.

6 June . . . . Operation Neptune: the Naval component of D-Day, in which the Royal Navy played a major role.

15 Aug . . . . Operation Dragoon: Allied invasion of Southern France.

24 Aug . . . . Aircraft from HMS *Furious* and HMS *Indefatigable* and two CVEs attack *Tirpitz* again causing damage.

19–21 Oct . . . . . Royal Navy bombards Nicobar Islands.

12 Nov . . . . *Tirpitz* (to the Navy's chagrin) finally sunk by RAF Lancaster bombers using 12,000lb 'Tallboy' bombs.

22 Nov . . . . BPF established under Admiral Sir Bruce Fraser. East Indies Fleet established under Admiral Sir Arthur Power.

1945

3 Jan . . . . Operation Lightning: Amphibious assault against Akyab.

4 Jan . . . . Operation Lentil: twenty-eight attack aircraft and thirty-two escort fighters target oil refinery at Pangkalan Brandan.

12 Jan . . . . Operation Pungent: Myebon assault to sever Arakan coast road at Kantha.

21 Jan . . . . Operation Matador: Ramree Island assault.

22 Jan . . . . Kangaw assault by 3 Commando Brigade.

24 Jan . . . . Operation Meridian: Fleet Air Arm strike on oil refinery at Palembang.

29 Jan . . . . Operation Meridian II: another strike against Palembang.

16 Feb . . . . Ruywa assault to block Japanese troops' escape route from Arakan.

1 March . . . . . . Three Japanese aircraft shot down by 804 Naval Air Squadron: first kills by escort carrier aircraft in the Far East.

13 March . . . . . Operation Turret: Letpan assault to cut Prome-Taungap road. Royal Navy supports landings by 4th Indian Brigade and one battalion from 71st Brigade.

15 March . . . . . . BPF ordered to assist in Okinawa (Operation Iceberg) as Task Force 57.

17 March . . . . . . Operation Transport: destroyers, including HMS *Saumarez*, bombard targets in Sumatra.

26–27 March . . . BPF carrier-based aircraft attack airfields and installations on the Sakishima Gunto.

1 April . . . . Operation Iceberg: D-Day Okinawa. Aircraft carrier HMS *Indefatigable* hit by Kamikaze aircraft and destroyer HMS *Ulster* badly damaged by a bomb.

23–30 April . . . . After experiencing intensive action BPF at San Pedro Bay for rest, maintenance, etc.

29 April–6 May . Operation Dracula: Rangoon invasion.

30 April . . . . . . Death of Hitler announced; Admiral Donitz becomes new German head of state.

7 May . . . . SS *Sneland* and SS *Avondale* are the last ships to be sunk by a U-boat (U-2336), while U-320 becomes the last U-boat to be sunk by British aircraft.

8 May . . . . VE-Day

4–25 May . . . . . Operation Iceberg continues: strikes by Royal Navy carrier-based aircraft on the Sakishima Gunto. Over 4,800 sorties flown expending 1,000 tons of bombs, 950 rockets and half a million rounds of ammunition. Forty-two enemy aircraft shot down, plus several more destroyed on the ground. Additionally, 186 enemy ships and small craft either sunk or damaged. Twenty-six FAA aircraft lost to Japanese fighters or AA fire, plus many more as a result of Kamikaze attacks on aircraft carriers or through accidents. Forty-one FAA aircrew and forty-four Royal Navy personnel killed.

10 June . . . . . . Operation Oboe: Borneo and Brunei assaults.

17/18 July . . . . . BPF joins in strikes against Japanese Home Islands.

31 July–3 Aug . . . Cable-cutting missions by S Class submarines from 8th Flotilla and X-Craft.

6 Aug . . . . Atomic bomb on Hiroshima.

9 Aug . . . . Atomic bomb on Nagasaki.

15 Aug . . . . VJ-Day.

Chapter One

Big Ships and Smaller Vessels

Historically the fleet comprised three types of warship: battleships or ships of the line, cruisers, and flotilla vessels. While the cruisers 'exercised control of our sea communications – supported by the battle fleets to prevent interference with our cruisers by more powerful enemy units ... the flotilla vessels acted as scouts for the battle fleet', as well as performing numerous other roles such as acting as escorts and providing local defence.[1] The onset of the Second World War changed this dynamic owing to the increased effectiveness of naval aviation, and the related requirement for aircraft carriers. According to the official historian, it was 'undeniable ... that some naval thought had rated the influence [of air power] too low and that a body on the air side had rated it too high'.[2] Yet he went on to highlight how 'shore-based and carrier-borne aircraft have shown themselves to be capable of carrying out a part, and in some circumstances the whole, of the duties borne for so long by one or other class of fighting ship'.[3]

For officers and ratings there was also a distinct contrast between serving on a capital ship, such as a battleship or cruiser, and on smaller vessels, such as destroyers, corvettes, sloops or minesweepers. George Mack, a seaman gunner aboard the destroyer HMS *Intrepid* from July 1937 to August 1940, remarked on experiencing a two-tier navy:

First, there were the Big Ship men, serving on battleships, battlecruisers, and carriers. These men always dressed in the rig of the day and always seemed to be falling in and out of divisions to a continuous blare of bugle calls. Their ships always seemed to be in harbour, swinging round the buoy, and on the rare occasions they went to sea, the whole navy went with them [the battle fleet]. They were held in disdain, but sometimes envy, by the second group – the Little Ship men – who worked and played harder, moved faster and shared greater hardships together. Their mess decks were crowded as the proportion of ship devoted to crew space was much less.[4]

Other large ships, such as armed merchant cruisers (AMCs) or depot ships, also offered a different experience from smaller ships. HMS *Tyne* was a

10,850-ton destroyer depot ship with a maximum speed of around 17 knots that served the Home Fleet before transferring to the British Pacific Fleet in 1944. As Petty Officer Douglas Bruce, who was part of the ship's company, recalled, *Tyne* was part of the 'Train ... that part of the mobile back-up force which was necessary to keep a fleet at sea. We had most of the logistical equipment to support ships away from any base. All ships carried armaments of sorts although we were not regarded as "Fighting Ships of the Line"!'[5] Likewise, many of those men serving with the Merchant Navy gained experience of larger ships. Londoner Leslie Beavan spent some of his war on the enormous liner *Queen Elizabeth*, after she had been converted to a troopship: 'She had her own newspaper, football pools, own bulletins, ... three cinemas, her own Pig & Whistle, like a real pub. And in New York they treated us like heroes. We were bringing over 15,000 American troops every trip, and taking back 3,000 wounded.'[6]

Personnel with Coastal Forces, operating a variety of small craft including motor torpedo boats (MTBs), again inhabited a different world from that of sailors on capital and other large ships. It was not just a question of the relative size and function of the various vessels, although clearly that had an impact. Rather the contrast was keenly felt in terms of the conditions and discipline experienced as well. Large vessels, such as the battleships HMS *Nelson* and HMS *Rodney*, were, as one officer explained, remembering his time as a midshipman, 'awe inspiring' even though these two 'looked very strange ... because they had the funnel right aft and these three enormous 6-inch turrets up front'.[7] On the other hand, Leslie Stevenson, an HO clerk, served aboard HMS *Nelson* from December 1940 until March 1944, and found that with a complement of over 1,300 men, this made for a distinctive environment. He cautioned: 'Conditions on board were good compared to small ships, but here is the rub: discipline at all times was very strict. Rig of the day always adhered to and woe betide any "scruffy Jack-me-hearty".'[8]

Life on Battleships

According to an official wartime publication, the names of some battleships, such as *Resolution*, *Revenge* and *Renown*, suggested 'their might and majesty, and the thunderous challenge of their guns'.[9] However, as author/historian Dan Van Der Vat intimated, the 'fixation on the big gun' was a hang-over from the First World War and earlier periods. Consequently, during the lead-up to the Second World War, the Royal Navy (RN) was guilty of downplaying the threat to battleships (and other vessels) posed by aircraft and torpedoes and the U-boat, not least because overmuch faith was placed on Asdic (the British version of sonar) to detect U-boats and on depth charges to destroy them.[10] Despite this, the RN differed very little from other major navies of the era in 'still regarding the battleship as the key to the command of the sea'.[11]

The idea of a battleship in the 1940s was essentially similar to what it had been when HMS *Dreadnought* was launched in 1906, albeit numerous technological advancements had occurred over the years since then. Like *Dreadnought*, any battleship required 'an all big gun armament to fire effective salvoes at long range, a secondary armament against torpedo boat attack [to this should also be added protection against air and submarine attack], good armour protection and high speed'.[12] Designs were additionally influenced by the various agreements forged between the leading naval powers during the inter-war years. For example, under the Treaty of London of 1936, battleships were supposed to be limited to 35,000 tons and 14-inch guns, although it was accepted that if Japan ignored these limits, guns could be increased to 16-inch, and that the 35,000-ton displacement would be raised or even removed, if any power built outside these limits.[13] The King George V class battleships introduced into the RN in 1939–1940 had a displacement of 35,000 tons, a maximum speed of 29 knots and a complement of over 1,500 men. Armament consisted of ten 14-inch guns, sixteen 5.25-inch guns, and forty-eight 2-pounder anti-aircraft guns. Armour protection included a main belt of around 5–15 inches thick, with 1–6 inches on the deck, and 9–16 inches of armoured plate on the main turrets.[14] There were numerous teething problems, and concerns over their guns in particular. However, protection was an area 'where the King George V class shone in comparison with their foreign contemporaries', as 'their heavy, simple and effective armour ... particularly the horizontal armour, was heavier than in any foreign equivalent'.[15] By comparison, many older capital ships went through refits in an effort to update them in line with contemporary standards. The venerable HMS *Warspite*, launched in 1913, underwent a modernisation programme costing £2,362,000 shortly before the Second World War, but even then her protection was 'much below desirable standard'.[16]

Whatever the age of the battleship on which they served, sailors' opinions of these leviathans varied or even changed over time in light of experience. Sailors on some battleships in the Far East, for example, had to endure unbearable heat and shortages of water in ships ill-suited to the tropics. A stoker who worked in the bowels of the battlecruiser HMS *Renown* reckoned most such larger warships were 'hopelessly overmanned, and all of these people had to be found jobs. The amount of time you spent in futile occupations like cleaning brass and holystoning [scrubbing] the decks. Well, it wasn't totally futile I suppose – in a sense it gave you a pride in appearance.'

As he found, stokers were basically there to operate fuel valves on oil-fed boilers, and this really didn't require the same levels of manpower as had been the case when ships relied on coal-fired boilers.[17] As a young midshipman, Commander R.A.C. Owen was drafted to HMS *Warspite*, and recalled that, like most new personnel on big ships, he was hit by a barrage of odours:

> obviously, on the upper deck of a ship, in the open air, all you'd smell is the fresh air. Occasionally you'd get a waft, which comes from a ventilation opening, because these ships were totally enclosed so, in principle, every compartment in this ship, of which there were many hundreds, were all served by mechanical ventilation. They had ventilation louvres into which air was blown. Some of them had extract ventilation, which was discharged somewhere on the deck through these – they were usually called 'mushroom heads', which was a device so that air could get out but rain and spray can't get in. So, of course, depending on where you were on the ship, you could smell all sorts of things. I remember particularly, if you were anywhere in the aft part of the ship, you'd probably smell the smell of the quarterdeck, captain's quarters, smell of Brasso, Royal Marines' boot polish, things of that kind. If you went a bit further forward, perhaps you'd smell an oily smell, which in harbour perhaps was coming from a generator room or something like that. You'd hear a distant thudding of machinery and then you'd go a bit further and suddenly you'd smell bacon, or eggs, or onions, because of course, the ship's kitchens, or galleys, were totally enclosed, and they were served with very powerful extract ventilation to make conditions tolerable for catering staff, so you'd get a waft of lunch or breakfast or whatever it was being cooked. Sometimes it wasn't so agreeable, you might have a waft of a fuggy bathroom, of a lot of men crowded together who'd perhaps not had the opportunities for washing.[18]

New arrivals often also had to rub shoulders with old hands, and become accustomed to navy life. Cliff Smith was drafted as an HO writer to HMS *Nelson* in December 1940 and initially experienced 'a lot of aggro' until accepting that he must do as 'instructed, *The Navy Way*'. Aboard he also encountered an experienced three badge AB or able seaman who was extremely happy with his lot, and did not seek promotion because he claimed 'he could make more money with his dhobying [laundry] firm and barbering, not forgetting his "Crown and Anchor" board circuit (strictly illegal) more than any chief petty officer's earnings inboard'.[19] In contrast, Sir John Harvey-Jones could not abide life as a midshipman aboard HMS *Duke of York*, one of the King George V class battleships, while stationed in Scapa Flow in the Orkneys, and this was one of the motivations for him joining the Sub-marine Service:

> I loathed the ship. It was a vast ship. Nobody really knew anybody else. There was a great deal of class distinction between both the ranks of officers and the troops [ratings]. You virtually never met the troops, didn't know anything of them. Apart from going out and firing practice, guns and so on, we spent most of the rest of the time swinging around the buoy where the midshipmen did their usual things – running boats, doing schooling ... *Duke of York* was a horrible warning as to what life could be like aboard large capital ships and certainly played a part in my decision to join submarines.[20]

As Captain Charles Fetherston-Dilke remembered, a midshipman's duties were many and varied, as part of a well-established routine into schooling very young men into becoming RN officers and having an appreciation of all the different aspects of life at sea. He served in this capacity aboard HMS *Rodney*, a 33,900-ton battleship with the Home Fleet during 1939–1940, and one of his duties was running the ship's boat to pick-up liberty men (ratings on shore leave), which provided an early 'taste of responsibility', and he soon learnt to 'always head into the wind to calm down drunken sailors'. Other tasks included acting as Midshipman of the Watch, in which case he would be on the quarter deck or have to run errands for the Officer of the Watch (OOW), and ensure that the routine pipes were made over the ship's broadcast system. Another function of midshipmen entailed acting as the 'commander's doggie' or assistant, which could be 'quite fun depending on the nature of the com-mander'. At sea he was frequently on the bridge, and had to 'write up the deck log, keep look out, run errands for officers', and basically 'keep his eyes and ears open, as it was learning all the time'. Essentially, like all midshipmen, he had also to compile a journal: 'Not only did you have to record everything you did, and the ship did and the fleet did, but you had at the end of each week to write up a resume of the international situation.'[21]

Like most members of the crew, midshipmen had a specific action station, which was part of their learning process as well. Aboard HMS *Warspite*, Commander Owen was Assistant Officer of the Quarters:

> An Officer of the Quarts of a gun was the officer who was entirely responsible for the performance of the gun's crew: that they were properly drilled, that they knew how to load the gun, they knew how to follow the pointers from the central control to get the gun pointing in the right direction, they knew how to provide the ammunition and handle

the ammunition ... and the quarters I was detailed for was the 4-inch anti-aircraft battery [starboard side]. There were two twin 4-inch guns, which were hand-worked; they had a crew of about eighteen men, nine for each gun. They were hand-loaded; the men had to pick up the shells from a hoist and load them into the breach by hand, and then, eventually, the gun would be made ready and then it would be fired by the central control, so I was put to be the assistant to the Officer of Quarters. He was an old style warrant officer ... He wore one thick stripe. He was what they called a branch officer ... a man in his forties. He'd been in the navy all his life, so I had much to learn from him.[22]

An ordinary seaman, on going to war aboard HMS *Howe*, another of the King George V class battleships, considered that he and his comrades had 'total confidence in her', despite the Germans possessing *Bismarck* and *Tirpitz*.[23] Similarly, as a youthful rating Arthur Rose joined the famous battlecruiser HMS *Hood* in the late 1930s, and explained how she was widely regarded as:

the most efficient ship in the Navy, she'd won all the sports, ack-ack [anti-aircraft], gunnery competitions, the manoeuvres competition. She was reckoned to be it. I steamed across Portsmouth harbour in a picket boat, and there was this magnificent ship ... the most beautiful thing you'd ever seen ... I went up the gangway carrying my kit bag, and my hammock ... I looked up and I couldn't believe it – she was enormous.[24]

However, when war was declared in September 1939 he was transferred to HMS *Nelson*, and experienced a 'terrible feeling of doom'; he wondered how his ship would fare in the upcoming struggle, especially as he had 'heard all the arguments about ships being obliterated by air power'. As he put it, 'there were some who said: "Oh, ships won't stand a chance"' and others who put faith in their equipment, such as 'our modern pom-poms [2-pounder anti-aircraft guns]'. Consequently, 'there was always that [uneasy] feeling in the back of your mind'.[25]

Arthur Rose and others were proved right to doubt how battleships would stand up to aerial attack. Experience during the war amply demonstrated that they and other types of vessel were vulnerable to enemy aircraft flown by well-trained air crew highly practised in anti-shipping techniques. A related challenge was documented by distinguished historian Correlli Barnett, in that the RN went to war with defective anti-aircraft arrangements, as the High Angle Control System (HACS) adopted in the late 1930s for the fire control of anti-aircraft guns aboard its ships was crude by contemporary standards. Rather than track the movements of enemy aircraft accurately, and pass that information on in the form of control data, as happened with a tachymetric system, HACS effectively guessed the movements of an enemy aircraft. Consequently, RN ships were 'firing at enemy aircraft with the hopeful wildness of aim of a tyro shot trying to bring down fast flying grouse', something that resulted in huge expenditure of ammunition 'without commensurate protection of the fleet or destruction of enemy aircraft'.[26]

This flaw played a part in many tragedies, including that which notably befell Force Z in December 1941. It comprised the capital ship HMS *Prince of Wales* and the battlecruiser HMS *Repulse*, and both were attacked and sunk by Japanese aircraft (34 high-level and 51 torpedo-bombers) off Malaya, although their escorting destroyers did manage to rescue 2,081 officers and men of the 2,921 on board the two ships. Petty Officer Frederick Hendy joined HMS *Prince of Wales* not long after she was commissioned, and was going to be second captain of the fo'c's'le but this role went to a veteran CPO. Instead he spent several months as coxswain of her motor-launch. He was one of those lucky enough to survive, and vividly remembered the moments when the Japanese attacked:

we were told to leave the turrets [his action station] to come on deck because they wouldn't use the big turrets for firing at the aircraft, and all the crew of 'A' and 'B' Turret were just standing around there on the fo'c's'le waiting for orders what to do ... An officer came along and ordered us to supply ammunition to the pom-pom gun. We heard every explosion, didn't realise what it was, it must have been a torpedo that went through the bows, the nearest point to us [HMS *Prince of Wales* was eventually hit by at least four torpedoes]. And we saw the pom-poms blazing away, and the 5.25s blazing away. We couldn't help them because they were self-contained. And the only thing we could do was supply ammunition and after the magazine was emptied we had nothing to do ... we didn't appreciate at the time what damage a torpedo could do.[27]

Subsequently, the ship suffered at least one more hit from a high-level bomber and was listing heavily. The destroyer HMS *Express* took off the wounded and those no longer required aboard to work the ship, before she eventually capsized. Afterwards PO Hendy was among those sailors who spent a nerve-wracking period desperately swimming together in the water, fearful of sharks, before the escorting destroyers eased their way through the slimy oil-coated sea to pick up survivors.

Large warships were also vulnerable to submarine attack. Famously, Günther Prien, the commander of U-47, skilfully succeeded in penetrating the naval base at Scapa Flow in what proved to be a carefully planned raid, and sank the ageing battleship HMS *Royal Oak* on the night of 13/14 October 1939, with the loss of over 800 lives.[28] As a teenager Stanley Cole had unsuccessfully attempted to join the RN several times, and eventually enlisted in the late 1930s aged 17 years and 4 months, once he no longer required parental permission. On completion of training as an ordinary seaman, *Royal Oak* was his first sea-going ship, and even when she was torpedoed he found it difficult to believe that she would sink:

> The first explosion woke all on the mess deck and we swung out of our hammocks to see what it was all about. The story was that it was either a CO bottle explosion, or something in the paint store – right forward – and some even said the anchor cable had snapped ... Believing the situation to be not serious many turned in again. [Shortly after] I heard two very loud explosions, separated by only seconds, and the ship listed whilst the secondary lighting failed.
>
> My abandon-ship station was to report to the port side whaler ... I was one of five men on the oars, in the charge of a coxswain, usually a leading seaman. The boat deck was several decks up and, still not thinking the ship would sink, although listing considerably, I struggled to get through the ladders ... [he managed to get there in the darkness] I soon established that I was the only one there, and wondered if I had heard no orders or instruction over the ship's tannoy. The whaler weighed about a ton and a half ... There was nothing I could do, and from the cries and splashes coming from the sea and the few heads I could just make out bobbing around in the water, I decided it was time to go ... I pulled myself through the lower gap of the guard-rail and launched myself in a half dive, half slithering movement down the ship's side. [He then trapped his foot in the guttering of the anti-torpedo blister, before eventually falling into the water.] I could smell the oil-fuel, but could not avoid getting some in the mouth, nose and ears, but keeping my eyes closed until I surfaced ... It was like trying to swim through liquid tar, and I was convinced I wasn't going to make it. The water was bitterly cold, and from all around me in the darkness I could hear cries for help from injured, burned, despairing bodies. [Eventually he desperately clung to items of wreckage for what felt like an eternity with other survivors.] ... My last view of *Royal Oak* was of her keel, silhouetted against the dark skyline. She appeared to have turned right over. Then, just as I had all but given up the struggle, along came a ship's whaler, and I felt myself hauled over the boat's side with two or three other lads dumped on top of me in a cold, sodden, oily heap.[29]

Another form of attack, notably pioneered by the Italians, entailed what were termed human torpedoes, underwater craft upon which two frogmen or divers sat astride and manoeuvred under enemy ships where they would place an explosive charge. On the night of 18 December 1941 the Italians launched a strike against Alexandria harbour. 'The submarine *Scire* surfaced in darkness and launched three human torpedoes which slipped quietly inside the harbour,' two of which approached the battleships HMS *Queen Elizabeth* and HMS *Valiant* and placed charges that subsequently went off successfully. 'In order to confound Italian spies, both battleships, which had been severely damaged underneath but looked all right above the water, carried on as if nothing had happened. Receptions were held, bands played, and steam was kept up, so it looked as if both ships were ready to sail at any moment,' when in fact this was far from the case.[30] Commander Tom Dowling, then a more junior officer on HMS *Queen Elizabeth*, recounted that 'there was oil everywhere in the harbour', plus 'the bows [were] right down and we had two submarines alongside. That was a give-away ... Anyway ... we used to move our guns to a different position each day, the main guns, and we used to fire at aircraft occasionally which we weren't supposed to do because it put off the army with their spotting but we did it just to show that we could and that was 4.5s but I think they must have known full well that we were out of action but they didn't know to what extent.'[31]

All of the above might suggest that by the Second World War era battleships were of limited value. In fact this was not entirely true. However, as distinguished naval architect D.K. Brown expounded, they were replaced in importance by the fleet carriers, which were even more vulnerable but with their aircraft packed a far greater punch. Consequently, it was not the battleships' vulnerability that led to their demise but rather because they were 'far less capable than the carrier of inflicting damage on the enemy'.[32]

Even so, battleships took part in many of the major naval actions of the war, plus they performed more routine functions, such as escorting convoys. At the Battle of Matapan (28/29 March 1941), HMS *Warspite*, HMS *Valiant* and HMS *Barham* from the Mediterranean Fleet helped to win a significant night victory over the Italians.[33] These ships had been extensively modernised since the First World War and although they were comparatively slow, they were still highly capable warships. An official wartime booklet gives a flavour of the action, which was brief and vicious, and succeeded in marginalising the Italian Fleet, as it remained in harbour until the following August.

> At 10.25pm two large cruisers and a smaller one were unexpectedly sighted by the *Warspite* steaming on an opposite course, about 2 miles

away. Although they were clearly visible through night-glasses, it was apparent, though incredible, that they were serenely unconscious of the presence of the Battle Fleet. They had presumably turned back in search of the *Pola* [an Italian heavy cruiser, damaged earlier]. The *Greyhound*, the screening destroyer nearest to them, switched her searchlight on to the second large cruiser in the line; the merciless glare revealed that her guns were trained fore and aft; every detail of her wood construction stood out vividly in the illumination of the *Greyhound*'s questioning stare. Almost simultaneously the *Warspite* and *Valiant*'s 15-inch guns opened fire. The enemy ship was seen to be the *Fiume* [another Italian Zara class heavy cruiser]. Both broadsides hit. She appeared to change into a sheet of flame that was only extinguished half an hour later when she sank.

The leading ship in the enemy line, as seen from the *Barham*, was silhouetted against the beam of the *Greyhound*'s searchlight. Captain G. Cooke opened fire and hit her with the first broadside. She turned away to starboard, a dull glow of internal fires partly obscured by smoke ... [Meanwhile] the *Valiant* shifted [her] fire to the second ship in the line ... This was the *Zara*. Fire from all three battleships was concentrated on her at 3,000 yards range ... in the terrible illumination of star shell, blazing ships and gun flashes, a number of enemy destroyers appeared astern of *Fiume* and fired torpedoes at the battleships before making off to the westward. The leading destroyers were hit by 6-inch shells from *Warspite* as the Battle Fleet swung to starboard to avoid the torpedoes. The Commander-in-Chief [Admiral Andrew Cunningham, later Viscount Cunningham of Hyndhope], with the battleships and the *Formidable* [aircraft carrier], then withdrew to the north-eastward ...[34]

Likewise, battleships were involved in the epic hunting of the *Bismarck* and were in at the kill when she was eventually sunk, after being crippled by FAA torpedo attacks. As Lieutenant Commander Peter Kemp, a wartime naval intelligence officer, explained, on the morning of 27 May 1941 HMS *Rodney* opened fire on the stricken German ship, rapidly followed by HMS *King George V*:

Another two minutes and the Bismarck replied to the fire. Her first few salvoes were accurate, the fourth straddling the Rodney without actually hitting her. The third salvo from Rodney hit the Bismarck, and after the German ship's gunnery deteriorated rapidly. A salvo from the Rodney knocked out both of her forward turrets, and one by one the others ceased firing as they were hit by shells from the two British battleships.

Her mast was blown away by a hit, and by 1000 hours all her main armament guns were silenced. For a few more minutes her secondary guns kept up a spasmodic fire; ten minutes later they, too, were silent.[35]

Significantly, battleships provided NGFS (Naval Gunfire Support), something that was particularly useful during amphibious landings, as a battleship could stand offshore and bombard enemy positions from a range of up to 25 miles. However, this was using 'low-trajectory guns, so it was difficult for them to fire over ships and men', plus 'a 15-inch shell could not be aimed within 1000 yards of friendly forces, because of possible inaccuracies and the spread of the blast'[36] On D-Day HMS *Warspite* was part of the Eastern Task Force, and played a part in the naval bombardment, firstly supporting the British landings in the Sword Beach sector, and later helping the hard-pressed American troops at Omaha Beach. One of her crew, Ordinary Seaman Ronald Martin, recorded how a situation arose whereby *Warspite* had to fire on German tanks hidden in woodland that had been spotted by an aircraft when someone carelessly lit a cigarette. 'We pinpointed the target and gave an order unique in naval gunnery history of "15-inch, fifty rounds, rapid fire. Commence."' This was difficult, owing to 'the time it took to load the one-ton shells, follow their pointers and so on.' However, 'the first broadside fell slap in the middle of the wood then succeeding ones started, because of human error and the time lag, the shells were chasing the Germans as they started to run away.' Later reports from aircraft were received stating that the shoot had been extremely successful. Martin claimed: 'We could knock a chap off a bicycle at 20 miles.'[37]

Serving on Cruisers

As indicated above, naval matters during the inter-war period were dominated by a series of treaties that set international limitations on the numbers of warships navies could possess and their size and armament. Consequently, most new warships during that period were built up to these limits, and with cruisers this entailed a demand for vessels displacing 10,000 tons, armed with 8-inch guns. In the RN these were termed heavy cruisers, and most were modified during the war to accommodate better crew protection, increased anti-aircraft armament and heavier directors, modifications that led to a reduction in the main armament on many ships to compensate for the increased weight. The introduction of radar had an even more dramatic impact. 'First came the aerials, often requiring tripod or lattice masts. Then there were the radar offices demanding more men and at the same time encroaching on accommodation space. The interpretation of the radar picture led to fairly elaborate action information organisation (AIO) spaces again increasing complement and reducing mess deck space.'[38]

Traditionally, cruisers had several roles: to protect maritime trade by hunting down enemy raiders, to support the main battle fleet by acting as scouts and to protect it from attack, especially by smaller torpedo-armed warships. However, by the Second World War aircraft and U-boats were a serious threat to heavy cruisers, and these powerful warships increasingly became deployed on tasks for which they were not designed, such as convoy protection/escort, NGFS, and naval blockading. Ironically, the very characteristics 'that made them perfect for their original functions – long range and endurance, seaworthiness, the ability to function as a squadron of flagships, and a formidable degree of firepower' ensured that they continued to play a significant role in the Second World War as 'the unglamorous workhorses of the fleet – until the very end of hostilities'.[39]

In January 1940 HMS *Hawkins*, for example, was sent to patrol the South Atlantic in search of raiders, a role she continued until the following September when she put into Durban for a refit. Leading Seaman Ronnie Turner from Liverpool complained in his diary that 'it's so damn monotonous this commission. We've done over 30,000 miles since we sailed, which is the length of six times a cruiser does in a two and a half years commission. And when we get into port it costs a month's pay nearly to enjoy oneself, everything is fairly dear. We are right in the traffic lanes meeting plenty of ships.'[40] Subsequently, HMS *Hawkins* operated in the Indian Ocean for lengthy periods, mainly escorting convoys and hunting enemy raiders, interspersed with returning to Britain for a refit and briefly being attached to the Home Fleet. In March 1944 she was recalled to Britain again and took part in the Normandy landings, providing fire support to American troops off Utah Beach, before undergoing another refit, this time on the Clyde, where she was when hostilities ended.

Another heavy cruiser, the Kent class HMS *Cornwall*, was part of 5th Cruiser Squadron on the China station when war commenced, and spent most of her service in Eastern waters before being sunk by Japanese aircraft off the Maldive Islands in April 1942. In her time she helped search for the *Graf Spee*, participated in operations against Vichy French forces in West Africa, and in the Indian Ocean destroyed the German raider *Pinguin* in May 1941. Petty Officer Robert Crick aboard *Cornwall* remembered this notable event, and the difficulties that were encountered in chasing down this wily foe:

We had a report that this raider had sunk a ship in our vicinity, and so we sent our plane up and found it but it claimed to be a Norwegian tanker

[*Tamerlane*]. We chased it and it still claimed to be a Norwegian tanker. It wouldn't stop, and we threatened to cross her bows but it still didn't stop. We chased after it, and perhaps rather foolishly got within 5 miles of her or less. And she dropped her flaps and opened fire on us and hit us before we could do anything. She could have put us out of action actually because one shell went through under the bridge into the flour store, went through the ring main which cut the power off. Also it damaged the engine room telegraph, so there was no communication between the bridge and engine room. And because we'd lost power, the guns couldn't train, the director wouldn't work, and we had to go back on hand control or quarters control they called it. As soon as they did that, the captain got his guns to bear on them, and we hit them, and she went up like a house on fire ... because she was carrying mines, a huge column of smoke.[41]

As a result of the London Naval Conference of 1930, and in order to save money, governments made new treaty arrangements concerning warships. Accordingly, Britain changed from building heavy cruisers to developing smaller, cheaper ones armed with 6-inch guns, dubbed light cruisers. As war approached, a new series of light cruisers was introduced, and with the wartime additions of fire control systems and radar, these proved to be extremely capable, versatile warships, and served in all the major theatres: the Arctic, Atlantic, Mediterranean, Indian and Pacific Oceans.[42]

Eric Hills was drafted to HMS *Manchester* as a young stoker in March 1941. She belonged to one of three groups of Southampton class cruisers built during the late 1930s, and saw action in the Mediterranean, where she was eventually lost. At the time Eric joined her, she was moored at Hebburn, and as he stood on the bank of the River Tyne and gazed up at her, he was in awe of the twelve 6-inch guns, plus an array of anti-aircraft weaponry. She was 'the biggest ship I'd ever seen' and 'looked terrific with all those guns on it'.[43]

According to one former officer who had served on HMS *Hood* and the light cruiser HMS *Fiji*, there was a difference in the atmosphere experienced aboard a cruiser compared with a battleship. 'Life in a cruiser was much more informal. There were only, I think, six midshipmen in the wardroom, instead of about twenty-five or more in a battleship or battlecruiser, so we all knew each other pretty well.'[44] The Leander class cruiser HMS *Ajax* that famously took part in the Battle of the River Plate, when *Graf Spee* was scuttled, was 'manned entirely by long service regular engagement officers and ratings; it would not experience any dilution of the ship's company by reservist and hostility only officers and ratings' until several months after the start of the war and after this famous naval victory.[45] Likewise, other cruisers gradually had more mixed crews. HMS *Edinburgh*, one of the third group of Southampton class cruisers, was a comparatively large ship with a complement of 850 men. As a young regular rating, specialising in radar, Commander William Grenfell was drafted to her in 1940, just after she had undergone a major refit in North Shields:

> And she had been fitted out with the most highly developed long range warning RDF. That was my first ship. She was a 6-inch cruiser. I believe the largest cruiser type we had in the navy, there were only two of them built. One was the *Edinburgh* the other was the *Belfast* [now preserved on the River Thames] ... The first thing that struck me was the discipline, and I liked it. I like discipline, I realise it is necessary, and I discovered that I had in fact by sheer accident, in a way I've the war to thank for this, that I had landed in the way of life that I really enjoyed most of all. A disciplined, clean way of life, with every opportunity for learning, we had instructor officers on board and even the higher ranked ratings, they all had an interest in the junior people, the PO and CPOs, you had every opportunity of learning as much as you wanted to. And I liked it.[46]

A year later Colin Kitching joined HMS *Edinburgh* as one of the first draft of HO ratings to serve aboard her:

> About two dozen of us [joined] and we were the objects of enormous curiosity amongst these time-served professional sailors, and it's interesting because to think I had just come down from Oxford, and expect I thought myself as quite a chap you know, but suddenly I found my real level there and I was a total nobody. I knew practically nothing. I mean the basic training was just to get you disciplined and march properly and not look scruffy and so on, and you were taught a bit about knots and all that, but there was so much to learn and I was, well, the six months I spent on board *Edinburgh* were most remarkable, and yes, the remarkable experience of my life, and there is absolutely no doubt. The professionalism of the whole thing was unbelievable and I was so impressed with, and I was so taken with the way I was treated, and the rest of the draft. They regarded us as strange beings who knew absolutely nothing, which was true, and we had the mickey taken out of us, but they weren't cruel and they weren't horrible. They just regarded us as slightly half-witted young men who had to be taken in hand and make sure that we didn't let the side down by doing something stupid when it mattered.[47]

The one-time anarchist, connoisseur of surrealist art, jazz/blues singer, writer and critic George Melly spent part of his naval service as a rating aboard the cruiser HMS *Dido*, and captured the crew dynamic and the outlook of the different branches of personnel on such warships:

> everybody in the ship's company held a different if partial view. For the stokers and engineers it was the engine-rooms and propellers which signified; for the gunnery officers and ratings, the neatly stacked shells and turrets; for electricians, the ship was a nervous system of cables and power points; for the writers, a list of names, each entitled to different rates of pay; for the cooks, the galleys and store rooms; for the Master at Arms, rebellious stirrings and acts prejudicial to naval discipline; for the Captain and senior officers a view of the whole, detailed or vague according to their competence ... there were tensions, tolerance, fierce vendettas fought out with the aid of King's Regulations or the sympathetic bending of the rules ... [It was] a steel village. At first enormous and confusing, it soon became cosy, not as intimidating as a battleship, not as cramped as a destroyer.[48]

Even so, not all ratings found the conditions favourable aboard cruisers. One who went to war with HMS *Southampton* commented that: 'Food was awful, with very little of it fresh due to sea time. And each man's living space became even smaller due to increased wartime complements and the need to pack in stores and new types of equipment.'[49] John Keller spent several years on HMS *Glasgow* as an artificer, and found that in cramped wartime conditions using a hammock was tedious owing to the amount of preparation needed to set one up, and then roll it up in the morning. Also the ship's company had to be prepared to always carry gas masks and anti-flash gear [protective clothing] wherever they went, and the need to routinely be at action stations half an hour before dawn was draining. This was because 'visibility suddenly increases at dawn, and you could be subject to surprise attack'.[50]

As with a battleship, crews aboard cruisers had their own action stations. On HMS *Fiji*, Commander Owen, then a youthful midshipman, 'was in charge of the anti-aircraft lookouts', but changed positions when she came under a series of heavy air attacks that would lead to her sinking south-east of Crete on 22 May 1941. The navigation officer:

> enlisted the midshipmen in turn; he called us there, I left my lookout and went to the bridge with him, and he said 'I want you to tell me the instant the dive-bomber opens his bomb doors, because that means that the bomb will leave the aircraft, and I know that if I give the order, hard a-starboard, the ship will have swung sufficiently when the bomb hits the sea [that] it won't hit us.' Unfortunately, the first planes that attacked

were not Ju-88s, which have bomb doors, but the Stuka Ju-87, which had a fixed undercarriage with the bombs carried under the wings. So the midshipman had to watch and see as soon as the bomb was clear of the aircraft and say 'Bombs Away!' whereupon Peter Norton [navigation officer] would give his orders and try to dodge it, dodge the bombs. There were several near-misses, and then we were hit by a small bomb, and the effect of this is a terrific jolt, and you feel the ship shaking and vibrating, and you hear splinters from the bomb and bits of metal that have been blown off the ship rattling about, and of course, if these hit you, you could be killed or wounded instantly. And after about two hours ... we were firing the guns all the time. Great anxiety that we would run out of ammunition, which indeed we eventually did – I think we had something like 20,000 rounds of ammunition for the 4-inch guns. And all of that was expended in about eight hours, so you can imagine that continuous noise, continuous firing; all the time we were getting further away from Crete. But eventually, sometime in the afternoon, we were hit – a very near miss, which caused one of the boiler rooms to flood. The ship stopped, all power was lost, and the ship started to list over to port, and then, looking up, I saw – I was back in the lookout position by then – I saw one plane approaching. I think it was a different sort of plane; it was a fighter-bomber, and I could see it had one large bomb underneath the belly, and he let it go, and there was no doubt that it was coming absolutely straight for us. So all I could do, and anyone near me, was to fling ourselves on the deck with our heads down – we had steel helmets, of course – and the bomb hit somewhere aft in the ship. I didn't actually see it hit the ship, as I was down on the deck, but we then heeled over even further, and the captain gave the order to abandon ship.[51]

Aboard HMS *Edinburgh*, Colin Kitching served as a communication number, and fuse setter in a revolving twin 4-inch gun mounting. Here he sat on a stool with a microphone in one hand to communicate with the 4-inch Director Top above the bridge, and in front of him there was a small handle. 'The shell would be put in with the fuse pushed into an aperture, and I would have a dial and the Director Top would say what range the fuse had to be set. I would lower my handle and the pointer on my thing had to meet the pointer which the Director Top had set. So then that fused the shell. Interesting, lively, and ... I enjoyed this ... my action station.'[52]

In respect to gunnery, the Royal Marines (RM) made a massive contribution, as they manned a main turret, plus a share of the secondary armament, in every battleship, battlecruiser and cruiser. As a young Royal Marine officer,

General Sir Peter Whiteley served aboard the Fiji or Colony class cruiser HMS *Gambia*, escorting convoys around the Cape and supporting the Allied invasion of Madagascar:

> we manned approximately a third of ship's armament ... in *Gambia*, for example, one 6-inch turret and two twin 4.5 mountings, anti-aircraft, as well as a number of close range weapons. This was an exceedingly useful adjunct to a, basically a soldier I suppose, and whenever we had the opportunity we would go ashore either for exercise, or in the case of Madagascar eventually we went ashore just to make sure that everything was peaceful and quiet.[53]

While off Madagascar *Gambia* took part in a significant bombardment of Tamatave [Toamasina], 'the object being to persuade them to surrender. We anchored in the bay, because there seemed to be no great opposition. Unfortunately the tide swung the ship round so that my director, which was the after director, was the only one capable of bringing guns to bear on the area. So it was my delight to be able to fire the first shots, and they were only the first shots because the moment we fired, the flag, white flags went up and a party of local dignitaries shortly came out in a boat to surrender. A very brief but significant occasion.'[54]

Since the First World War the action station for musicians of the RM band on larger warships was in the Transmitting Station (TS) situated in the depths of the ship, where they operated the fire-control table, effectively a forerunner of the computer. It was their task to manually make the appropriate connections to provide a firing solution for the guns. Typically, in a gun director above the bridge operators monitored the movement of a target, and kept their director trained on it. Another operator worked out the range using an optical range finder. These actions were passed via electrical circuits to pointers on dials in the TS. This gave 'the movement of the target relative to their own ship, and the target's elevation. As the range-taker spun the screws on his range finder to match the images of the target, the range was transmitted to the table in the TS.' Other data would be fed into the table such as outside temperature, wind speed and direction, and the temperature of the guns because as they heated up their ballistic properties altered. All the information would be linked so as to continuously alter pointers in the TS, which were carefully monitored by RM personnel, and employed to generate the final settings to be conveyed to gun turrets through electrical circuits. 'Here each turret trainer swivelled the turret to place his pointer in his dial over the one being controlled from the TS, while each gun layer elevated or depressed his gun by following the pointer on his dial.' Often individual guns, even in the same turret, would have slightly different characteristics, and these required specific variations in elevation to hit a given target, which would have to be 'pre-calibrated and the gun layer's pointer adjusted accordingly. The firing solution computed by the TS enabled the guns to be aimed in such a way that twenty or so seconds after the guns fired, shells and target would arrive in the same piece of sea.'[55]

Like battleships, cruisers were also deployed to provide NGFS, especially during amphibious operations, and systems had to be employed for effectively orchestrating this fire. Having trained as a telegraphist, William Bradshaw volunteered for special duties and in April 1941 was drafted to Combined Operations, that branch of the navy that dealt with amphibious warfare. Subsequently, he worked as a Naval Gun Spotter, helping to direct fire in Norway, Madagascar (where he won the DSM), Burma and at Anzio, Italy. His was an eventful career, as by 1944, as well as contracting dysentery, he had even briefly been held prisoner in the Far East. Effectively, he was a sailor-soldier, his role similar to a Forward Observation Officer's team in the Royal Artillery (RA). As if to emphasise this, personnel wore khaki and were issued army boots, but retained their naval insignia and headgear. 'Going ashore, you picked up targets, tanks or troops, whatever ... We had an officer, leading telegraphist, telegraphist and a signalman ... Targets were located using a six figure map reference, and you'd ask for a shot.'[56]

Men aboard cruisers also experienced some of the major events of the war. George Burridge served as a seaman radar operator on the Southampton class cruiser HMS *Belfast* in Home Waters, the Arctic and off Normandy during 1942–1944. Known affectionately by her crew as the 'Tiddly B', tiddly being naval slang for something good, she was built by Harland & Wolff and launched in 1938, and proved to be an extremely successful ship. Notably, Burridge remembered the Battle of the North Cape in late December 1943 in the Barents Sea. Here, together with the cruisers HMS *Norfolk* and *Sheffield*, the battleship HMS *Duke of York* and the cruiser HMS *Jamaica*, plus a number of destroyers, *Belfast* was instrumental in sinking *Scharnhorst*, a ship that would have posed a grave threat to the Arctic convoys had she remained operational.[57] Burridge recalled:

We were called to action stations, and my action station was the radar plot just under the bridge. And we were simply doing our job of plotting reports from the radar sets, and we were eventually told that we were in contact, they thought with heavy German ships or a ship, and we were likely to be going into action fairly soon. And we had several skirmishes ... The ships were reported as being close enough to cause us problems, bearing in mind the *Scharnhorst* was a very powerful ship, 11-inch guns versus our 6-inch guns. It was on 26 December that I remember Admiral Burnett coming on to say that we were in contact almost certainly with the *Scharnhorst* and we were about to start firing star shell to identify the ship. And this carried on for some time, star shells were fired and our guns opened up ... We had reports that the *Norfolk* was temporarily put out of action, and I think they lost six, it was hit aft. And then we had a further report from the *Sheffield* to say that they were having engine problems and couldn't keep up with the high speed action. Admiral Burnett came on to say that we were alone, and were going to take on the *Scharnhorst*, which frightened the life out of everyone I think.[58]

Subsequently, the armoured door to the plotting room was blown off by the firing of the *Belfast*'s own guns, providing George with a view of what was happening as well as the information from the radar plots:

The firing continued [from *Belfast*] and then of course *Duke of York* started firing and I can see it now, the entire *Scharnhorst* was on fire from bow to stern ... a mass of flames. And we in due course went in with torpedo attacks two or three times, and then there were so many other ships there, destroyers and cruisers that we pulled away, and the destroyers went in to finish it off. And we didn't pick up any survivors but we did see little red lights in the water ... and the destroyers picked up about thirty-six survivors. [During the pursuit it had been] tense, everyone was as tense as they could be because we knew we were in real danger, but we still had confidence in the ship that we could survive. There was no panic, just concentrating on the job in hand. There was elation at [*Scharnhorst*'s] sinking, and relief to have survived. [The order was then given to splice the main brace, i.e. issue rum.][59]

Experiences on Smaller Ships

Something of the character and qualities of destroyers was captured in an official wartime booklet, which stated:

In proportion to their size they are more powerful than any other warship; the engines of a 1,900-ton destroyer develop nearly 50,000 horsepower. This gives them manoeuvrability as well as speed. They can turn sharply to leap forward and ram a submarine suddenly sighted on the beam. They are so strongly built that they can stand up to the heaviest sea, and yet so easily handled that they can manoeuvre in narrow channels, harbours and fjords, or go alongside another ship to rescue survivors or even to board her.[60]

This versatility ensured that destroyers were often in the thick of the action, including escorting convoys, mounting anti-shipping sweeps, providing shore bombardments and taking part in naval battles. Correspondingly they took casualties. Sydney Greenwood joined the H class destroyer HMS *Hero*, part of Captain Warburton-Lee's 2nd Flotilla, as a stoker shortly before the outbreak of war. The flotilla consisted of eight other destroyers, plus *Hero*. These were *Hardy*, *Hasty*, *Hunter*, *Hereward*, *Hostile*, *Hotspur*, *Hyperion* and *Havoc*, and 'they would all soon be involved in violent action, most of them sunk or heavily damaged within two years'.[61] Likewise, destroyers and their crews had to endure the worst the world's oceans could throw at them, and this could lead to alarming incidents, such as when HMS *Aldenham* off Malta rolled so far to starboard that she nearly capsized. As one of her crew described, with destroyers 'there was always a danger of "broaching-to" – that is the sea getting under the quarter and heeling over so far that she could be in danger of capsizing'.[62]

While officers had bunks, ratings had to learn how to use hammocks, which was not easy in rough seas. If the ship went 'down into a trough of a wave just as you were swinging up, you would end up flat against the deck head, pinned to it by the pressure of the ship going down, and when it stopped you would of course drop back again'.[63] However, once safely in a hammock, one sailor on destroyers explained how 'rolling or pitching, it doesn't matter, the hammock keeps you in a nice reasonable position'. Conversely, 'on cruising stations or such like you don't sling your hammock, you sleep where you can, [and given space was at a premium] those that are not on duty sleep on the deck or on the lockers or something like that'.[64]

Various classes and ages of destroyer were deployed by the wartime navy, and it is worth highlighting some of these.[65] HMS *Windsor* was a W class destroyer of 1,100 tons, launched in 1918; with a maximum speed of around 34 knots, she was intended as a short-range escort. One of her crew recounted how she had a 'funny little long slim funnel forward and a fat one aft, so you could spot a V and W class destroyer anywhere'.[66] In contrast, HMS *Havelock*, launched in October 1939, was part of an order intended for Brazil but instead acquired by the RN. Owing to Brazil's long coastline and shortage of suitable ports, these destroyers 'had to have an exceptionally high fuel capacity' and, according to Eric Denton, who served aboard her, this ensured 'that whereas the ordinary destroyer would normally stay at sea in the Atlantic for approximately twelve days, the destroyers of the Atlantic Advanced Striking Force [including *Havelock*] could stay at sea for approximately four-teen to fifteen days, and the record whilst I was on board was seventeen days!'[67] This increased fuel capacity ensured that at least two would always be operating to escort in-bound and outward-bound convoys.

As George Mack explained, HMS *Intrepid* was one those I class destroyers authorised under the 1935 programme, and so still comparatively new when war was declared. She was 'built in the Isle of Wight by J.S. Samuel White at a cost of £259, 325 ... and launched on 17 December 1936. Her statistics were: 330 feet in length, breadth 33 feet, depth 19 feet 7¾inches, displacement 1,370 tons ... speed 34.396 knots, and she was manned by a crew of 145'; she was armed with 'four 4.7-inch guns, two sets of quadruple 0.5-inch machine-guns' and 'two sets of quintuple torpedo tubes'.[68] Other types of destroyer built in the late 1930s were the J and K classes, initially serving in Home Waters before redeploying to the Mediterranean where losses were heavy during 1940–1941. One of these ships, HMS *Jersey*, was eventually mined off Malta; interestingly, long before this one of her crew observed that 'she had a peculiar noise signature, we seemed to be particularly attractive to mines'.[69]

The Tribal class also appeared in the late 1930s, with double the gun armament of the A-I classes at the expense of halving their torpedo capacity, while simultaneously being provided with increased anti-aircraft weaponry. As a sub-lieutenant in the RNVR, Ludovic Kennedy was posted to HMS *Tartar* in February 1940 for watch-keeping and other duties. She was 'one of the famous Tribal class destroyers, completed a year before the war, the fastest, biggest and most modern destroyers in the fleet, formidably armed and superbly appointed and commanded by the cream of the Navy's destroyer captains'. She belonged to the 6th Flotilla, based at Scapa Flow as part of the Home Fleet, and had 'a complement of around a dozen officers and 250 men. Of the sixteen built, only four would survive the war.'[70]

The Hunt class, replete with anti-submarine and anti-aircraft armament, arose from the need in the late 1930s and on into the Second World War for a fast ship 'to perform the work of a modern escort vessel and be capable of carrying out the manifold duties of a Fleet destroyer with the exception of attendance on the Fleet'. Once the war started, the programme for construction of the Hunt class was increased, and the initial design was improved to produce the Type II, followed in March 1940 by the Type III, which carried more depth charges, was equipped with MF DF (Medium Frequency Directional Findings), and had a respectable speed of 27 knots.[71] HMS *Beaufort* was one of the Type II Hunts, and according to Commander Tom Dowling, who served on her as a junior officer in the Mediterranean, she had:

Six 4-inch guns ... When they launched them initially they were just a bit too narrow and lacked stability. So they broadened them by I think it was about 2 feet and we had the full armament of six 4-inch. One fore-mounted four barrel pom-pom and [two 20mm anti-aircraft guns], which was actually a jolly good armament for a ship of that size. We were only about 1,000 tons and we did about 27 knots. Not quite the full speed of a destroyer but still pretty good and my job as officer of the quarts was A mounting. That is the far one. There were four guns aft and two forward. One twin and actually the aircraft virtually always attacked from the stern because it made the target easier to hit and so A mounting was nearly always in what they called independent [mode]. You could fire barrages. The main thing was just to fire your gun and make a lot of noise and bangs in the sky because it was pretty conspicuous ... the enemy attacks when they succeeded and I was with about nine that did. Didn't see, I didn't see necessarily the ships sinking ... but they did sink in company because a lot of these things were at night but what I noticed was that it was always the ship that wasn't firing its guns that got hit. Firing guns had a colossal morale effect on the Navy and it was when a ship was caught by surprise that it got hit.[72]

Typically on destroyers, a small ship routine existed that was based around meal times. Remembering conditions on HMS *Ilex*, built in 1937, another of the destroyers he served on, Stanley Greenwood explained what this was like. There 'was generally a cup of tea for breakfast, a tot of rum about 11.00am, main meal at mid-day, and a spartan supper at 6.30pm. The tot of rum, after seventeen hours of fasting, tore into the vitals. One hour later the dinner of meat and two veg, deceptively weighty on its heavy plate, looked as tempting as a king's banquet and was devoured ravenously.'[73] Conditions could be even more severe on older destroyers, including HMS *Malcolm* of First World War vintage. Thomas Jones served on her, including during convoy work in the North Atlantic, and recalled:

> The mess decks was the worst, in heavy weather there was always three or four inches of water on the mess decks, and the potatoes, sprouts and cabbages smelt like a horse's stable. How the crew managed to exist in it, put up with it, it was absolutely terrible. If you were at sea more than ten to fourteen days you went on corn dog [slang for corned beef]. That probably was the worst of wartime conditions – it was very, very bad.[74]

Another important aspect of the routine was keeping watches. The system employed by the RN 'was four hours from midnight till four in the morning known as the middle watch, followed by the morning watch from four till eight, and the forenoon watch from eight to twelve. The afternoon watch was twelve to four, and this was followed by the dog watches. These were two hourly periods, the first one from four to six, and the second from six to eight, followed by the resumption of the four hour watches from 8.00pm to midnight.' As the watches resumed after the two hour breaks it ensured personnel changed their watch daily so they were not stuck covering the same periods all the time. This took time for the body to adjust, and was a 'weird system of getting one's rest'.[75]

Aside from the routine, personnel had to be prepared for their action stations. For Eric Denton on HMS *Havelock* this entailed acting as masthead lookout from a position not dissimilar to a large dustbin secured to the front of the mast near the yardarm, where he had a grandstand view of what was happening in the Atlantic, and 'had to report everything before anybody else saw it' which needed 'a great deal of alertness'. However, just getting to the lookout post, especially in rough weather, was complex, as the ladder did not stay still, often leaving the climber to hang on desperately. 'With experience, one discovered that it would be stationary in one position for a few seconds, and those were the few seconds when one would take another two or three steps up and hang on tight again.' Thus sailors tended to reach the position exhausted. As they would be relieving someone already there, the climber usually went round to the right of the mast, while the incumbent 'climbed out and went round to the left'. Then 'the previous lookout could start going down the ladder as soon as the climber was clear of it'.[76]

In contrast, while on watch stokers, including Sydney Greenwood on HMS *Ilex*, working in the engine room would try 'to obey telegraph orders of: Increase, Decrease, Stop Making Black Smoke, etc.' Simultaneously, he found you had to control via 'another telegraph system the number of oil fuel sprayers on the other two boilers', a task that invariably proved tricky. Then off watch, like most engine-room ratings, Greenwood would join a Fire and Repair party, and was in charge of 'a team manhandling shells and cordite from the magazines to the guns'.[77]

The 4.7-inch guns that equipped destroyers were good weapons but, as one member of a gun crew cautioned: ' to keep an absolute clear head, and to think clearly in the midst of all the racket around, with the roar of aircraft engines and bursting of bombs, only comes after many hours of weary drills'.[78] Bert Blackmore served on HMS *Jersey* prior to being commissioned and becoming a bomb disposal officer.[79] His action station 'was on "A" gun, which is the turret on the forecastle' and 'I was the cartridge man ... we didn't have fixed ammunition, we had a shell and a cartridge ... my job was to put the cartridge on the tray ready to go into the breach' and 'they came up from down below on a hoist' and could be fired as quickly as possible.[80]

Lieutenant Commander C.H. Knollys spent the latter stages of his war serving on the 1,730-ton S class destroyer HMS *Saumarez*, part of the 26th Flotilla with the British Pacific Fleet (BPF). In May 1945 she was engaged in a dashing action, one of the few occasions during the entire war when destroyers attacked and sank a superior enemy at night with torpedoes and guns, in the classical pattern for which they were designed. The Japanese cruiser *Haguro*, returning to Singapore having abandoned attempts to relieve the Andaman Islands, was spotted to the north-east of the 26th Flotilla:

The Flotilla increased speed to 27 knots and turned to a course of E.S.E. going 'like a rugby full-back for the corner flag'. It was essential to cut *Haguro* off but then, as we steamed through a calm sea with the blue distant hills of Sumatra on our starboard side, the full realisation came up on us. *Haguro* was a heavy cruiser of nearly 14,000 tons, with a speed of 33 knots, armed with ten 8-inch guns whose range was 32,600 yards, eight 5-inch guns and eight torpedo tubes. If we encountered her in daylight, we would be silhouetted against the western sky. Now for five destroyers to meet a cruiser of this type under such conditions is not a very hopeful proposition. With her great speed and overwhelming gun power she could destroy the Flotilla before we could even get close enough to retaliate. But in case we missed her altogether, we could not afford to slow down and so pressed on, hoping for the best.

[Subsequently, the night was dark, filled with storm clouds and no moonlight] ... We were ready for the enemy but would he appear? By 10.00pm ships' companies had been at action stations for 12 hours and were feeling the strain. In the chart house, which was the Action Information Centre, where I was, the atmosphere seemed heavy and oppressive. The dim red lights and the monotonous ticking of instruments had a mesmeric effect and it was hard to keep awake ... suddenly, just before we were due to turn back, over the R/T came a report: *Venus* [one of the other destroyers] had a contact away to the North East. [Each destroyer was allotted their sector for a star attack, whereby each would converge on the target from their appointed position.] It was like a net closing in and we were expecting the quarry to begin snapping at any moment. [Despite] ... close ranges – 6,000 yards closing – not a shot had been fired. We must have been detected ourselves but the enemy gave no sign of alarm. Perhaps he thought we were friendly, coming as we were from the South. That was the last quarter from which he need expect an enemy. It seemed uncanny to be chasing this silent and so far invisible monster around his own backyard without once being bitten.

[Confusion then reigned as both sides opened fire.] From the chart house I heard our own guns firing. There was another noise rather as though we were going through a tunnel ... this was the noise of 8-inch shells passing overhead and around us ... Salvoes fired at almost point-blank range were landing all round the ship and the splashes were drenching everybody [and hindered visibility] ... Then we got hit amidships. We felt a bit of a blow and there was a rush of escaping steam. In the chart house we felt the ship heeling over and all the lights went out. [The air was thick with steam and shell fumes. Then there was a] rather eerie quiet and it seemed we had stopped ... owing to heroic work by the engine-room staff, the ship had [in fact] barely faltered in her stride and was only heeling over because we were turning at high speed.

On the bridge the captain had turned the ship quickly and fired torpedoes as the massive shape of the cruiser went by less than a mile away. Her sides could be seen glistening wet by light of the star shell; [to judge] by her huge bow wave, she must have been going pretty fast ...

[Later the other destroyers] *Venus*, *Virago* and *Vigilant* all fired their torpedoes but *Haguro* was a tough cookie, still afloat after six hits. *Venus* closed in and fired her two remaining torpedoes and *Haguro* eventually sank. *Saumarez* transmitted: 'Vs for victory' and led the Flotilla away from the scene as it was well within range of enemy airfields.

On 21 May the 26th Flotilla entered Trincomalee harbour in Ceylon [modern day Sri Lanka], cheered by men lining the decks of every ship ...[81]

As the above demonstrates, destroyers of all classes were fast and capable ships, but most lacked the endurance to make them fully effective Atlantic escorts. Nor were they suited to such a role, especially offensively, as their 'low-angle guns were of no use against aircraft, [their] torpedoes no use against submarines', and furthermore their 'speed was in excess of requirements' and they were not as seaworthy as other vessels.[82] Once the war extended into the Atlantic, therefore, a requirement existed for adequate numbers of effective ships with suitable weapons systems, especially for anti-submarine warfare, plus improved habitability, endurance and seakeeping qualities. Ultimately the RN relied on various types of ship to act as escorts, as an ideal vessel for this role was never developed. Instead the following were deployed: 'two classes of corvette, a variety of destroyers, several types of destroyer escort [small destroyers without features not needed on escort work, such as torpedoes and high speed], frigates of both British and American design, and sloops of pre-war types'.[83]

One of the most successful designs employed were the Black Swan and Modified Black Swan class sloops of 1,250 to 1,350 tons. They had a complement of 180–192 men and a speed of around 20 knots, which was fine for escort work and marginally faster than a surfaced U-boat. They were armed with ten 20mm Oerlikons, six 4-inch guns suitable for surface or anti-aircraft firing, and aft had four depth-charge throwers, often with as many depth charges as could be carried.[84] As an HO signaller, Denis Logan served on HMS *Starling*, skippered by the famous anti-U-boat ace Captain Frederic Walker, who commanded the 2nd Support Group. *Starling* was one of the Modified Black Swan class sloops, and:

> Our job was to get between the wolf packs and the convoy routes and to break up them up ... For example, RAF Coastal Command used to fly the Sunderlands [flying boats] out and if they made sightings they used to send us after them ... The system was that the moment they broke the surface, the guns opened up because they could fire off torpedoes. It was unfortunate for them they had no ways of showing a surrender really.[85]

Another small type of ship that did sterling service as an escort was the Flower class corvette, albeit at 16 knots it was too slow to catch a surfaced U-boat and its ocean-going qualities were far from ideal. The following extract gives a vivid impression of what conditions were like for the men who endured early models of these vessels:

> It was sheer unmitigated hell. She was a shore fo'c'sle corvette and even getting hot food from the galley to fo'c'sle was a tremendous job. The mess decks were usually a shambles and the wear and tear on bodies and tempers was something that I shall never forget. But we were young and tough and, in a sense, we gloried in our misery and made light of it all.[86]

Although the design was subsequently improved, conditions remained tough. Having trained as a radio mechanic, Jack Cole served on HMS *Sweetbriar* in the Atlantic and off Normandy during 1943–1945. It was extremely cramped, but then he 'was put into a miscellaneous mess with all the stokers and store assistants and sick berth hands and people like that. And it was a very friendly mess actually ... it was amidships and didn't pitch and toss as much as that in the fo'c'sle, where all the poor sailors were.'[87] For corvette crews, life revolved around watch-keeping, sleeping and eating meals when not at action stations. However, those in positions of responsibility could never fully switch off. Sir Robert Atkinson commanded a number of corvettes with B7 Escort

Group in the Atlantic during 1940–1943, and gives a snapshot of what this was like:

> There were long periods of doing nothing. I even did a couple of tapestries during the war. You never had a bath and you slept mostly with your clothes on. And to be alert you were on edge all the time, some more than others. Some with responsibility would be alert all the time. Ordinary members of the crew would be getting on with their job, and not know what was happening in the Asdic cabinet etc.[88]

Mines and Minesweeping

Both sides employed minefields at sea that were a threat to naval and merchant shipping. Offensive minelaying was carried out close to enemy shorelines with the intention of sinking shipping in their home waters and/or restricting their movements. In contrast, defensive minelaying aimed to protect friendly coastlines and shipping. Mines could be laid by aircraft, warships, submarines or specially converted merchantmen, such as the 5,396-ton *Port Quebec*, which laid more than 33,000 mines as part of the 1st Minelaying Squadron.

The unglamorous but important job of minesweeping was another area heavily reliant on the smaller vessels of the RN. Some units, including the 8th Minesweeping Flotilla at North Shields, employed paddle-steamers, which, as Lieutenant James Reeve (RNVR) found, were well suited 'because of their shallow draught, which was about 7 feet, and their extensive decks, which allowed them to be fitted with powerful steam winches from which sweeps could be streamed on either quarter', albeit their large decks were vulnerable to enemy aircraft, especially when 'scrubbed to please a zealous first lieutenant', which 'made the ship a conspicuous target on a moonlit night'.[89] Similarly, a number of fishing vessels, such as trawlers and drifters, were pressed into service as minesweepers, often crewed by the same men who had manned them in peacetime. They 'put on His Majesty's uniform, and changed their routine to naval routine' and set out to 'fish for the deadliest and most devilish pieces of machinery that the wit of German scientists can devise'.[90] Again, these vessels could be readily converted, as they already had the necessary gear for lifting nets that could be applied to equipment for sweeping mines, but there were disadvantages. Being deep-hulled meant that they were more likely to hit mines themselves, and their steel-hulled construction made them vulnerable to magnetic mines.

'Smokey Joes' – coal-burning minesweepers and relics of the First World War – also posed problems because they emitted 'huge columns of smoke by day and spectacular sparks by night'.[91] HMS *Ross*, a Hunt class sweeper launched in 1919, saw action, notably off Dunkirk. One of her crew recounted that:

> there were about sixteen hands in the mess deck, and only room for one man to sling his hammock. We all used to sleep on the deck. She was a coal burner ... and she had flames coming out the top of her funnel 15 feet high when she was steaming at full speed ... The food was terrible, 'nuts and bolts' we used to call it, stew with about an inch of fat on the top of it.[92]

In contrast, the Halcyon class comprised fleet minesweepers of around 800 tons, built in the 1930s, and as the war progressed these were joined by the new Bangor class of around 600–670 tons, originally designed as a coastal equivalent of the Halcyon class, and 'the smallest ships in the Navy to be classed as "major war vessels" – as many a man who served on their crowded decks would willingly testify'.[93] Production subsequently switched to the larger Algerine class of 850 tons, many of which also proved useful as escort vessels.[94] There were additionally motor minesweepers, ideal for local operations such as clearing harbours, which had diesel engines and wooden hulls in order to reduce their vulnerability to magnetic mines. Likewise, British American Minesweepers (BAMS) and British Yard Minesweepers BYMS) were American-built vessels for the RN, the BAMS along the lines of the Algerines, while the BYMS were smaller and known only by their number.[95]

According to an Admiralty minesweeping summary, issued shortly before the end of the war, 'the total mines swept in all areas since the outbreak of hostilities [was] 25,000'.[96] Despite its importance, minesweeping was not a recognised specialism for RN officers, like gunnery. Nor was it a separate manning division akin to the Submarine Service, nor did it have non-substantive badges, which would have marked out ratings as being qualified in it as a particular trade. Bernard Maher, a wartime RNVR officer, noted that minesweeping nonetheless, as a potentially risky duty, did qualify personnel 'for a modest payment of danger money', plus crews on small minesweepers were eligible for 'hard lying money, an allowance given to all for service in ships that lacked many of the normal amenities of larger ships'.[97]

Ultimately, whatever ship they served on, personnel involved in minesweeping were engaged in 'a deadly chess game ... in which the advantage changed hands as new devices were introduced and changed again as the other side figured them out and developed ways to sweep them'.[98] There were distinct types of mine, as Lieutenant Commander Ted Maughan RNVR, who served on the Bangor class HMS *Beaumaris*, including during Operation Neptune, explained:

> there are two categories of sea mines. Those that are moored to the sea bed with a sinker and a wire or chain, the length of the mooring wire determines the depth of the mine below the surface [known as contact mines]. These are laid from the stern of large mine-laying ships. The second category is mines that are laid on the sea bed. They are either dropped by aircraft or from fast coastal craft such as German E-boats. These are laid in harbours, estuaries or shallow coastal waters. [Then there were influence mines, such as the acoustic and magnetic.] Acoustic mines, these are detonated by sound waves from a ship's engine. [There were also] pressure mines, known as 'oyster mines'. These were lowered onto the sea bed and the pressure waves set up by a ship passing over the mine will detonate the mine.[99]

Various counter-measures were developed. For moored mines, a streamlined towed float was employed, known as an Oropesa after the ship (HMS *Oropesa*) on which it was developed. The idea was to keep the towed sweep at a deter-mined position from the sweeping ship. As Lieutenant Commander Maughan outlined, 'you either had a 100 per cent sweep or it could come down to about a 50 per cent clearance of an area ... But to sweep channels it was always a 100 per cent sweep, where the ships were in echelon ... but two cables behind each other and astern on the quarter of the ship ahead. So it's rather like cutting the lawn.' Having swept in one direction, the sweepers would then turn round and widen the channel, which was marked by 'Dan buoys, which were laid by trawlers coming up astern of the ships'.[100] Likewise, a seaman who served on HMS *Ross* described how the Oropesa was:

> a grid with bars across it at an angle, and when this was thrown over the side of the ship, the bars were made in such a way that as soon as the water pressure coming onto them hit them, the thing went down and it was arranged at whatever depth you had to sweep mines ... from there wires led out to the stern of the ship to port or starboard, depending which side you were sweeping, to another thing [kept at a certain level] and attached to it were cutters, and attached to it were floats you could see from the ship ... As you went along, if this wire hit a mine's wire it guided it along to a place where it could cut it. The mine then came up to the surface and your job was to shoot at this mine with rifles and sink or explode it.[101]

In contrast, acoustic mines were eventually swept successfully by a device known as 'a Kango hammer in the bow of a ship which sends the sound waves ahead to explode the mine'. Pressure mines were more challenging, but could be countered by controlling 'the speed of ships, so most of our heavy ships moved about at very slow speeds of about two knots in shallow' areas that were affected, 'and larger ships were towed slowly out to deep water'. Alternatively, efforts were made to sweep these mines by towing 'barges filled with concrete by small craft with a very small displacement', the aim being 'to explode the mine under the barge rather than the towing craft'.[102]

Magnetic mines were best dealt with by wooden-hulled minesweepers, such as the BAMS. One method used a generator to produce electrical current, and on the stern winch were two lengths of thick, insulated electrical cables, each with a bare copper electrode on their outer end:

> When the sweep began, the generator was switched on to transmit an electrical current down one of the cables to its exposed end; as salt water is a good conductor of electricity, the current was conducted horizontally across the surface of the water, thus creating a magnetic field that could detonate a magnetic mine beneath the water … [During the sweep] the generator alternated the direction of current from one to other end of the cables [and] the change in direction of the flow of electrical current reversed the polarity of the magnetic minefield. [This was vital as mines tended to be sensitive to only one or other polarity.][103]

Royal Naval Patrol Service (RNPS) and Coastal Forces

The RNPS was effectively a navy within the Royal Navy, with its own silver badge worn by all sea-going personnel, and headquarters known as the 'Sparrow's Nest' at the municipal pleasure gardens in Lowestoft. It operated a wide variety of trawlers, drifters and whalers, many of First World War vintage or even earlier, along with requisitioned craft such as yachts and paddle-steamers. Initially most vessels were operated by former fishermen, as members of the RNR, but as the war progressed crews were diluted by floods of HO personnel, many of whom had little knowledge of the sea. As indicated above, some men of this rickety fleet embarked on minesweeping. Others served on the bleak Northern Patrol, between the Faroes and Iceland, principally tasked with monitoring any German raiders looking to prey on Atlantic convoys, or patrolled in the Channel and 'E-boat Alley', that stretch of the North Sea from Grimsby to Dover. Anti-submarine operations also relied on the RNPS, and it supported Atlantic and Arctic convoys, plus operating in theatres as diverse as the Mediterranean and Indian Ocean. Eventually over 60,000 men fought with the RNPS, operating at least 3,000 small vessels, and by 1945 the service had suffered over 3,200 killed.[104]

As Commander D.A. Rayner of the 14th Anti-Submarine Group observed, most trawlers tended to develop 'little idiosyncrasies of their own'.[105] *Lady Shirley*, a 470-ton Hull trawler of mid-1930s vintage, was typical of the sort of vessel operated by the RNPS. At the outbreak of war she was requisitioned by the Admiralty, and after a period of working up in Tobermory was sent to Gibraltar in 1941 on convoy escort and anti-submarine patrol duties. The crew consisted of a mixture of RNR and RNVR personnel, commanded by Lieutenant Commander Arthur Callaway, an Australian who had previously been the managing director of a bedding factory. They always knew when full speed (10 knots) had been reached 'because the bridge windows began to rattle. Nine knots was when the bridge flag locker shook; eight knots down to five produced minor shakes in the bridge ladder. An extra burst of speed needed in an emergency shook the whole bridge works in harmony.'[106]

On 4 October 1941 *Lady Shirley* encountered and, amazingly, sank a U-boat (U-111). After firm Asdic contact, she launched a pattern of five depth charges which forced the U-boat to the surface, and there followed a bitter firefight lasting around 23 minutes. Acting Sub-Lieutenant Allan Waller, the young signals and navigation officer, noted 'our only other guns besides the point-fives and the four-inch were a Hotchkiss .303 each side of the bridge' and when they both fired at each other 'there was a flash of tracers all over the place' which added to the 'nightmarish experience'. Presumably U-111 was damaged by the depth charges, and she suffered at least nine direct hits from *Lady Shirley*'s 4-inch gun before slipping below the waves. 'Everybody lined the ship's side with whatever arms they'd got – rifles, revolvers – as we hauled the Germans aboard one at a time.' It took them a while to appreciate that they were Germans: 'We'd thought them Italians as they were all so dark, but instead they were just deeply sunburned.'[107]

A well-publicised and seemingly glamorous aspect of the RN, especially when compared to minesweeping, was Coastal Forces, again a branch reliant on small craft. From virtually nothing in 1939, it grew to over 20,000 officers and ratings by September 1944, many of who were RNVR or HO. Commander Christopher Dreyer was a regular naval officer who served with a number of Motor Torpedo Boat (MTB) flotillas in Home Waters, at Dunkirk and in the Mediterranean during 1940–1943. On taking command of the 24th MTB Flotilla, despite being only in his mid-twenties, he was one of the oldest in the unit and:

the only RN officer in the whole outfit. Some of the coxswains were RN petty officers, but almost the whole of the crews were HO sailors of different sorts. Most of the boats had a motor mechanic rather than an

ERA which is the naval rank, and the motor mechanic was a wartime HO rank of PO or Chief Motor Mechanic ... a skilled motorman from garages, engineering works given naval training in operational boats. The Chiefs of practically all our boats by the middle of the war were motor mechanics. And not only our boats, of course, but in the base staff, practically, the whole of the technical staff in bases were Wrens. By 1943 one's engine, hull, radio, torpedoes and guns were all looked after by Wrens, with a smattering of sailors together with them.[108]

According to one authority, Coastal Forces, using predominantly MTBs, Motor Gun Boats (MGBs) and Motor Launches (MLs), 'played a major role in keeping open, and moving, Allied sea communications' and the importance of these craft 'exceeded their size and they were a considerable part of that combination of arms by which sea power is exercised'. Most were of 'wooden construction and so utilised the building capacity of many boat yards, in both the UK and abroad, which could not otherwise have been kept fully employed', notably the British Power Boat Company and Vosper.[109] MTBs in particular were useful for attacking German convoys in areas such as the English Channel, where they might wait 'like little wasps' desperate to strike, and simultaneously avoid being shot up themselves.[110] Additionally, Coastal Forces craft helped land agents in enemy territory and rescued downed aircrew, notably during the Battle of Britain.

The MGBs were intended to counter the awkward and crafty German E-boats that often hid alongside buoys, making them hard to detect with radar or even by eye, and typically used their superior speed to outdistance RN craft. John Davies, who served on MGB 320, provides an idea of what they were like: '[She was] 110 feet in length, with a 17 feet beam; ... three Hall-Scot engines that were supposed to give us a speed of 26 knots maximum and an average of speed of 23 knots [usually more like 18 knots in a fully loaded boat]. The armament was good for the size of boat. On the fo'c's'le we had a two-pounder manually operated pom-pom, on either side of the bridge' further aft 'were power operated twin .5 machine-gun turrets' and aft 'a two pounder Rolls-Royce gun, plus a supply of depth charges'. There was also a Holman projector for launching hand grenades, although this proved highly unreliable and unpopular.[111] In contrast, motor launches, such as ML 137, a Fairmile B-class motor launch, were, according to ML 137's navigator, 'the maids of all work of Coastal Forces' and were deployed on anti-submarine duty, as convoy escorts, for minelaying and minesweeping, air-sea rescue and as ambulances, and were 'navigational leaders for the D-day landings'. They proved 'excellent sea-boats capable of long voyages under their own power' and had a maximum speed of around 20 knots. ML 137 'was 65 tons displacement; 112 feet long; 18 feet in the beam' and armed with 'two twin Oerlikon 20mm, one 3-pounder gun and two twin Vickers machine guns'.[112]

For one youthful naval officer, fast craft like MTBs were 'every young man's dream'.[113] Consequently, Coastal Forces attracted high-quality manpower, the sort of young men who might otherwise have tried to fly with the RAF. They included some famous names, notably Peter Scott, son of Scott of the Antarctic, who went on to become a leading nature presenter on TV. Another veteran found that combat with Coastal Forces had its thrills as well as its horrors. As part of a flotilla, 'the sight of a number of fast, well-armed small craft heading out to sea, ready for anything, is really impressive' and 'our officers in the main were dare-devils', despite most having come from civilian life shortly beforehand. Boat crews also got to grips with the enemy in an intimate manner, very different from the experience on larger warships, where sailors might not actually see their foe. Correspondingly, casualties were high and 'inevitable with the risks they had to take'. In mitigation, personnel received 'one shilling per day extra; sixpence of this was supposed to be "danger money"'.[114]

The sea-keeping qualities of Coastal Forces craft were another distinctive feature, and they could be particularly demanding in rough conditions. For John Davies and many others, seasickness was a concern, although after six months on an MGB he found that he stopped suffering, and was 'accepted as a real sailor'.[115] An officer on an MTB caught in a storm off Sardinia described the conditions:

> [There was] a huge swell like the Atlantic. That is really quite common in the Gulf of Lions and you find yourself sort of being carried up a mountain of a wave. Then at the top, I think it was a half moon. You look down into a sort of black abyss. I could be accused of telling a fisherman's story but really not. Anyone who was on that trip will never ever forget a little 70-foot MTB in this sea and then you would go downhill at a high speed. Crash in the bottom and then climb, climb. So you had to have someone on the throttles all the time. You couldn't set them at a given speed.[116]

MTBs clearly had to be capable of carrying torpedoes and operating at speed, and able to attack warships or merchantmen in coastal waters. Typically, those built during 1942–1944 'were of 37 tons on a length of 72½ feet' with 'a speed of 38–40 knots … two torpedo tubes, a 20mm gun and two machine guns and were operated by a crew of thirteen'.[117] In 1940 one of Commander Dreyer's boats was MTB 30. She was 'much less yacht-like [than earlier models], rather more robust, and not nearly so comfortable. Our wardroom went half-way across the ship and was quite cramped. Accommodation for two officers and ten men now, we had a rather bigger wireless office and more effective radio. We still, of course, didn't have any radar in those days and only a magnetic compass, so we were fairly primitively equipped. But compared with the prototype we carried much more fuel.'[118]

However, as one veteran cautioned, they used '100-octane petrol, which, if you were hit in your tanks, you didn't stand much chance, whereas the German E-boats had very large effective diesel engines ... So we always had this handicap of having to have petrol.'[119] This feature ensured MTBs were best employed by night otherwise, as one officer ruefully remarked, they were 'too easy to shoot up'.[120]

But these flaws did not stop Coastal Forces craft being employed in significant actions in Home Waters, the English Channel, the North Sea and the Mediterranean. Shortly after Operation Husky, the Allied invasion of Sicily in July 1943, Commander Dreyer's 24th MTB Flotilla was lying off Messina when one night:

> We heard the dumph, dumph, dumph, noise of a diesel engine coming down and we started engines ... and suddenly saw a shape coming and a wash and a bow wave. And it was quite clear it was coming very close to us indeed. So we all went astern to get out of the way, and the U-boat passed about 50 yards across our bows, much too close to fire at, and we were just going to turn and follow it to attack it when we heard another one coming behind the first, so we continued to go astern and made enough space between us and him to clear the torpedo warhead safety mechanism, which in that elderly type of torpedo we had at that time was only 100 yards. But I think we were about 200 yards away when we fired, and one could hardly miss. And the U-boat blew up, bits landing all over us ... It was a very satisfactory outcome. We then chased after the first one ... we fired one or two more torpedoes at that one which missed because he was hurriedly submerging, [and] they dropped across his bow. We all dropped depth charges, and hoped we'd at least frightened him. And then we went back to look to see if there were any survivors of the first one, [but] we didn't find any. But while we were doing that two E-boats came down, and stupidly we fired our remaining torpedoes at them, thinking they were U-boats doing 18 knots [on the surface] but in fact they were E-boats doing 30 knots and we missed.[121]

Chapter Two

Naval Aviation and Aircraft Carriers

Britain was a pioneer and leader in the field of naval aviation during the early part of the twentieth century. The employment of aircraft on board the protected cruiser HMS *Hermes* during the Royal Navy's 1913 Naval Manoeuvres, for example, 'bore witness to the fact that virtually all the basic ingredients of carrier-borne operations and equipment, albeit in embryonic form, had been identified' prior to the First World War.[1] By 1915 seaplanes were being used for spotting and reconnaissance during naval bombardments of land targets, although these had to be launched from ships too slow to stay on station with the Fleet, and so were best suited to independent operations such as these. In November that year Flight Sub-Lieutenant Towler successfully took off from HMS *Vindex* in his Bristol Scout, and this paved the way for future use of wheeled aircraft from ships, better suited than seaplanes to roles such as intercepting airships because they did not have drag-inducing floats.

In August 1917 Squadron Commander E.H. Dunning DSC of the Royal Naval Air Service (RNAS) bravely became the first man to successfully land an aircraft (a Sopwith Pup) on a moving ship (HMS *Furious*), although he was killed not long afterwards attempting the same feat. By the end of the First World War the RN had also demonstrated the viability of the modern-looking aircraft carrier with its characteristic flat top when in December 1917 HMS *Argus* was launched 'with an unobstructed, full-length flight deck'.[2] A converted liner, *Argus* was too slow to accompany the battle fleet but served in a useful training role, and during the Second World War saw action with the Mediterranean and Home Fleets, particularly in trade protection, as a training carrier and for ferrying aircraft, before ending her days in reserve as an accommodation ship during 1944–1945 moored at Chatham. According to George Melly, who served as an HO sailor, in this role 'the *Argus* ... was a den of skivers, misfits and lunatics, a floating, tethered thieves' kitchen', presided over by a captain who was an elderly lieutenant, a 'scrawny religious maniac risen from the ranks'.[3]

After the First World War aircraft carriers continued to be built, progressing from conversions of the 1920s to the purpose-built *Ark Royal* launched in 1937, and the Illustrious class fleet carriers of the 1936–1939 programmes. During the war the Implacable and Colossus class carriers were also produced, the latter proving particularly effective as light fleet carriers with the RN post-war. Notably, HMS *Ark Royal* acquired a legendary status within the navy, until in November 1941 she was torpedoed by *U-81* off Gibraltar, leading to catastrophic flooding that eventually sank her. Seaman Stanley Reynolds served aboard HMS *Ark Royal* in the Mediterranean during 1940–1941, before subsequently being drafted to the destroyer HMS *Petard*, and experiencing further action in the Mediterranean, Atlantic and Indian Oceans. He contrasted the sea-going characteristics of these two very different types of vessel:

> It was very hard compared to being on a carrier. The carrier was more like a hotel compared with the destroyer, and the different movements in the *Petard*, the destroyer, than the carrier. In rough seas there was more being thrown about in the destroyer, movements, turning port to starboard, than there would be on the carrier, which was more graceful on her turns.[4]

Although the RN had aircraft carriers, for the best part of the inter-war period the operation of naval aircraft was governed by a messy compromise between the Admiralty and the Air Ministry. This 'only worked at all thanks to the fundamental goodwill and common sense that prevailed in both services', and resulted from the Admiralty effectively giving up control of naval aviation in 1918 when the RNAS became part of the newly established RAF. A corollary of this was that it hindered the development of suitably designed aircraft, especially 'for offensive and defensive work from carriers' as although the Admiralty provided the funds and specification, the Air Ministry was responsible for design and production at a time when it was already hard pressed meeting the demand for land-based aircraft. Likewise, the situation hindered the development of a dedicated, experienced body of naval aviators. Captain Stephen Roskill, summing up the position extant during 1918–1937, stated, 'the Admiralty was thus in the anomalous position of being responsible for the design and construction of aircraft carriers, but was dependent on another department for the aircraft which would work from them, and on another service to provide a proportion of the aircrews who flew on and off their decks'.[5]

Ultimately during the war FAA personnel experienced a variety of bases and aircraft carriers, and operated a range of aircraft types, some of which proved more popular and effective than others, not least because until modern American aircraft became available under Lend-Lease, naval aircrews had to use obsolescent designs or those that had been adapted from land-based aircraft. The FAA also became engaged in a variety of theatres, ranging from flying patrols in the gruelling, bitter Atlantic and Arctic seas, to mounting carrier-borne operations against a determined Japanese enemy in the sweltering heat of the Far East.

Life on Aircraft Carriers

Aircraft carriers are effectively floating airfields. This presented their designers and builders with a distinctive challenge. 'On a hull possessing most normal warship features, provision must be made for the operation and maintenance of several squadrons of aircraft' which, had they been operated ashore, 'would require an airfield extending over several square miles with air control, hangar, maintenance shops, petrol stowage, bomb dumps, barrack blocks and messes, transport and runways thousands of feet in length. In the carrier this had to be compacted into a ship about 800 feet long with a flight deck area of less than two acres.'[6] Typically, on the flight deck there would be arrestor wires for helping to decelerate an aircraft to a standstill. By 1944 a fleet carrier had nine of these, 'designed to stop an aircraft of up to 20,000 pounds in weight at a speed of up to 60 knots'.[7] Additionally, there were large nets that officialdom termed safety barriers, although most crews appreciated that these were effectively crash barriers. These were raised during landings to stop any wayward aircraft that had missed the arrestor wires, and lowered again to enable aircraft to clear the area. Many carriers also had an accelerator or catapult to help launch aircraft, depending on wind conditions.

A pilot with 890 Naval Air Squadron (NAS) flying from the Attacker class HMS *Battler* found that:

> We had to learn how to judge our approach to the deck to land ideally within fifteen seconds after the aircraft in front of us [then] taxi fast forward over the lowered crash barrier seconds before the pilot behind cut his throttle to catch one of the arrestor wires ... If he missed all the wires ... it would be catastrophic if the crash barrier had not come up again in time to prevent him crashing into the aircraft already landed. It was all split second timing and co-ordination between pilots and the crewmen and engineers of the flight deck.[8]

On some carriers there was even a 'goofers' gallery', with a view over the flight deck; here, as wartime naval pilot Norman Hanson outlined, off-duty officers and ratings would muster to watch 'pilots dicing with death' and this was 'no exaggeration', given the hazards associated with a deck landing.[9]

Given their distinctive role, some personnel developed a particular affinity with their carrier. HMS *Argus* was sometimes known as the 'Flat Iron' owing to her appearance, with her distinctive 470-foot flight deck on top of her hull. She was described by George Amyes, an FAA air mechanic who served on her in the Atlantic early in the war as:

> a chunky little ship, almost box-like, and that was where she got her [other] nickname from, 'The Ditty Box', just like a huge ditty box floating on top of the water. [A ditty box was a lockable box/container in which a sailor kept his most valuable and/or unusual possessions.] The canteen messing on there was really fun, that was where the individual mess could have been anything from a dozen to forty people and had to cater for themselves. They were allowed a certain amount of cash that they could spend but that cash was to be spent inside the ship. And it was all on paper. It wasn't actually money that changed hands. They drew their stores from the purser's mess, and did their own catering feeding each other. If you spent more than your allowance it was docked off your pay. If you were more frugal and you saved a little bit, then you got that back as a bonus on pay day.[10]

During 1940–1941, Amyes explained, it was *Argus's* job to ferry aircraft from 'England to Gibraltar … a club run, a regular trip, so regular that we almost dug a groove in the water way. I was not attached to a squadron at the time. I was attached to the ship's company as aircraft handling party. We took on the aircraft in England, lifted them by crane onto the *Argus*, packed them down into the lower deck with their wings folded, and then went out to Gibraltar and did the whole thing in reverse.'[11]

Similarly, HMS *Eagle*, launched in 1918, was another conversion, this time of an ex-Chilean battleship, and was noteworthy owing to being built with an island superstructure and double hangar. At the outbreak of war she was serving in the Indian Ocean, escorting troop convoys and mounting anti-raider sweeps, before moving to the Mediterranean and then the Atlantic, mainly covering convoys, before being sunk during Operation Pedestal, supplying aircraft reinforcements to Malta on 11 August 1942.[12] As an Air Mechanic (O) – ordnance mechanic – with the FAA, Robert Cosh was serving on her during what proved to be her last voyage. It was 'very crowded. Mess decks were shared, and there was no room to sling a hammock in the recognised areas. I slept the first night in the hangar, and lay there in wonder. Rats were trotting along the steel girders at the deck heads … the bread was infested with insects.'[13] Similarly, one youthful FAA pilot drafted to *Eagle* experienced pretty basic conditions. Instead of being allowed to share a cabin, together with another officer he used the Captain's secretary's office. 'We each had a camp bed on the floor and the use of a small desk and two chairs for our clothes. Otherwise we lived out of our kitbags. There were no chests of drawers, wash basins, fans, wardrobes, mirrors or such luxuries.'[14]

HMS *Courageous, Glorious* and *Furious* were all conversions of battlecruisers and all were launched during the 1920s. They generally proved successful, and crucially 'enabled the RN to experiment in the use of airpower at sea' during the inter-war period, an area in which the British lagged behind other leading naval powers, notably America and Japan.[15] All three soldiered on into the Second World War until *Courageous* was sunk by U-29 west of Ireland on 17 September 1939, and *Glorious* was sunk by gunfire from German warships west of Narvik, Norway, on 8 June 1940. *Furious* remained with the Home Fleet throughout 1939–1944, before being placed in reserve 1944–1945. Commander 'Mike' Crosley was stationed aboard her for a period with 880 NAS, and vividly recalled being shown an antiquated but effective piece of machinery by the Officer-in-Charge of the flight deck machinery, which:

> worked the aeroplane-shaped lifts, the aerials and arrester wires by driving a hydraulic pump. It was a double-expansion, double/acting, horizontal steam engine. It was fascinating to watch this latter-day piece of high quality British workmanship as it turned two huge flywheels almost silently, at 60 times a minute at full throttle, with its mahogany-lagged cylinders, drip-feed lubrication and its brightly polished gunmetal pistons ...[16]

In contrast, the Illustrious class carriers launched in the late 1930s and early 1940s had armoured hangars, a design feature that proved especially bene-ficial when they were deployed to the Far East and faced Kamikaze attacks. This included making 'the deck 3ins thick which would stop 500lb bombs from dive bombers or similar bombs from level-flying aircraft at over 7,000 feet. The sides were 4.5ins thick and would resist shellfire beyond 7,000 yds.' However, carrying armour came at a cost as these carriers could only field thirty-three aircraft compared with a nominal sixty on *Ark Royal*.[17]

Like battleships, these were big ships, all well over 20,000 tons and with complements of over 1,000 men. John Brown, a supply assistant in the accountancy branch, remembered his first encounter with HMS *Formidable*: 'The sight was forbidding. I walked gingerly over the brow, complete with hammock, kit bag, etc., and found myself in a labyrinth. I was bewildered ... I was sure I would never find my way round the ship, a feeling I had for a fortnight.'[18] Similarly, as a youthful observer with the FAA Gordon Wallace was posted to 831 NAS aboard HMS *Indomitable* in September 1941. He was feeling nervous and, looking out of a rain-splattered train window at the greyish expanse of the Clyde, suddenly he 'saw the silhouette of a large aircraft carrier anchored about half a mile off shore, camouflaged in grey and blue, it dwarfed all shipping nearby. My anxiety increased.'[19]

Another naval aviator who experienced HMS *Indomitable* in the Far East highlighted a flaw common with many RN vessels operating in the tropics, for which they were not designed, namely, 'the heat on board was ... difficult to bear' with no 'air conditioning or anything of that sort. Fresh water for drinking and for showers too was in short supply' and most personnel suffered 'from prickly heat, which could drive a man dotty with its irritation but, at least, in my opinion was not as bad as the mosquitoes ashore'.[20] On the other hand, conditions could still be pretty good, especially for officers. Gordon Wallace, who spent some of his war aboard HMS *Indomitable*, commented, 'apart from flying, life was just a round of sleeping and eating'. This included first class food, even when the cook resorted to 'deep fried rice balls' when potatoes were short. 'There were always prunes for breakfast and 'an everlasting supply of pickled walnuts' with lunch, while in the bar his taste 'shifted from dry sherry to crème-de-menthe frappe or whisky'. However, socialising tended to be confined to within squadrons, and between pilots and their observers, rather than mixing with members of the ship's company or other FAA personnel.[21]

Despite their size, aircraft carriers could also be crowded environments, depending on operational circumstances. When HMS *Implacable* set sail for Norway in late 1944, most of her crew expected to soon be bound for the Far East. She had on board almost double the number of aircraft she'd originally been designed to operate, and 500 extra crewmen. Many of the ratings from the extra squadrons 'had to take pot luck with the left-over messdecks' or 'sling their hammocks in the passageways', which was not conducive to getting much rest with other crew members rushing about, and 'junior officers had to treble up'.[22]

Conversely, sometimes measures were taken to improve conditions, even if accommodation remained basic. Charles Hawthorn trained as a telegraphist/air-gunner (TAG) and saw action with 810 NAS flying from HMS *Illustrious* in the Indian Ocean during 1942. The TAG's quarters were:

so low down in the ship, we were underneath the capstan machinery flat, that it was jokingly said that if we were two foot lower down we could have claimed submariners pay ... At Madagascar the hierarchy suddenly realised that TAGs had no facilities for having any food, so that if you were out on a dawn anti-submarine patrol or out bombing early, and they got back after 8 am, there was no breakfast for them. So they opened up, and we were allowed to go into the wardroom [despite not being commissioned officers] where they had a buffet, so each time you landed you could have coffee or tea or sandwiches.[23]

As well as accommodation, below decks in an aircraft carrier was typically dominated by large hangars, plus the necessary workshops, storage areas and offices for the administration of the ship and smooth running of the air department side. As a young rating working in the clothing stores accounts on HMS *Formidable*, John Brown found this could lead to rackets being established. One he encountered entailed the following process: 'items would be returned as unserviceable and renewable without charge to accounts. So you had articles which could then be sold without appearing in the accounts ... I was offered £5 to do this job per month [fill in the appropriate documentation etc.]. I refused, and was not asked again to prepare it.[24]

One Air Mechanic (Electrical), who served on a number of escort carriers during 1942–1946 in Home Waters and the Atlantic, observed that during operations: 'When they were flying some of us were [always] up on the top or ready for emergency work ... Anything serious that needed to be done would be done down below in the hangar ... The worst thing was crashing down too hard on the flight deck and hitting the arrester hook back into place and of course they sailed straight on into the arrestor wire and smashed the propeller up.'[25]

Escort carriers, as the designation implies, were intended to accompany convoys and provide a degree of aerial protection, particularly against the long-range Focke-Wulf Condor, as one of the challenges facing Britain from mid-1940 was dealing with the threat to merchant shipping that sailed within reach of German air bases along the European coastline. They were smaller than fleet carriers, and correspondingly operated fewer aircraft. Those in the Archer class, for example, had 'a wooden flight deck 442 feet long, a tonnage of 8,200 and a speed of 16 knots. They carried an air group of 15.' These were 'followed by the eight ships of the Attacker class, which entered service in 1942–1943' and were bigger at 11,420 tons.[26]

Robert Cosh served on one of these, HMS *Stalker*. Affectionately known as 'Spam Cans', they were not 'ships as we knew them but floating ditty boxes, welded together and even more cramped and uncomfortable than usual, with bulkheads that wouldn't stand a good whack from a liberty boat without denting'. More worryingly, 'loaded with aircraft, ammunition, TNT and thousands of gallons of fuel oil, they were floating bombs', although crews gave scant heed to that at the time owing to being too busy.[27] Another air mechanic, who served on the Archer class HMS *Biter* and Ruler class HMS *Ravager* and HMS *Trumpeter*, noted that on these escort carriers space was at a premium. 'Bunks about 18 inches apart, I didn't like that at all, so always went upstairs in the hangar with a hammock, which was a lot more comfortable, and you were above the water line.'[28]

Before becoming a legendary test pilot, Captain Eric 'Winkle' Brown served with 802 NAS aboard HMS *Audacity*, one of the earliest escort carriers, 'a most extraordinary ship ... The "bridge" was simply a little metal tray stuck on the ship's side level with the flight deck on the starboard side about a quarter of the way back from the bows.'[29] Commissioned in June 1941, she was a conversion of the *Hannover*, a cargo ship captured in the West Indies. 'Her superstructure, funnel and masts were stripped off, her uptake diverted to discharge horizontally, and two arrester wires aft, a safety wire amidships and a crash barrier forward were installed on the flight deck.'[30] There was no hangar or lift, so *Audacity*'s aircraft were permanently kept exposed to the elements on the flight deck, parked forward near the bows on landing, and right aft for taking off. Initially, as Captain Brown recalled, the ship's company 'were half Royal Navy, half Merchant Service. All the squadron personnel were of course RN as well as deck officers and key technicians. Most of the seamen and all engine room staff were Merchant Navy men. It threatened to be an impossible mixture, oil and water ...'[31]

At nearly 23 years old, John Wellham was promoted acting lieutenant commander and appointed to the Archer class carrier HMS *Biter* in 1942 as Commander of Flying. (*Biter* was another conversion from a merchant ship.)

Now I had only vaguely heard of an escort carrier, I knew nothing about it, I hadn't been on the carriers as I had been on *Eagle*, and thought 'this is great, I haven't a clue how you run this sort of thing, have I?' However, I joined *Biter*, discovered what she was, and everything else, and fortunately, my predecessor was still there for a few days, and gave me a run over the thing, passed the bumph on and so on of the ship, and then I discovered to my alarm that *Biter* was the sister ship of *Dasher*, which was blown up and sunk in the Firth of Clyde, and the Captain had been Captain of *Dasher*, which had repercussions afterwards. [*Dasher* was sunk by a petrol explosion during aircraft refuelling in March 1943.] However, we then went out, we did some exercises in *Biter* in the Firth of Clyde, deck landing training for people. I discovered that everything worked extremely well, and I quickly learned to get my own ideas, changed a number of things, altered some things, but found I seemed to be able to do the job all right.[32]

During 1943–1944 a number of American-built escort carriers dubbed CVEs entered RN service. Those of the Ruler class were 11,420 tons, had a maximum speed of 17 knots and could carry up to twenty-four aircraft. These proved versatile, being employed on a variety of other operations as well as convoy escort. Later in his wartime career John Wellham was posted to one of these, HMS *Empress*, which served with the British Eastern and Pacific Fleets. Unlike Robert Cosh, he was impressed with this type of ship. She 'was virtually a miniature aircraft carrier ... the Americans I must admit had made a very good job of that. Apart from the fact that we had to have them anglicised [adapted to British requirements and standards], which they did for a month, and then we had to have them made safe under British rules, another month before they were operational ... so we did that, and we ended up with the *Empress*, where we had Avengers and Hellcats ... a marvellous aeroplane, and after doing a bit of waffling around doing some pranks and things in this country, we went out to the Far East.'[33]

Merchant Aircraft Carriers (MACs) were a similar concept to HMS *Audacity*. During 1942 it was decided to convert six grain ships, which did not have to load their cargo vertically so a flight deck could be placed on top of them. They were provided with a hanger 142 feet long, a single lift and four arrester wires, but no barrier or catapult. This was followed by conversions to a number of tankers, so that they too could fly a limited number of Swordfish aircraft. The MAC ships arrived too late to play a decisive role in the Battle of the Atlantic, but still escorted over 200 convoys and mounted 4,174 sorties.[34] They were full-scale merchant ships, and operated as such, with the addition of the air element.

According to John Shoebridge, a pilot with 836 NAS, relations between the RN personnel and Merchant Navy crews on MAC ships were 'harmonious'. The RN personnel would eat with MN officers, and enjoy drinks and playing bridge in the smoke room when off duty, as there was no ward room. Other off-duty activities included holding debates, putting on plays and games of deck hockey. Notably, he fondly remembered his 'riotous 21st birthday celebrations in the mid-Atlantic', culminating in 'dancing a conga on deck'.[35] Additionally, Shoebridge outlined something of the organisation he experienced while flying from MAC ships, and how they operated in practice:

'B' Flight was the first real routine flight that was formed. Now, a flight on grain ships would consist of four pilots, four observers, four air gunner/wireless operators [AG/WOP], four Swordfish [aircraft] ... There would be a petty officer in charge of sixteen ground crew, who'd maintain the aircraft on the ship. Grain ships had four aircraft and a hangar [whereas] tankers had three aircraft and no hangar, and they remained on the flight deck all the time ... The tanker had a safety barrier and three aircraft but no hangar, so when the aircraft landed on, the two aircraft had to be ahead of the barrier. Then the barrier would be lowered down and they'd all be pushed back again, and one would take off. [In contrast] the grain ships had a hangar but no barrier, so one aircraft would land and had to be stuck down first, and aircraft were in the hangar at all times [except when flying].[36]

Another emergency measure, introduced in the spring of 1941 before escort carriers became widely available, were the CAM ships – Catapult Armed Merchantmen – merchant ships converted to launch a single expendable Hurricane fighter in an effort to provide convoys with aerial protection. This required a particular mind-set. As the Official Historian Captain Stephen Roskill expounded, 'the pilots knew that, once they had been catapulted off, their patrol would probably end by a parachute descent into the sea, hoping to be picked up by a surface escort vessel. Their sorties demanded a cold-blooded gallantry.'[37]

Henry Gostelow joined the RNR in early 1939, saw action as a seaman aboard the anti-aircraft ship HMS *Curacoa*, and after being commissioned trained as a Fighter Direction Officer in 1941, before moving to the Merchant Ship Fighter Unit at RAF Speke, Liverpool. He was then drafted to the CAM ships *Empire Franklin* on Atlantic convoys and later *Empire Morn* on Russian/Arctic convoy duty. Regarding the Atlantic, he explained how CAM ships 'were used to much better advantage because the Focke-Wulfs, ... they recognised that they couldn't possibly cope with a Hurricane fighter and they never tried to bomb a North Atlantic convoy plying between Halifax and the UK ever again. Churchill himself described this as a positive negative unit. Positive in that no ships had been lost through aerial attacks on convoys by Condors, and negative in that we hadn't shot any of them down.'[38]

On Arctic convoy PQ 18 *Empire Morn* found that she was the only ship available able to offer any form of aerial protection en route to Archangel, because the aircraft carrier that had been escorting them left to join a homeward-bound convoy. Eventually the moment came when it was deemed necessary to launch their single Hurricane:

we were attacked, I think it was by fifteen Heinkels from astern, and we launched Flying Officer Jack Burr (RAF) in the Hurricane and he fired off forward because you had to have the ship's speed into the wind to assist him with his take-off from the catapult. And as he took off all ships [in the convoy] having seen the flashes [from the rocket-propelled catapult] thought a ship had been hit, so they all fired at us. And so he said: 'Will you stop these bastards firing at me!' And I thought I didn't know how to do that because we were getting hammered on our ship of course. Anyway he got round again, he couldn't fail to see the target, and it came in, and unfortunately the whole flight launched their torpedoes before he got to them. And he shot at least one down, probably two ... and the torpedoes came towards us but fortunately for us they were more or less spent by the time they got to us, and we were able to avoid them. Then he orbited the convoy for a while and there were no further radar reports of aircraft in our vicinity so I said: 'What are you going to try to do, Jack?' He said: 'I think I'll make for Archangel' ... which was about 240 miles away. And of course he only had a magnetic compass and we were virtually over the magnetic North Pole or very close to it, and variation in those circumstances is a very difficult thing to calculate, so I went down to the chart room and gave him a vector of 180 I think. And I came back up and gave him that because he was getting out of range, he was on his way by this time, going out of R/T range, and I thought I'd better just check it and a better course would be 170. And I gave him 170 and he came out of a cloud right over the airfield, so I was a bit lucky there. Anyway, saved the aeroplane and saved his life perhaps, because it was freezing cold by this time.[39]

Impressions of their Aircraft

Towards the end of the war the Admiralty examined the feasibility of helicopters, as under Lend-Lease America supplied Britain with forty-five Sikorsky R-4 B helicopters (known to the British as the Hoverfly 1), and most of these went to the RN.[40] However, for the bulk of the war the FAA was reliant on two types of aircraft: float planes and flying boats able to operate from the water, and fixed winged aircraft capable of flying from an aircraft carrier. Notably, the former category included the Supermarine Walrus, 'a biplane with a hull for landing in the water, an engine mounted well above the fuselage to keep it clear of the sea, and a "pusher" layout in which the engine was ahead of the propeller'. It had a retractable undercarriage as well, so was technically an amphibian as it could be landed like a conventional aircraft, or operated from water as necessary. With a maximum speed of 135mph, and good handling characteristics, it proved popular with crews, who affectionately dubbed it the 'Shagbat'. There was a crew of three: the pilot sat in an 'angular enclosed cockpit', while the observer's position was deep within the fuselage, but he also had access to a forward-firing machine gun mounted ahead of the pilot; a telegraphist sat behind the observer with a rear-firing machine gun aft in the fuselage. During 1939–1944 the FAA used the Walrus to mount coastal patrols in West Africa looking for German commerce raiders, and it equipped several battleships, battlecruisers and cruisers, where it was operated via catapult flights, and employed 'for ship-to-shore communication flights, spotting for its parent ship's guns, and in an attack role using its capacity to carry 760lb (345kg) of bombs or depth charges on underwing racks'.[41]

In contrast, fixed wing aircraft, used for deck landings and take-offs, proved more of a mixed bag. While some designs used by the FAA were rugged and reliable, others were rather less so. The antiquated-looking Fairey Swordfish biplane, for example, proved effective and was purposely designed as a reconnaissance and torpedo/bomber aircraft. As such it had the cockpit raised to give the pilot a better view during deck landings. Aircraft that were adaptations from land-based designs, such as the Seafire (a naval version of the famous Supermarine Spitfire), did not enjoy such advantages. As Commander Crosley explained, with the Seafire 'the naval pilot's solution to the poor view over the nose was to approach in a steady, left-hand turn, all the way down to the deck. With hood open, locked in position by half unlatching the small side door, with goggles on, with the head to one side and seat raised, it was possible to see part of the flight deck and the batsmen through the haze of the port engine exhaust.' Even then the situation could be complicated in heavy rain or if the sun was at a low angle and reflecting off the sea, making proper sighting of the carrier very difficult, and liable to lead 'to a heavy arrival, an off-centre, or one-wheel, yawed arrival, or a hasty "go round again"'.[42]

Another challenge in the lead-up to the war was that some designs of naval aircraft seemed somewhat ungainly, with a wide fuselage, owing to the requirement to have a full-sized chart table for the observer similar to those employed on ships for navigation. Typically, they were also slow, often powered by the same engine as would be suitable in a single-seat fighter, yet they had to carry a pilot, observer and TAG. Whether multi-seaters or single-seat fighters, naval aircraft had also to have foldable wings, so they could be stowed on a carrier successfully. There were various ways that this was achieved, such as folding upwards or twisting and folding backwards, as on many American designs, but this was an added complication to the design process.

As indicated above, the development of naval aircraft suffered owing to the awkward relationship between the Admiralty and the Air Ministry during the inter-war years. An upshot of this was that the FAA had often to rely on obsolescent designs. One of the aircraft that John Wellham encountered in his naval service, while acting as a pilot for trainee observers, was the

Blackburn Shark, a biplane of 1930s vintage with a top speed of 150mph, intended as torpedo bomber/reconnaissance aircraft.

> it was a perfectly chronic aeroplane; it was nothing like as good as the Swordfish [its replacement]. It looked neater, but its great advantage was that it had a canopy so it kept you warmer in the British weather, but otherwise it was frightful, and I think [I spent] most of my time flying around the country trying to collect spares for the Sharks, because they kept falling to pieces, you see. Well, they flew all right provided you didn't try to make them do anything but fly straight and level ... it was poorly designed, but I think one must give a certain amount of credit to both Fairey and Blackburn [aircraft manufacturers] because of the difficulties they were presented with. The Admiralty knew absolutely nothing about flying and they gave impossible specifications. I mean, you can't design an aircraft which is a cross between a torpedo-bomber, a dive-bomber, flying over the sea long range, reliability, everything, you can't get that in one aeroplane, and so they produced things like the Shark. It was the dog's breakfast.[43]

By comparison most aircrew had a much more favourable opinion of the Swordfish, a two/three seat torpedo-bomber/reconnaissance biplane, which although approaching obsolescence by 1939, gave admirable service throughout the war. One former pilot commented: 'It was an aircraft with no vices whatsoever, I think the only one ever built. No vices. It was quite incredible. I mean, you couldn't make it spin without trying. Also quite illegally you could do aerobatics with it. I've got as far as doing a loop and a roll off the top, I think we did that. Completely illegal, one wasn't supposed to do it. But it was a remarkably fine aircraft to fly. That's why it was never taken as a trainer. It was never a trainer because it had no vices, so you couldn't tell whether the chap was any good or not, you know, but that was the principle.' Its slow speed (138mph or 128mph in seaplane configuration) was a disadvantage compared with most contemporary aircraft, 'but not always, because when people started getting unfriendly and shooting at us, they nearly always shot in front of a Swordfish ... Because they didn't calculate, particularly I think loaded with torpedoes and whatever else, and having dived steeply onto the water to attack them, they just didn't believe it could be going that slowly,' which possibly saved a number of aircrew.[44]

Likewise, Vice Admiral Sir Hugh Janvrin, who served as an observer with various naval air squadrons in Home Waters, the Atlantic and the Mediterranean, noted of the Swordfish that: 'Of course it was old ... We had great affection for it, and it was a remarkably versatile aircraft. [It had] the discomforts of an open cockpit and was very cramped, especially for the observer, trying to wield a chart board at the back.'[45] Designed as a replacement for the Swordfish, the Fairey Albacore was faster (maximum speed 161mph) and had an enclosed cockpit but was still generally outclassed by its predecessor. A member of the FAA considered the Albacores appeared 'robust' owing to 'their metal-clad fuselages' when compared to 'the fabric-covered Swordfish', plus they had 'lovely Perspex-covered cockpits with the luxury of a door for entry into the observer's domain'. Yet just like the Swordfish, they were slow biplanes and were 'sitting ducks to an enemy fighter'.[46]

The Fairey Barracuda was a monoplane designed to replace the Swordfish and Albacore as a three-seat torpedo/dive-bomber. The Mk II, the main production variant, entered service in 1943, with eventually over 1,600 being built. Crews converting to it 'must have thought their new mount an extremely complicated machine. It was at least more streamlined than its predecessors, although with landing gear down and full radar array its appearance was distinctly odd.'[47] According to Gordon Wallace, 'it was impressive and just missed being a good-looking aircraft by having a strut braced, high mounted tail-plane', although importantly from his perspective, the observer's position 'under the long Perspex canopy was everything one could desire'.[48] It suffered from being overweight, particularly when additional equipment was added that was not part of the original specification, and the airframe was strengthened, leading to a poorer performance than intended. One pilot complained that it had an 'in-line engine and was underpowered, so it was bit of a wash-out', especially when flying in the tropics. Moreover, it seemed that 'bits were put on as an afterthought' and he reckoned 'you didn't stand much chance' in one if you had to ditch in the sea.[49]

By comparison, the American-built Grumman Avenger was a well-designed torpedo-bomber, notably used by the FAA in the Far East during 1944–1945. It was:

> so much more comfortable and powerful. It had a radial engine and it felt totally different to the Barracuda. It was a nice aircraft to fly. They were second-hand planes from the Americans. The model was the TBF, whereas the Americans had the more powerful TBMs and occasionally while out in the Pacific they'd come and formate on you with their gunmetal blue, cheekily ... The Avenger looked like a flying beer bottle. It was fat and had a conventional tail as opposed to the Barracuda which had a high-level tail. It was a much better, more serviceable, very tough aircraft. You had a chance with it if you were to come down [in water], it would float for a bit ...[50]

The Blackburn Skua which entered service in the late 1930s had the distinction of being the first operational monoplane with the FAA but again suffered limitations owing to attempting to combine the functions of a fighter and dive-bomber in the one airframe. Similarly, a development from it, the Blackburn Roc, suffered numerous flaws, notably a slow maximum speed, and tried unsuccessfully to marry a power-driven four-gun turret with a fighter intended for naval deployment.

To protect bombers on long-range operations, the Admiralty considered that a two-seat fighter with an observer was necessary. The Fairey Fulmar, adapted from a light bomber, was the result, and it saw service in all theatres during the war, although by early 1945 was being replaced by the Firefly. According to one FAA pilot, the Fulmar was 'too awkward compared with say [an American] Hellcat, which was easier to deck land'.[51] Douglas Parker, who commanded 1842 NAS on HMS *Formidable* with the British Pacific Fleet (BPF) during 1944–1945, highlighted its good points, as well as noting deficiencies with the design:

> The Fulmar, good aircraft though it was, could barely catch several of the aircraft raised against us unless one had a height advantage and could build up some speed before getting on the tail of the enemy. The chances of shooting him down were pretty slight. [However] the Fulmar was a delightful aircraft, absolutely free of vice, a gentleman's aircraft to fly. Unfortunately it needed at least another 1,000 horsepower and better aerodynamic characteristics to get the performance required. But it could absorb quite a deal of punishment and was a comparatively easy aircraft to deck land, and was very, very reliable.[52]

The FAA also deployed a number of British- and American-manufactured single-seat fighters, and this was an area that saw huge advances in technological sophistication during the 1930s and 1940s. The Sea Gladiator, an adaptation of the Gloster Gladiator biplane flown by the RAF, served in the 1940 Norwegian Campaign and in the Mediterranean, despite being at least 100mph slower than its monoplane fighter adversaries. Similarly, the Sea Hurricane was adapted for naval operations from the land-based Hawker Hurricane, but was a modern monoplane fighter with high performance, maximum speed of 342mph, and four 20mm forward-firing cannon. While operating in the Mediterranean, a pilot based on HMS *Eagle* commented: 'We had no doubt that the Sea Hurricane ... was the master of any Italian aircraft and we hoped that when we had to meet a Ju 88 [Junkers Ju 88] snooper, that we should have the height advantage and be able to catch it up by diving on it.'[53]

The Seafire was another high performance single-seat fighter adapted for carrier operations from a land-based design. It had a top speed of over 350mph, was armed with two 20mm cannon, four .303-in machine guns, and could heft up to 500lbs of bombs. Although an impressive aircraft, it was not without its problems and invariably proved frail as a naval fighter. When Allied forces landed in the Gulf of Salerno in September 1943, around a hundred Seafires were deployed, some even flying from HMS *Unicorn*, a maintenance carrier hurriedly pressed into service. 'With only a light wind blowing and the carriers operating 1,000 yards (915m) apart, conditions for the Seafires were unfavourable and an unusually large number of deck-landing accidents occurred.'[54] Some considered that the Seafire's undercarriage was far too weak for carrier work and, despite its speed, it could not catch low-flying German FW 190 fighter-bombers at Salerno, which was its primary task. However, as Commander Crosley explained, the poor interception rate resulted from 'our radar suffering the "robbing effect" of ground clutter and the ships and thus the aircraft received little or no warning of the low-flying approaches of the FW 190 fighter-bombers by radar'. Put simply, the Germans fully understood that to avoid detection by ship radars they had to keep high ground behind them in-line with their sea-level approach. Another criticism was that the Seafire 'lacked endurance to remain on CAP [Combat Air Patrol] for the necessary two hours in spite of the 45-gallon slipper tank'.[55]

As the war progressed, a number of American-built single-seat fighters were also employed by the FAA, and generally proved popular. The Grumman Wildcat (known as the Martlet to the British) was a fast (300mph), sturdy monoplane. According to Captain Eric 'Winkle' Brown, 'she was blunt-nosed, square-tipped, and looked like an angry bee' but was nonetheless 'a tough, fiery, beautiful little aeroplane', albeit until it was remedied, initially 'there was a very fierce swing on take-off and landing which needed some handling'.[56] It was replaced by the Grumman Hellcat, 1,100 of which were supplied to the British, most seeing action in the Pacific. Again it was a tough aeroplane, and fast: it could reach a speed of 380mph. Pilot Norman Hanson 'was certainly enamoured of it', with its 'roomy and efficiently laid out cockpit' and overall good performance, plus it was relatively easy to land, owing to 'its superior visibility and better stall characteristics' when compared with many other naval fighters.[57]

Another American aircraft that saw action with the FAA, notably in the Pacific, was the large Chance-Vought Corsair with its distinctive inverted gull wing to allow for a shorter undercarriage, and a maximum speed of over 400mph. 'It was a rugged machine which could take any amount of punishment on the flight-deck … The cockpit was meticulously arranged with all dials readily visible and every lever and switch comfortably and conveniently to hand, without any need to search or grope.'[58] However, the Mark 1 had one significant flaw, in that the undercarriage had 'built-in bounce' leading to the aircraft behaving 'like a jack rabbit. If the pilot didn't catch a wire on his first contact with the deck, the odds were that he would finish up in the barrier.' Some 'were burned to death', others 'thrown over the side', while 'others didn't need even an aspirin. It was all a matter of luck.'[59]

Geoffrey Hyde served with 898, 790 and 1770 NAS, before training as a test pilot and eventually working as a test and maintenance pilot with No. 1 Transportable Aircraft and Maintenance Yard in Brisbane, Australia, in 1945–1946. Based on his experience, he made some telling observations about the relative merits and drawbacks of British and American naval aircraft:

> They had nothing like the Spitfire or Hurricane. [Theirs] were very robust. The USN were streets ahead of us in carrier work. They had aircraft that could bang on the deck, and were very robust. Towards the end of my career when I was testing Seafires and Corsairs they were so different. The Seafire is a wonderful plane, the Rolls-Royce engine never let you down. The Pratt and Whitney would – the only engine failures I ever had were in American planes.[60]

Training Aircrew and Trade Training

Clearly, for the FAA to function effectively, it needed not only trained pilots and aircrew but the necessary administrative and support staff to keep those men flying. Air Mechanic George Amyes grew up in Hull and worked in the grocery trade before enlisting in the RN in 1939. After basic training, he was sent to HMS *Kestrel* at Worthy Down near Winchester, a RN air station that had been taken over from the RAF.

> They really worked us ... They taught us the basic elements of using tools, cutting tools such as chisels and drills, fine tools, sanders and emeries, and technical tools such as micrometers ... We began to get our designations as: Air Mechanic Second Class; Air Mechanic First Class; Air Mechanic Engine Branch; or Air Frame Branch; or Electrical Branch. We were beginning to get segregated and that was really hard work because apart from the fact that we were doing the work in the workshops during the day, we also had to go to night school to learn basic arithmetic, the values of metals and various other attributes. On top of that we had sentry duties around the camp.[61]

Subsequently, Amyes was drafted to HMS *Condor*, an airfield at Arbroath in Scotland, where he worked on real aircraft for the first time, notably the

Albacore with a Taurus engine that was larger and more powerful than anything he'd previously encountered.

Likewise, after basic training most aircrew underwent a process of study as well as learning to handle aircraft and equipment. TAGs were generally recruited from ratings physically fit enough to fly but deemed to lack the necessary education to become a pilot or observer. At HMS *Kestrel* they were taught gunnery, 'mostly with single machine guns on flexible mounts in the rear cockpit', and fired at a drogue towed by another aircraft, and worked on simulators. They also learnt the telegraphist part of their designation with an accent on Morse code, 'radio telephony was not reliable at long ranges'.[62]

At No. 2 Observer School at HMS *Condor*, Gordon Wallace from Heddon-on-the-Wall, Northumberland, initially found more time was spent in the classroom than in the air. 'It had never occurred to me to wonder how one set off from an aircraft carrier, flew in all directions, blown by unforeseen winds, and arrived back to whatever spot in the ocean the carrier might have sailed to in the meantime.' Navigation was central to the observer's role in an aircraft, and it was not straightforward in the early 1940s 'without the assistance of radio beacons and radar, and continually blasted by the cold air and noise which numbed the fingers and dulled the brain'' Additionally, observers had to be able to operate the wireless telegraphy W/T or radio set, and the relationship with pilots, who had been posted on training duties, could be awkward, as invariably these considered it a bore and had been 'either passed over for operational flying or [were] too old for it'.[63]

Captain Eric 'Winkle' Brown learnt to fly with the pre-war RAF before transferring to the FAA. At HMS *St Vincent*, Gosport, he was inducted into the RN before he and his draft were classified as potential fighter or torpedo-bomber pilots. 'The older and steadier ones went for bombers, the suicidal types like me for fighters.'[64] Another naval pilot who underwent a similar process with RAF instructors recalled, 'I have no knowledge on what basis the selection was made or who made it' but he was mightily relieved 'for whatever reason' to have been 'considered ... suitable to be a fighter pilot'.[65]

Similarly, John Wellham left the Island of Bute in the Western Highlands of Scotland aged 17 in 1936, and was commissioned into the RAF before transferring to the FAA two years later, and becoming a naval officer and pilot with war on the horizon. His pre-war flying experience was on biplanes of the period, predominantly the Hawker Hind light bomber with 50 Squadron at RAF Waddington, near Lincoln. On joining the navy:

> there was a considerable amount of training actually. The first thing they
> did which really caused a lot of amusement, we were all sent down to

Gosport, the torpedo training unit, and they hadn't a clue about us, they'd never heard of us before, you see. So they didn't know anything about our experience at all so they took us up in a Swordfish and said that's how you fly it and so that just took about 20 minutes, easiest aircraft in the world to fly. We then flew round a bit and then they said, right we'll teach you to formation fly, you see, and they then took us off in formation to show us how to do it and said now all right, four of you go up and be very careful, don't get too close, and we looked at each other and said look we've to get them on the right frequency here. So we went up and disappeared down to one of the Martello towers, got into absolutely close formation tight together and then with a roar about 50 feet across the middle of Gosport, you see, all the trimmings and tricks, all of us having been in fighter or light bomber squadrons and we'd been doing aerobatics in formation, and so the instructors sat back and said oh dear we've got this a bit wrong haven't we? So we said, right, what we want to do is we want to learn how to drop torpedoes ... how to be catapulted ... Well after that we want to go into ships and we want some naval people to come along and tell us about the navy so that we're not walking along like a lot of clots not knowing which is the sharp end, and which is the blunt end of a ship. So we got organized and it became a very good course in the end.[66]

Commander Crosley enlisted in the FAA in 1940, having been allowed to leave the Metropolitan Police, where he was a probationary constable, if he volunteered for the armed forces. As he discovered, learning to fly was a progressive process, lasting around nine months in his case. At No. 24 Elementary Flying Training School (EFTS), Luton, he undertook three months' instruction under the auspices of the RAF on the Miles Master, one of the first monoplane trainers, which proved 'good at getting itself into spins, as it had a vicious wing-drop at the power-on stall'. This was followed by a period at RAF Netheravon near Salisbury, effectively a 'half-way house' in flying training, as it taught trainees to perform 'basic skills in much more powerful and sophisticated aircraft' as well as some navigation, dive-bombing, formation and night flying. Subsequently, at RNAS Yeovilton he went on a three or four month course designed 'to learn to fly, fight and deck land an operational fighter aircraft'. Successful completion of the course led to him being appointed to HMS *Eagle* in late December 1941 as a 'spare fighter pilot'.[67]

Henry Adlam experienced RNAS Yeovilton as well, and noted there was a big difference here compared with his previous RAF instructors. While the training was conducted just as seriously, 'at Yeovilton we were all officers and pilots together and [instructors] were prepared to talk with us on equal terms' and 'as a sprog pilot and midshipman ... there was so much to learn from talking and listening to them'.[68] The temperament of a flying instructor could also impact on his pupils. While training with the RAF earlier in his career, Adlam had an elderly sergeant instructor who disliked aerobatics, and only allowed him limited practice of a loop and a roll. Years later he confessed: 'That lack of instruction stayed with me all my life.'[69]

Many other naval pilots trained in Canada or in America under the Towers Scheme orchestrated by the USN. Many of the American instructors were very good. At Pensacola, Norman Hanson recorded his instructor was 'quiet, reserved and gentlemanly', all agreeable characteristics, and in the air only spoke when 'strictly necessary'. This enabled trainees to make mistakes and learn from them, whereas, had he jumped in straight away to correct something, they would have missed out on this learning experience, and would be liable to repeat the error because they did not appreciate what they were doing incorrectly. The basic training aircraft was the N3N-3, a biplane with dual controls that was 'remarkably uncluttered and had a fixed undercarriage and no flaps'. It had an alarming feature in that the carburettor had a chamber and a float, so if the aircraft was 'in inverted flight at the top of a loop, the float was apt to fall from the bottom of the chamber to the top', hindering the supply of petrol to the cylinders and causing the engine to cut out until the aircraft resumed normal flight. On these biplanes trainee pilots would learn and practise all the necessary skills until they could perform such manoeuvres as a 'three-point landing ... where all three wheels touched the tarmac simultaneously'.[70]

Having mastered the basics, further flying training was conducted on what the British knew as the North American Harvard, a 'modern advanced trainer; all-metal, dual-controlled and highly manoeuvrable ... with retractable undercarriage, constant-speed propeller and flaps'.[71] With its 700 horsepower engine, Owen Smith, who experienced it at 31 EFS, RCAF, in Kingston, Canada, found the Harvard: 'A very stable aircraft but very noisy. The engine used to make a real whine, you could hear it fast revving. You had to concentrate a lot more' compared with the Tiger Moth elementary trainer he had experienced previously.[72]

Most naval pilots returned to Britain for further operational training but, as Norman Hanson discovered, while in America he gained an appreciation of fighter tactics and skills such as ground strafing. At Miami he converted to the Brewster Buffalo (F2A), a stubby, chunky aircraft with a 1,200 horsepower Wright Cyclone engine, and trainees started to receive instruction from

British personnel. They were shown 'how to shake off enemy fighters' and conducted exercises such as when an instructor would 'set us patrolling on a certain course and then himself appear out of the blue, streaking in with all the menace of a true enemy. It was up to us to turn towards him at the right time to parry the attack.'[73]

Obviously deck landing was a crucial skill for all FAA pilots to learn, and a factor that set them apart from other aviators. ADDLs or Aerodrome Dummy Deck Landings were used to prepare pilots, and entailed using a runway with white lines painted on it to simulate arrestor wires. Pilots would then be expected to land on it under the direction of a batsman as would be the case on a real carrier. Generally landing on a carrier was more challenging than taking off from one, although with both there were risks, and numerous accidents occurred throughout the war. Matters were complicated by factors such as a carrier being 'at its most vulnerable from air or submarine attack when committed to steaming into the wind'.[74] A pilot training with 890 NAS in America described how he 'failed to take sufficient account of the carrier moving in my opposite direction and my crosswind turn was too late ... by the time I had made my final turn into the wind, I was too far behind and having to drag along after it'.[75] Recalling his training, John Shoebridge explained how you had to make at least five successful take-offs and deck landings on the ageing carrier HMS *Argus*:

> You would start at the end of the flight deck, of course, and she'd be into the wind and off you go. The main thing was you had to keep straight or you could hit the bridge, although *Argus*'s bridge was extremely low as I recall. Anyway you take off and my big fear was I was convinced that this aeroplane would never take off. The deck was much too short. The aeroplane would never get in the air at all, which of course it did. And I was so relieved I think everything else didn't really matter, and went round and landed again ... You did your normal circuit as you'd been trained to do at Arbroath over and over again, and came in on a curve much of the way, which didn't make it any easier because the nose of the Swordfish would obscure your view. But your batsman would direct you with signals: up, down, right, left, you're too fast, etc. You'd watch the batsman like a hawk, especially when you were new, and hoped you'd be all right.[76]

The size of carrier made a difference, too. One pilot likened landing on HMS *Audacity*'s flight deck to 'perching on a cliff ledge in a blizzard'.[77] In contrast, when compared with escort carriers, the pilot William Fenwick Smith reckoned the fleet carrier HMS *Indomitable* had 'a nice big deck, plenty of room'.[78] Comparing deck landing on HMS *Argus* with HMS *Victorious*, another pilot commented:

> Landing on *Victorious* was a great pleasure because earlier we'd done some of our first deck landings on *Argus*, which was a very, very small carrier, a converted merchantman with a deck about 50–60 per cent of the area of *Victorious*. So we were able to carry out deck landings on *Victorious* with relative ease. We had so much speed and distance, and of course the aircraft carrier was able to give us much more wind over the deck for landing, so our relative speed was lower than it was possible in HMS *Argus* whose flat-out speed would be around 20 knots as compared with 30 knots in the big fleet carriers.[79]

Another factor was that different carriers could have differing systems of landing aircraft. Recalling his service aboard HMS *Illustrious*, Vice Admiral Janvrin outlined how she:

> was the first carrier to work the barrier system of landing aircraft. In the *Ark Royal* [which he had experienced previously] when you landed on her you taxied into the wires and onto the lift, and the lift went down before the next aircraft landed on. When you landed on the *Illustrious* you landed on into the wires and you had a wire mesh barrier in front of you rather like a badminton net. And this was raised and lowered and the moment you landed this was lowered and you taxied over it, and the next aircraft landed on immediately. So there was a much faster rate of landing on.[80]

Operational Experiences

The FAA was involved in some of the epic actions of the war, including helping to sink the German battleship *Bismarck* in May 1941, when, as a result of a torpedo hit aft, her steering was so badly damaged as to leave her virtually unmanoeuvrable, and a relatively easy target for gunfire and torpedoes from RN capital ships. However, such successes were not necessarily viewed with any jubilation by pilots and aircrew. Lieutenant Commander John Moffat, then a sub-lieutenant (RNVR) flying from *Ark Royal*, took part in the strike and was widely credited with launching the torpedo that damaged the battleship. During his 'second trip over the *Bismarck*' he was deeply disturbed at the sights encountered, which remained with him into old age.

> She was smoking like fury, and just as I approached, the ship turned on its side. I flew across and there were all these bods in the water, hundreds of them; there were heads in the water. It was a terrible thing, a terrible

sight really. That haunts me, the hopelessness of life. When we all got back we had a drink, and nobody said great or anything. That was why we had a drink, because we all thought, 'There but for the grace of God ...'[81]

On 11 November 1940 the FAA undertook Operation Judgement, an audacious and highly successful attack on the Italian naval base at Taranto, while all the enemy's capital ships were in harbour. It was launched against an enemy alert to the possibility of attack and capable of putting up significant anti-aircraft defence. The attack relied on the training, skill and courage of those involved. One of the participants recorded that: 'We used to practise night torpedo attacks, so we were working up for it for quite some considerable time.'[82] Prior to the operation, aerial reconnaissance was extremely important, while during it various technological innovations, notably radar and torpedoes fitted with the Duplex pistol, played a part. The latter could explode either under a ship's hull or on impact with it, and for Taranto were set to 33 feet and 27 knots. According to an observer involved in the raid:

> The situation when dropping was that the torpedo had to enter the water nose first. It had horizontal rudders which would take it down to the preset depth, but it would initially go beyond this, then porpoise up and down until it reached the correct depth. As we would have dropped at about 30 feet, we had to have a good deal more than 5 fathoms of water in which to drop.[83]

Ultimately, the plan 'called for two strikes, of twelve and nine aircraft respectively, with six torpedoes in each flight. *Illustrious* and her escorts would steam to [a] position ... 40 miles from Kabbo Point, Cephalonia, from where they would launch the first strike at 2100, giving them a total distance to Taranto of 400 miles on the round trip. The second strike would be launched at 2230, and the first recovered at about 0100 on 12 November, 20 miles from Kabbo Point. Each wave would be formed around one of *Illustrious*'s squadrons: a toss of the coin decided which.'[84]

An observer with 815 NAS explained how his Swordfish was one of those employed as a flare-dropper to help illuminate the attack. By the time they arrived over the target, the enemy were:

> already firing. There was no need for accurate navigation, you could see where to go. We arrived over Taranto, and the strike leader detached the two flare-droppers ... and we went and laid our string of flares, and he led his torpedo aircraft down in order to be in a position to attack the battleships silhouetted in the light of the flares ... We dropped our flares

at about 8,000 feet and we were fired at considerably, a fair amount of ack-ack fire, the most extraordinary things that looked like flaming onions. But otherwise one just went through it and it made no great impression – didn't think they would ever hit you.

[Later they went on to dive bomb oil tanks, although they were unsure of the results. And after the raid] I think we had a feeling of euphoria that some major damage had been inflicted. But we didn't know how much or what [in fact six Italian capital ships and a destroyer were sunk or damaged, thus severely weakening the Italian naval presence in the Mediterranean.] I remember after we landed we had eggs and bacon and whisky laid on, then off we went, turned in, only to be told the same operation was planned for the next day. [This was called off owing to poor weather, and later he remembered witnessing Admiral Cunning-ham's famous flag signal from HMS *Warspite* that the operation was 'A manoeuvre well executed.'][85]

One of the Swordfish pilots in the second wave was John Wellham, who was tasked with mounting a torpedo attack against the outer harbour and battle-ships. He successfully negotiated the Italian anti-aircraft defences, despite his aircraft suffering serious damage in the process, launched his torpedo and made it back to his carrier with 'a god-awful bump as I caught the wire and hit the deck'. Remembering the raid, he noted:

There was a tremendous barrage over the harbour, low level barrage which was up to about 3,000–4,000 feet perhaps, and a high level one. Well that didn't worry us at all. I never heard of anyone being hit by high level anti-aircraft fire ... I thought if I go round to the left, I can get behind the balloon barrage, come down nicely in there and there was a nice sort of hole in the barrage ... By the time I got there unfortunately it wasn't a hole any longer ... the only thing you can do is shut your eyes and dive. With a barrage you must keep your nerve and dive straight through it ... Well I was busy doing that when to my surprise [at 4,000 feet] I met a barrage balloon ... Obviously it had been shot away, because as a result I had to do a very violent manoeuvre, to the alarm of my observer, and just as I was avoiding this wretched balloon, there was a tremendous thump and the stick ... jammed absolutely solid ... I was out of control ... so I applied brute force and ignorance – there's nothing else you can do in the circumstances – found I could get it over slightly to the left and fully to the right, and while I was trying to sort this business out I had completely forgotten the fact that I was diving straight into the middle of Taranto city ... So I hauled everything back to pull out of the dive ... and that brought me over the town, where we had no intention of being, and still slightly turning to the right, because it was very difficult to make the aircraft fly straight ...

[Eventually] I came round back onto the harbour, by which time of course after the diving I was going much too fast to either drop a torpedo or ditch the aircraft ... so I did all the things you can do to slow the aircraft properly, the throttle [and with a calm sea and lots of reflection it was hard to judge direction and height, except by eye] ... as I got near the water down there, saw ... a huge battleship to the right and thought, well I wasn't going to cart the torpedo all the way back home ... so did a pretty violent steep turn towards it ... Straightened the thing out by which time the battleship had woken up and they were firing at us, but fortunately they couldn't depress the guns far enough, they were shooting over the top ... I dropped [the torpedo] and hoped it would go somewhere. But if you drop 2,000 lbs of weight off the aircraft it rises and there's nothing you can do about it. By which time I was in a very steep turn to get out of it, and we got hit again, because ... we went into the barrage from the ship ... I was still flying, to my amazement, and then we ducked out in between the barrages ... and out to sea and we were still flying ... So I climbed to about 1,000 feet ... and shouted to the observer, are you still alive?, and ... he was.[86]

Important as these actions were, a great deal more of the FAA's wartime activities centred on less glamorous matters. As John Shoebridge, who spent much of his war on convoy protection with a MAC ship, explained, flying in the Atlantic and Arctic typically entailed what were dubbed either Cobra Patrols or Mamba Patrols. In a Cobra, 'one aircraft was always flying round and round a convoy, usually morning and evening', in order to 'keep U-boats' heads down and protect the convoy'. This would usually be mounted by a Swordfish armed with rockets or depth charges. In contrast, a Mamba involved an 'aircraft being sent out by the Senior Officer of the Escort to a known U-boat location' based on intelligence information or an actual sighting.[87]

Of course, although protecting convoys was a form of routine activity, there was always the chance that a naval pilot might experience action when engaged in this duty. On 26 May 1944 Stephen Mearns, a Sea Hurricane pilot with 835 NAS flying from HMS *Nairana*, a Ruler class escort carrier with the 2nd Escort Group, intercepted a German Junkers Ju 290, a large four-engine maritime reconnaissance aircraft:

I shot down a 290 ... We'd had several stabs at them but they'd escaped into cloud which was rather a frustrating activity. This occasion we had a perfect interception and made what we used to call the classic quarter attack, that is a form of attack with a fighter that gives you the maximum opportunity of shooting somebody down without being shot down yourself, in that you are coming in on an angle of deflection at the target. The Ju 290 was quite heavily armed with machine guns and 20mm rearward-firing cannon but they were a big target, and in that respect somewhat easier to hit than a smaller one, perhaps. We were armed with 20mm cannon, a highly effective weapon with semi-armoured piercing rounds and high explosive incendiaries. You only need one or two of these rounds to do vast damage to an aircraft. In fact you could see them striking the target. They explode on impact and are very lethal. In this case the aircraft went down and ditched, and the crew took to their rubber life-rafts. I took a photograph of them with my camera, [as] we had a camera in the wing of the Hurricane. I am afraid the poor chaps in the water thought I was going to shoot at them because I was diving at them, because you operate the camera like the guns but with the guns switched off. They were all picked up by an escort, quite a useful exercise for intelligence purposes.[88]

Naval aviation was vitally important in the Far East as well. During 1944–1945 the East Indies Fleet supported the seaward flank of the Fourteenth Army as it advanced through Burma using several types of warship, notably escort carriers. It was also tasked with containing Japanese warships in Singapore, and denying them the freedom to operate in the Indian Ocean, plus degrading Japanese air forces based ashore. By doing so, the enemy garrisons in the Andaman and Nicobar Islands would be isolated and prevented from threatening the seaward flank of the Fourteenth Army. In contrast, the BPF was tasked with operating alongside the Americans in the central Pacific as the war against Japan headed towards its conclusion. Based around the 1st Aircraft Carrier Squadron, the BPF was essentially an attempt by Prime Minister Winston Churchill to ensure that British forces had a role in the defeat of Japan and that Britain would exert an influence in the region after the war.

In both theatres British ships were subjected to Kamikaze ('Divine Wind') attacks. A sailor aboard the aircraft carrier HMS *Formidable* described how this was a horrifying experience, albeit the armoured decks on British carriers ensured the damage was not perhaps as bad as it might otherwise have been. On 9 May 1945:

at 18.00 a Kamikaze Jap plane made a suicidal attack on us. We were fortunate in some ways as although the bridge was peppered and flames licked all around, only one rating was killed and four injured. The flight deck was dented again, sets riddled with shrapnel, aircraft became a complete write-off, and there was danger of fire spreading to the hangar. Another attacking plane was shot down before it could crash on the deck ... The *Victorious* was also hit. *Uganda* signalled: 'Deepest admiration.'[89]

Perhaps one of the more unusual jobs that fell to Owen Smith while flying from HMS *Ruler* was to mount simulated Kamikaze attacks on ships from the BPF in order to help prepare them for such an event. 'I was asked to do dummy Kamikaze attacks on three of the ships of the fleet ... you approached them and did all the things a Kamikaze pilot would do, and at the last minute you'd pull out. In the meantime they'd be firing at you with real bullets but on an off-shoot angle, aiming at you but firing to miss you, so that was a bit hairy.'[90]

Initially the BPF underwent a period of training and replenishment in base areas, before supporting American operations at Okinawa. By July 1945 it became a fully integrated Task Force serving with the American Third Fleet, primarily geared up for strikes against Japan itself. As part of the British contribution a series of strikes were launched on strategic oil targets in Sumatra. Those against oil refineries at Palembang were code-named Operations Meridian 1 and 2, and were designed to demonstrate to the Americans that the RN had the capacity to conduct sustained operations against the Japanese. Launched on 24 and 29 January 1945 respectively, FAA personnel were under no illusions as to how tough these operations might prove. One pilot stated: 'The air strike would have to cross 150 miles of high mountain ranges and dense jungle ... The inestimable value of the target to the Japanese was calculated to bring into action their full force of interceptors.'[91] While fighters provided cover/support, Avengers did most of the actual bombing. Simultaneously, other fighters mounted what were known as Ramrod sweeps, strafing runs of enemy airfields. These probably destroyed many enemy fighters on the ground, although several were still present to engage British aircraft, and in the process of strafing the FAA suffered heavy casualties.[92]

During the Palembang raids William Fenwick Smith flew a Hellcat with 1844 NAS with the 11th Carrier Air Group, 1st Aircraft Carrier Squadron, based on HMS *Indomitable*. His experience readily illustrates the confusion and sense of isolation that were common features of aerial combat during the period:

> I suppose there must have been about 100 aircraft in the air. It was quite a sight for the FAA. And off we went. We were escort to the Avengers. We were in flights, four aircraft in a flight. And I was the last one because

I was on the outside of our flight, and just when we were getting near the objective we were going to bomb, the oil tanks, we were attacked by Tojos [Nakajima Ki-44, a Japanese single-seat fighter/interceptor] or something. Anyway I had to turn to meet this chap who was coming towards me. And we had a little go together, and he went down. Whether it was my shots that put him down, I could never get it confirmed, of course, because when I turned back there was not an aircraft in sight, not one. I thought: 'Jesus, what happened now?' But we'd all been given a vector back to the ship, of course, which was a long way away … so I didn't quite know what to do. I followed this fellow as far as I could, this Japanese, and he was smoking a bit, and I thought I am going to leave you. I am not going to follow you anymore. And I turned and went right down close to deck as I could get … Then there's the big mountains the other side, got over those, got to the other side, and asked for a vector.[93]

Chapter Three

Underwater Warfare and Anti-Submarine Warfare

According to a wartime booklet, submarines – or boats as they were usually known by their crews – were one of 'the dark and secret methods of waging war at sea', and together with mines they conducted 'a guerrilla war against the sea routes'.[1] This was especially relevant in areas where it was difficult for surface forces to harass enemy convoys, such as the coastal waters of Norway or the Sicilian narrows, prior to the defeat of the Axis powers in North Africa. Indeed, as Dan Van Der Vat observed, British submarines made the most of their limited wartime opportunities, notably in the Mediterranean, 'sinking an average of 9.3 ships for every boat lost (seventy-five British submarines were destroyed)'. This equated to 'a rate of exchange' second only to the USN in the Pacific, where the Japanese had neglected anti-submarine warfare (ASW) and failed to impose a convoy system.[2]

Yet submarines did not only attack enemy shipping with torpedoes and gunfire. Some became involved in mine-laying, not always a popular operation among submariners who feared that these weapons might damage their own boat. Another task entailed bombarding targets ashore with their guns. While on patrol in the Mediterranean, HMS *Roach* reportedly fired on a railway viaduct, an action that 'blocked the line and caused a great congestion of railway trucks at a nearby junction'.[3] In various theatres, submarines proved useful on clandestine operations, particularly by inserting agents or sabotage parties behind enemy lines and extracting them after they had completed their mission. Submarines also ferried supplies at times, notably during the relief of Malta, became involved in rescuing Allied airmen downed at sea, and undertook various training roles throughout the war.

Another facet of underwater operations involved the X-craft or midget submarines that 'brought their unorthodox talents to bear upon the war', including during daring raids against Japanese warships in the Far East.[4] A related activity was that of frogmen or divers, who had an important role to play in clearing obstacles such as mines from harbours, as well as attacking enemy shipping in hostile waters. Notably, this was sometimes done via

'Charioteers', where frogmen sat astride what was effectively a two-man torpedo. Additionally, many submarines contained men trained as divers among their crew, who could disentangle their boat from underwater obstacles such as fishing nets, which risked clogging their propellers.

Countering enemy submarines was important too, and by 1943–1944 the Royal Navy could justifiably claim to be a world leader in the field of ASW. Together with the efforts of RAF Coastal Command, this naval capability was crucial in winning the Battle of the Atlantic. However, it was only developed through hard-won operational experience and the assimilation of the relevant lessons, because during the inter-war years ASW had been seriously neglected, initially leaving the Royal Navy ill-equipped to counter the U-boat menace at the outbreak of the Second World War.

Submariners and Submarines

The Submarine Service was in some ways a navy within a navy, with its own distinctive identity and highly developed sense of esprit de corps. During the war submariners experienced action in a diverse range of theatres, including the North Sea, the Mediterranean and the Arctic, Atlantic, Indian and Pacific Oceans.[5] While many men volunteered for submarines, it was far from being an all-volunteer service, and as the war progressed, HO, RNR and RNVR personnel all rubbed shoulders with regulars in many boats. To outsiders, submariners might have appeared as a non-conformist group. At least one experienced submarine commander disputed this impression. Submariners may have appeared like 'a gang of pirates who never wore proper uniform and never shaved', but 'we were pretty standard naval officers and our ships were just as smart as surface ships, and we took a great pride in running them along proper naval lines'. However, 'we developed an enterprising nature and the life in submarines developed it, particularly in war you became very independent'.[6] Positions of command usually became available more rapidly in submarines compared with other branches of the navy, and there were plenty of wartime submarine skippers who were still in their twenties.

Many submariners agree that the intense comradeship enjoyed in the confines of a submarine was a notable feature of their war service. Having trained as a signalman, Des Radwell served on the T class HMS/M *Taurus* on patrols in the Arctic, Mediterranean and Far East during 1940–1944. There was:

> such a great crowd of fellas and such a mix from all over the country and they're all part of the crew, and you lived together so closely. It's just a terrific life to me, I think because I'd never had any brothers or sisters, so this was fantastic to me. I had loads of brothers, they were always

good. If you went ashore, you went ashore as a family. And if you came back and you'd had a few too many, you'd crash and your money belt would be on the table, and they'd put it away for you, and it would all be there in the morning. No one would ever think of stealing anything like that ... It was such a great family life.[7]

Similarly, for Sir John Harvey-Jones, service aboard submarines, notably as third officer aboard HMS/M *Sea Scout* in the Far East, was a formative experience that shaped his later life and outlook:

Aboard submarines we were very close to our men, and like many middle class people, I had very little understanding or knowledge of the conditions under which the working class had lived before the war ... we were on watch a great deal, and, of course, when you were submerged you had plenty of opportunity to talk to your men and I really ... It made a profound impression on me. First of all how miserable their lives had been. Secondly the tremendous capability they had when they were given any training and any responsibility. I must confess it made my political views left-wing. It gave me an enormous belief in their capabilities and reliability and excellence of ordinary Englishmen if given any chance of any training. And that has really been the cornerstone of the whole of my subsequent life.[8]

A submariner's experience was also influenced by the nature of the discipline that he was subjected to, and this tended to differ considerably from that on surface vessels. The cook or chef aboard the submarine HMS/M *Taku*, deployed as a training vessel in British waters during 1944–1945, provided a slightly different impression to that given by the submarine commander quoted above. Rather than working along standard naval lines, according to him, 'If you didn't do your job, you got a kick from your mate and that quickly resolved it. There was no, I'll put you on a Captain's Report, and that sort of thing ... It would have to be something serious for that ... In the boat it was self-discipline all the time.'[9]

Coupled with this was the overall dynamic within a boat or submarine's crew. William Douglass grew up in Sunderland, enlisted in the Royal Navy in 1942, trained as a stoker at HMS *Kabul* near Wetherby, then volunteered to become a submariner, having grown weary of the routine at Chatham Barracks. By his own admission, he never regretted his decision. He served aboard three submarines and experienced action in the Mediterranean:

A submarine crew, it's got to fit, the right people have got to fit in. I am a bit of joker really myself, and I like a laugh. And I was glad they put me

aboard the *Tudor* because it was exactly what I thought it would be like . . .
The crew have got to blend otherwise it don't work . . . You've got to
look after the man next to you and so on . . . On a surface ship you
wouldn't get the seamen mixing with the stokers, the engine room
branch. I don't know why but that's the way it used to be. The submarine
is different because they're all on one level. You've got the seamen up
front and the stokers at the stern end. You see the same people everyday sort of thing, and that's it. That's the way it should be and that's the
way it was.[10]

As Des Radwell recounted, under such circumstances it was virtually an
unwritten law that submariners never talked about religion or politics so as
to avoid arguments and maintain harmonious relations on patrol. This was
especially important given that crews often comprised men from a variety of
backgrounds and faiths. Typically, submariners were a superstitious bunch as
well. When HMS/M *Taurus* was commissioned at Barrow in 1940 she was
allocated the pennant number 313: this was swiftly rejected by her crew and
had to be changed.

There were numerous reasons why officers and ratings joined the Submarine Service, including a loathing of bigger vessels. As a midshipman,
Sir John Harvey-Jones spent a brief period aboard HMS *Duke of York*, a King
George V class battleship that served with the Home Fleet and had a displacement of 35,000 tons. 'It was a vast ship. Nobody really knew anybody
else, and there was a great deal of class distinction between both the ranks of
officers and the sailors. You virtually never met the sailors, didn't know anything of them.'[11] On completion of his officer training, Chris West decided
that he 'did not want to serve on big ships, and was given three choices: Fleet
Air Arm; Combined Operations [which primarily entailed operating landing
craft] and submarines. I gather that if you put down for submarines you were
posted there.'[12] Likewise, submarine commander Captain Mervyn Wingfield
'didn't relish the prospect of being a watch keeper in a big ship, which was the
fate of many a young officer, endless watch keeping. We called it tramping the
teak, and I thought submarines gave one a more interesting career.'[13]

For others, including the chef Alec Wingrave, there was a financial
incentive in becoming a submariner. As he remembered, Submarine Pay was
two shillings and sixpence, with a further one shilling and sixpence if a boat
was on combat operations, plus nineteen pence for every night a rating spent
aboard the boat. Additionally, there was a clothing allowance of nineteen
pence as opposed to only sixteen pence in small ships, and this was generous
by contemporary standards.

For others, submarines appeared to offer a more active role as part of the war effort. One young officer aboard a trawler in 1941 remembered that with a comrade 'we looked through the Admiralty Fleet Orders – the AFOs – and they were asking for volunteers for this and that and that one was an appeal for people to join the Fleet Air Arm and the other was submarines, and I'd always had a fascination for submarines ...'[14] Submarine commander John Bromage similarly highlighted that:

> The attraction of submarines was that for the whole war we were offensive. There was, practically speaking, no other branch of the Armed Forces [except arguably RAF Bomber Command] that for the whole war was offensive. And you can put up with a lot of hardship, and a lot of danger, if you are being offensive and morale is much improved by success. If you sink a ship and so on it is a tremendous fillip to people. If you are endlessly on defensive patrols, it is so much harder to keep morale going and the rest of the Armed Forces during 1941–1942 were largely on the defensive.[15]

The technical nature of submarines and submarine warfare held an appeal as well. Vice Admiral Sir Ian McGeogh became a submariner in the late 1930s, after attending Pangbourne Nautical College and embarking on a career as a naval officer:

> The reason why I specialised in submarines was that I had become dedicated to offshore yacht racing, and used my then elementary knowledge of navigation to help navigate yachts. It so happened that in those days sailing yachts were not very fast and they were subjected to the tides and currents to a great extent. This also happens to diesel-powered submarines when they dived on their electric motors and proceeded very slowly at about the speed of a sailing yacht. Hence part of the navigational problem for offshore racing was reflected in navigating a diesel/ electric submarine. So I thought I would improve my ocean racing capability if I joined HM Submarines.[16]

Crucial to the performance of submarines was the training of their crews. The importance of the signalling training that he received was neatly summed up by Des Radwell:

> You had to take this all in because when I joined submarines I was the only signalman on the boat because they only had one signalman on the boat, so it's all down to you. You are on that boat and any visual signals were all your responsibility, so you've got to be really on the ball. You

just couldn't afford not to be on the ball in a submarine because you've got no one else to rely on except yourself. It's quite a responsibility but I loved it.[17]

All trainee submariners were also subjected to the escape tank at HMS *Dolphin* at Gosport, where they were instructed on the use of the Davis Submerged Escape Apparatus (DSEA). This comprised a breathing bag, a metal canister containing soda lime, plus rubber mouthpiece, oxygen containers and valves. It was designed to deliver oxygen to the wearer's mouth, and could also be employed as a smoke or gas mask. If an escape from a submarine was necessary, men were to gather by one of three hatches, either under the gun, forward or aft, and don their DSEA. The compartment was then flooded, and the men would escape one after the other, with a senior officer or rating present working the valves. This might have been good for morale, but in practice most submariners probably privately knew that there was only limited chance of escape from a stricken submarine. William Douglass recalled what it was like to be in the escape tank and use the DSEA: 'that was the old one ... the clip on the nose, the tube in the mouth and a pair of goggles, and that was it. And a bottle underneath and a thing that used to go over your shoulders ... and an apron, which was rolled up ... It was good actually because I enjoyed it, I am a good swimmer. You'd undo the apron in front like a skirt, and it'd stop you coming up too fast, slow you down.'[18]

It was part of the general ethos on submarines that everyone could do each other's job where practical. Although he was a chef, Alec Wingrave performed numerous other duties. He recounted how one of his skippers took great pride in the fact that his chef could also operate the periscope effectively. Typically, crews were split into three watches, and, as Des Radwell explained, 'you'd be on the helm or if you'd dived, you'd be on the hydroplanes ... That would all be part of your duty.'[19] Routine largely centred around meals and the issue of the rum ration, usually done at 11 o'clock, unless the crew were at dive stations, equivalent to action stations on a surface vessel. As Alec Wingrave recalled: 'Lunch was always 11.30 for the change of watches. The watch changed at 12 o'clock, so the early people had their lunch at 11.30 then went and relieved those who'd done the morning watch and they sat down and had their meal ... There was a pot of tea made at teatime about 3.30 to 4 o'clock everyday then supper was 6.30 always.'[20]

Alec Wingrave always tried to produce food that was wholesome, such as casseroles, roast beef and dumplings which proved immensely popular, plus used potatoes that each mess had peeled. Yet cooks or chefs were not always so competent. Aboard one submarine the role was taken by an ex-miner who also served as part of the gun crew. One day the gunnery and torpedo officer was summoned by the coxswain (the senior petty officer responsible to the first lieutenant and in charge of discipline and the general running of the boat) and told to come and look at something. 'We went along the passage past the diminutive galley to which he pointed his thumb. Black [the cook] was trying to fill macaroni with jam using a teaspoon. I asked the Coxswain what he was doing. Oh, he said, I told him that the boys would like macaroni jam for sweet. (The Coxswain was responsible for deciding the menus.) About half an hour later the Cox'n again summoned me. As we went past the galley Black dipped a tube of macaroni into a jar of jam. Having sucked it full he slid his finger under the end, lifted it out and carefully laid it onto a small pile on a plate on the counter!'[21]

Everyone had a particular dive station. On HMS/M *Taku* Alec Wingrave's was at No. 5 Tank, conveniently situated by the galley. However, if it was a surface attack, he recalled:

> I might be on the 4-inch gun, and that was No. 7 on the gun, sight-setter because you have to set the sights on order from the gun layer or the bridge to what the sight setting should be, and you had to make sure you got that right. [They were trained to fire their first shell within 24 seconds.] When you cleared the gun the call came from the bridge: 'Check, Check, Check.' And everybody would dive for the gun tower hatch, two hatches you had on S and T class boats, and I was always next to last down because behind me was the gun layer.[22]

Important to all crews were Engine Room Artificers (ERAs). Petty Officer William Pook joined HMS/M *Truant* on commissioning at Barrow at the start of the war, and served aboard her in the North Sea, Mediterranean and Far East during 1939–1942, by which time he had become her Chief ERA. 'I had a watch in the engine room, and for diving stations I had the after diving stations which meant I was in charge of the after hydroplanes, aft steering, the air compressors and so on, the stern glands. As a Chief ERA, I was in charge of the engineering right throughout the whole boat.'[23] In contrast, the navigation officer in the control room was tasked with keeping a careful check on the position of a submarine. Depending on the conditions at sea this could be challenging. HMS/M *Snapper* of the 3rd Submarine Flotilla operated in the North Sea during 1939–1940. Her navigation officer described how: 'We were required to be within 5 miles of the Dutch coast and in the winter it was extremely difficult, you could never see the Dutch coast, the water was very shallow, and the only aid you had was a light vessel which was on station that winter making underwater sounds which we could pick up.'[24]

Ultimately, the commander of a submarine bore sole responsibility for the success or failure of any patrol. As indicated above, he required a degree of individualism, and was the only person who knew what was happening during an attack because only he employed the periscope. John Bromage served in submarines throughout his war, including commanding HMS/M *Sahib*, which served with the 2nd Submarine Flotilla in the Arctic during 1942 and later with the 10th Submarine Flotilla in the Mediterranean. He reckoned that 'a submarine captain is more individualistic than the captain of a big ship, where everyone is aware of what is going on and what decisions are being made, where the captain himself has to make them. The captain can hide things in a submarine, really the crew know no more or less than what the captain wishes to tell them is happening.'[25] As Petty Officer Pook commented:

> One problem with being crew in a submarine is that you don't see any-thing. The captain is really the only man who sees what's going on and knows what's going on, unless it's a gun action then the gun crew do see what's happening. But the normal crew inside the boat, you have to judge by remarks passed as to what's happening.[26]

Another important characteristic for submarine commanders was self-control. John Bromage emphasised that: 'You don't shout, you do keep calm, you can be severe if you like, and you can be positive but you must keep the temperature down, as it were. You can't go shouting at people and all that, in my book you can't ... It's a quiet atmosphere, there's a feeling of stealth when you're dived ... you're trying not to be detected.'[27]

During the war British submarine production centred on three types: the large T class, the medium S class and the small U class.[28] In the 1930s, when the T class was originally conceived, the Treaty of London dictated sub-marine design. At 1,573 tons submerged, it was still smaller than some pre-existing designs then in service, and it was envisaged that it might have to play a role in the Far East. The Chief ERA aboard the T class HMS/M *Truant* commented that: 'The T Class submarines were to my mind the best class of their time. She was a Vickers-built boat, and Vickers are the submarine builders, her engines were excellent.'[29] According to Admiral Christopher Hutchinson, who commanded *Truant* on patrol in the North Sea with the 2nd Submarine Flotilla during February–June 1940, the T class had:

> ... more room for your creature comforts, such as eating at table or sleeping in a bunk. And at least we had one bunk each, whereas in previous submarines you always worked with what was called a hot bunk,

so that one chap was on watch and the other was in the bunk, then they changed round.[30]

The S class was discovered to be ideal for operations in the North Sea, and fifty were built from 1942 onwards when the design was reintroduced to complement existing pre-war boats. Chris West joined HMS/M *Sleuth* while she was being built at Cammell Laird's yard in Birkenhead, and noted:

The S class, first built in 1929, were small submarines, with an interior diameter of 16 feet. They had been designed for operations in the North Sea and the Mediterranean and to patrol for two to three weeks. Patrols in the Far East, [where] we were bound, would last for three months. Some of the main ballast tanks were converted to carry diesel fuel to extend our range to 6,500 miles. If these tanks were holed, the leaking oil would make it easy to follow us. We had a 4-inch gun because it was expected that there would be a lot of gun work in the Far East, but we did not have radar.[31]

In contrast, the U class was conceived during the 1930s as a training boat, both for submariners and for ships engaged in anti-submarine work, where the friendly submarine would act as what was known as a 'clockwork mouse' for the destroyers to practise against. Coastal patrolling was deemed a secondary function. However, the design was found acceptable for operations, and once war was declared it was given production priority as the U class was relatively simple to manufacture. By 1945 over sixty had been launched, and because of their small size these proved especially suited to service in the confines of the Mediterranean. Another of the smaller submarine types to serve was the V class, described by one submariner who experienced one during a long voyage from the Mediterranean to Colombo, as 'very cramped and pretty uncomfortable'.[32]

Living conditions could vary depending on where a submarine was serving, but typically crews all ate the same and smelt the same. Space was invariably at a premium. Aboard HMS/M *Sleuth* the crew had 'problems with the storage of food, our vessel being so small. When we sailed we had crates of food all over the submarine. In the passageways you had to bend double climbing over them. Our magazine only held 75 shells, so we put them all over the place – on the bunks, under the wardroom table. They had safety clips on them which would fall off as the shells rolled around the floor.'[33]

As Sir John Harvey-Jones found aboard both HMS/M *Voracious* and HMS/M *Sea Scout*: 'We were very short of everything, including water. We didn't wash. We had about a gallon a day for cooking, drinking, washing, the lot per man. The only combined washing and toilet facility was smaller than a phone box, no showers or anything like that.'[34] Usually human waste could be jettisoned from a tank only with permission, so as not to give away a submarine's position, and kitchen waste could be blown out of a torpedo tube.

A corollary of the lack of water was that hygiene could prove problematic, especially in hotter climates. Des Radwell remembered arriving in Malta after one patrol, when on his submarine:

> We were all down with scabies and crabs. We were lousy. The infection scabies came on the boat, don't know how, but once one of them got it, it just went through the boat like wildfire ... So we all had that and we all had crabs. We were in a mess. You didn't wash, you could clean your teeth, but you couldn't wash or change your clothes. Water was precious or unavailable.[35]

Similarly, in the Far East the heat was terrific, leading most submariners 'to wearing almost jock-straps, as little as possible regarding clothing on. There were problems with heat rash. We had no air conditioning in those submarines ... so you just lay on your bunk and you sweated, there's no doubt about it, it absolutely poured off you. If you had to work, then it was very bad conditions for working in.'[36]

Another feature of submarines was that they were often damp environments to work in. The crew of HMS/M *Taku* serving in Home Waters during 1944–1945 found that they:

> always had water dripping down and all the bulkheads, when they painted them, they splashed caulk on that prevented a certain amount of condensation but not a lot. You were always dripping with water in hot areas or where there was no proper ventilation. The only time you got any ventilation was when the control room or the gun tower hatches were open, and the diesels sucked the air in. That's how the diesels ran fresh air ... and of course stokers never got any because the air was taken up by the engines forward of the stokers' mess deck.[37]

In contrast, the Arctic was an intensely cold and miserable area for submariners to endure. On an Arctic patrol in 1941 the crew of HMS/M *Taurus* found that they were constantly wet and their boat was:

> covered in ice, the periscope stands were thick with ice. And even after we'd dived for a few hours, the ice was still there. And it was so difficult to see or hear anything or listen for anything out there. You'd surface in the evening to charge batteries but it was still miserable. Then when you

surfaced you'd have a hot meal because that's when they could cook ... and the boat's rolling all over the place and you can't put the tables up, so you sit with a pot mess in between your legs and grab a spoonful of it as it went past, and that sort of thing.[38]

Likewise, the various seas or oceans in which submarines operated had varying characteristics that could impact upon operations. Comparing the waters off Scandinavia with those of the Mediterranean, one experienced submariner expounded how: 'One of the big differences is the matter of the water. It's clear water in the Mediterranean and aircraft can see you very clearly. Apart from that it's the same. Waters are still rough at times. The Mediterranean can be quite rough. Further to go than in the North Sea, especially up the Adriatic.'[39]

Patrols tended to start along similar lines. Although submarine crews were not necessarily told a great deal, they knew something was about to happen because they'd be loaded with torpedoes and rations. Eventually, the orders 'Harbour Stations' and 'Sea Duty Men Close-up' would be given as a submarine was about to depart. Next, as William Douglass described: 'All the seamen are up on the fore ends ABs [Able seamen] and Killicks [Leading seamen], letting go of this, letting go of that. Skipper's on the bridge, First Lieutenant up on the bridge, and probably another officer, possibly the Navigation Officer, then you know you are going to sea. The only man that steered the boat was the Coxswain, and he was the policeman, he was the doctor, you name it, it was the Coxswain ... He was Master of Arms of the boat ...'[40]

Once at sea, the captain would usually address the crew over the tannoy and provide some indication about the nature of the ensuing patrol. Subsequently, submariners faced numerous challenges, including the threat of friendly fire, as it was relatively easy for a Royal Navy submarine to be mistaken for a U-boat. During the course of his wartime career as a submariner, Captain Mervyn Wingfield was attacked by Norwegian, German, French, Italian and British aircraft, although miraculously he never suffered serious damage from air attack. However, while in command of HMS/M *Umpire*, he suffered the indignity of colliding with an armed trawler off Blackeney during July 1941, thus illustrating another danger facing submarines. This was particularly a concern in areas such as the east coast of England, where there was heavy convoy traffic in a comparatively narrow stretch of sea, so that the risk of a collision could potentially pose more danger than the enemy.

Mines were another hazard. According to one submariner, they were a 'constant fear ... never any let up, if you were in mined waters you never knew when there was going to be a bang'.[41] Sometimes crews could even hear the eerie sound of the wires of moored mines scraping against the hull of their submarine. When HMS/M *Voracious* was operating in the Aegean to interdict German supplies and reinforcements, extensive minefields had to be negotiated both to enter and exit the area. Her navigation officer found that this usually 'took about three hours and was certainly a moderately hairy sort of experience'. Simultaneously, he recorded that it 'was all quite exciting because in those days we had no particularly good methods of detecting mines ahead and if you were to go through the minefield you were running a sort of short transmission Asdic [equivalent to sonar] and you picked them up about 50 or 60 yards ahead and just had time, if you were lucky, to avoid hitting them, which of course would detonate them.'[42]

An early lesson that had to be appreciated by many submariners was night adaption. As one experienced submarine commander outlined: 'We hadn't realised how important night vision was and how badly ordinary light affected your eyes. It was certainly 15 minutes before you were night adapted, and then you really could see in the dark.'[43] Conversely, if an officer came straight from the ward room to the bridge, he was at a distinct disadvantage. This could be significant because if the Officer of the Watch called for the captain, he would clearly be hampered for some time, and no submarine was allowed to dive in an emergency without the captain's permission. Comfort with night operations was also an issue because most submarine commanders faced the decision of whether or not to attack a target at night rather than in daylight. As another wartime submarine commander explained, 'it is quite probable you will meet a target at night, not quite so probable in daytime because you can't detect them so far away'. Darkness also helped hide the submarine, particularly when the British aped the German practice of surfaced torpedo attacks by night, and in the absence of radar, Asdic, the British equivalent of sonar, could be used to detect targets. Additionally, 'a submarine trimmed down is a small target from the point of view of visual observation and if you were careful and kept end on and it was reasonably dark, it would be very difficult to be sighted, unless the enemy was using star shell or something like that.'[44]

Another issue, according to Vice Admiral McGeogh, was that unlike the Germans who employed electrically fired torpedoes with no track, the Royal Navy was heavily reliant on a firing system using air and dubbed hosepipe firing. This ensured that all the torpedoes fired by a British submarine followed 'approximately the same track. They were fired one after the other.' In contrast, 'the Germans were able to fire a fan of torpedoes at short intervals, so that they were spread with a short 5-second interval between them, in a sort of fan shape, so they could cover a certain error, high or low target speed'. For the British, achieving the spread of a salvo had to be done via timing, 'that's to say if the target was going at 12 knots from our plots or Asdic listening, [how far] the target would move in so many seconds had to be calculated. And when you fired say four torpedoes, you started aiming the first one say half a length ahead of the target through your periscope. And if by then you had to dip your periscope and go deep, the remaining torpedoes in the salvo were fired at a time interval, which might be as long as 12 or 15 seconds.'[45]

The above could all take time, particularly against a usual target such as an enemy merchantman, plus the tracks of the air-fired torpedoes were visible to any warship escorting a convoy, which could then follow them to their source in order to locate the submarine. If the torpedoes were launched at significant range, their tracks also provided ample warning, giving ships plenty of time to take avoiding action. Similarly, enemy aircraft could easily spot these torpedo tracks and alert shipping.

Torpedoes could also be employed against enemy warships. On 9 April 1940 the submarine *Truant* achieved a notable success when she sank the German cruiser *Karlsruhe* off Kristiansand, Norway. Admiral Christopher Hutchinson was then a more junior officer, and serving as her captain. He remembered that it took some time and patience to manoeuvre into an attack position:

> I went down to about 60 feet to get a burst of speed, so as to get inside the screen [of at least three or four destroyer escorts] and ahead of the oncoming cruiser. After I had eased down the speed and it was safe to raise the periscope without showing a lot of feather in the water, I found that I was in an ideal position to be able to fire in about 2 minutes time. Down periscope and in about 2 minutes I raised it, hoping I would be able to give the order to fire quickly.[46]

Unfortunately, the cruiser and her escorts had altered course so that they were now on the starboard quarter and rapidly moving away from *Truant*. However, as they turned away Hutchinson was fleetingly presented with an unbroken line of four ships, the cruiser and three escorts. Ten torpedoes were fired, despite the danger that expending so many in one action might lighten the bows and risk the submarine breaking the surface:

> I thought I'd better fire a large salvo with the first torpedoes set shallower to catch the escorts, and the middle torpedoes a bit deeper to catch the cruiser. And then the last torpedoes set shallower to catch the escorts that appeared now to me to be astern of the cruiser. Well, fire

I did, with the range of about 2,000–3,000 yards, just over a mile, a far from ideal attack angle ... As I regained control of the submarine, we heard two explosions at the time I expected to hear them and I was hopeful that we had scored at least one hit.[47]

In contrast, gunfire could be used by submarines operating on the surface. This had particular resonance in the Far East, where the Japanese employed a lot of small supply ships and wooden junks to support their various garrisons. In the spring of 1944 HMS/M *Sleuth* started operating with the 8th Submarine Flotilla out of Freemantle, near Perth, Western Australia, under the overall command of the American Rear Admiral J. Fife. One of her officers illustrated the typical gunnery tactics that were employed, frequently with two submarines cooperating together, which achieved better results:

We would surface 300 yards astern of the escorts so our shells hit them with the first round. Once the escort had been dealt with, the supply vessels would be sunk by gunfire or sometimes blown up. I would go on board them with 1¼ pounds of dynamite, place it where the cooling water goes into the engine. When the dynamite exploded, the ship sank. In all my time in the Far East we never sank a ship with a torpedo.[48]

Having engaged in an attack where escorts were present, many submarines faced the challenge of being depth charged. This was never a pleasant experience, and something that frequently had to be endured for a prolonged, nerve-wracking period, during which all kinds of damage might be suffered, potentially crippling a submarine. Essentially it was a sort of deadly game of cat and mouse or a battle of wits between the attacking destroyer/s and the submarine desperately trying to hide or evade the situation. One submarine commander vividly remembered being depth-charged in the Tyrrhenian Sea, an event that ultimately led to his submarine being lost.

the first pattern of depth charges didn't do much harm ... I was talking to the navigator ... We weren't the slightest bit worried about being sunk, because we had been depth-charged so many times before ... So we went on down to what was then regarded as maximum safe operational depth of 300 feet and settled down very quietly and there he was. And then he came in with a second lot of depth charges. About twelve at a time ... and this again didn't do us any harm because they were obviously set well too shallow and I was beginning to feel quite confident about this. However, because of the isothermal water [the Tyrrhenian Sea was notorious for this] we could hear very clearly his sonar banging away, and I realised after about another 10 minutes that he was in contact and he was coming in on a steady bearing … the third attack opened up and I think about the third depth charge … must have gone off extremely close to the stern of the submarine at about the right depth, about 300 feet, and clearly serious damage occurred. We took water in astern and the stern went down at a terrific angle, and of course, we then started going down, and I found that we couldn't speed up on both shafts because one shaft was jammed. So we only had power on one side and the submarine was twenty degrees down by the stern and the deep depth gauge goes down to 500 feet, and of course, the shallow depth gauge at 100 feet were both shut off. Then the deep depth gauge needle hit 500 and of course, after that I had no idea how much further on we were going down, and clearly a crushing depth would be fairly soon … I wasn't able to do anything about it, and I told the chaps to get ready to abandon ship.[49]

Chariots and X-Craft

The Royal Navy made use of divers/frogmen, particularly in clearance work and/or rendering explosive devices safe. For example, to support the D-Day landings in June 1944 specialist diving teams were required to clear obstructions in front of landing craft, assist landing craft that had run into difficulties, and later clear captured ports of booby traps and mines so that Allied units could be kept supplied. This was hazardous work, not least because explosive blasts underwater could be deadly, and contemporary technology ensured that diving while breathing oxygen under pressure was not easy either.[50] Another facet of underwater warfare that employed trained frogmen was as crews for Chariots, effectively a form of two-man or human torpedo. The British machines aped Italian developments as by 1942 the Italian Navy had already used this type of weapon in the Mediterranean, particularly in successful attacks on HMS *Valiant* and HMS *Queen Elizabeth* while they were moored in Alexandria Harbour.

The men selected to become 'Charioteers' were soon embroiled in a brand of warfare where they 'were operating in a new world, a world of mystery and unseen dangers – the weird underwater world'.[51] Most responded to notices asking for 'Volunteers for Special and Hazardous Service', little knowing what they were letting themselves in for, albeit they often already had some significant naval service under their belts. Petty Officer Len Berey was in Gibraltar at the start of the war, and as a member of his ship's water polo team was physically fit. He volunteered in the summer of 1940 but heard no more about it until he returned to Britain over a year later. Subsequently, he received training in coping with the escape tank at HMS *Dolphin*, and rapidly found that it was a man's ability rather than his rank which was all-important.

He then underwent instruction in diving techniques in the Portsmouth Harbour area, although at this stage still knew little about the role for which he had volunteered. Work included helmet diving, plus an introduction to oxygen breathing. Trainees had to be made especially aware of 'Oxygen Pete', as the signs of oxygen poisoning, such as trembling lips, were dubbed, because in the 1940s comparatively little was known about oxygen diving.

Under the dynamic Commander G.M.S. Sladen, a distinguished submariner and the driving force behind the Chariot concept, and his second-in-command Lieutenant Commander W.R. Fell, training continued in Scotland, based around the submarine depot ship HMS *Titania*. Ultimately, as one volunteer who had successfully completed his training remarked, he was introduced to the Chariot:

> It was a machine of about 21 inches diameter and about 21 feet long, with a hydroplane and a rudder at the stern. Coming forward you had a locker at the rear end for carrying tools/cutting tools, any spare magnetic mines, anything like that you wanted to carry. Then you had the position of the No. 2 and forward of that you had the ballast tank, which was a tank blown to bring the machine up rapidly or when you gained your trim, you expelled the air and filled it with water. The machine then sank with, you hoped, a neutral buoyancy achieved, but it was a handy piece of kit to get you up in a hurry.
>
> Forward of that was the No. 1 and in front of him was a shield to break down the water pressure, which wasn't great as the top speed was only about 3 knots. The controls consisted of a rudder combined hydroplane and one control such as you'd find in an aeroplane but it was a bit more robust, plus a control for pumping water to the ballast tanks fore and aft. There was another control to pump water from forward to aft to achieve a level stability. And there was also a control for speed ... a clock, compass and a depth gauge with the minimum amount of numerals on any of them because they were luminous and we found at night when diving ... you lost your night vision looking at the dials, so we reduced it down to the minimum you could have on the actual dial.
>
> Forward of that shield you had an explosive head which was filled with around 500 lbs of Torpex at that time, which was a very high explosive piece of plastic [explosive] but it was very dormant. In other words you had to have a dynamite charge to set off the main charge. The dynamite was set off by an electric charge, the whole being controlled by a clock with a maximum 8 hour delay ... The head was attached to the body of the machine by a handle which you lifted and which released a ratchet

gear and the head became detached, which you proceeded to put under the target and hold in position with magnets. And you hoped that there weren't too many barnacles on the ship's bottom otherwise you had a long job in scraping them all off.[52]

Typically, a Chariot would have to be towed or somehow ferried into a position from where its crew could hope to successfully complete a mission. One way of doing this, used when surveying beaches ahead of Operation Husky (the Allied invasion of Sicily in July 1943), was for them to be 'carried in special chocks on the after casing of U class submarines. The principle of the operation was for the Chariot to be released about 3 miles from shore, the submarine submerging to allow the Chariot to float off; folboat canoes [collapsible canoes] then led the Chariot to within half a mile of the beach that needed surveying.'[53] The Chariot crew would then proceed inshore, complete their survey and return astride their machine to the submarine, guided by the canoes that employed infra-red gear to contact the submarine.

Like their Italian counterparts, Royal Navy 'Charioteers' were brave and determined, although this did not necessarily translate into operational success. During Operation Principle against enemy shipping at Palermo, Sub-Lieutenant Dove and Leading Seaman Freel made a bold and highly successful attack against the SS *Vimina*, seriously damaging her. Other actions achieved less dramatic results. In January 1943 Lieutenant G.W.J. Larkin (RNVR) and Petty Officer Berey were one of the crews involved in an attack on Tripoli harbour. Their hydroplane was damaged, probably on leaving HMS *Thunderbolt*, the submarine that took them into action, rendering their Chariot useless. Having abandoned it, the pair subsequently endured a tense period evading capture in North Africa.

Berey was again in action in February 1944 in an attack on La Spezia, Italy, which in his case failed owing to a faulty battery, leading him once more to abandon his machine. Again he had to evade capture, this time by going on the run in Italy, an experience that made him wryly comment after the war that it was his two epic evasion attempts that were an achievement, rather than any of his active service as a 'Charioteer'. Batteries were supposed to give a range of around 8 miles, but this was not always borne out in practice, as Berey discovered. As well as mechanical flaws or damage, navigation was another significant challenge for 'Charioteers', as once released they had to make their own way to a target. Additionally, entering hostile waters and harbours was clearly fraught with danger, and potentially increased the possibility of being captured if something went wrong. 'Charioteers' did sometimes make successful attacks, as occurred when the Italian light cruiser

Ulpio Traiano was sunk in Palermo harbour during January 1943, but afterwards 'none of the "chariot" crews' on this operation 'reached the rendezvous with the rescue submarine'.[54]

Another possible reason for the mixed results of British Chariots was highlighted by Berey when he was interviewed in 1990. He reckoned that the Royal Navy effort simply had not been launched early enough in the war. By late 1943 'the tide of war had turned ... and the X-Craft had disabled the *Tirpitz*, the Italian Fleet had gone from the Mediterranean because they were out of the war, the Germans didn't have a lot of ships left to attack. And I think generally it was just too late.'[55]

In contrast to Chariots, X-Craft were properly functioning submarines, albeit midget ones. They were 'about 57 feet long, about 13 feet from top to bottom, and the actual hull was about 6 feet ... they could stay at sea for up to three weeks', and had a diesel engine and motor giving an effective range of approximately 1,000 miles when surfaced.[56] Each X-Craft had a crew of four: a captain responsible for commanding it and navigating it to where it was required for an attack; a first lieutenant who operated the motor and hydroplanes control; a rating who was almost invariably trained as a shallow water diver and acted as helmsman; and an ERA in charge of all the mechanical machinery and who also assisted the other three. However, twelve men were required to operate each X-Craft. This was because they were invariably towed to their operating area by a larger submarine, so an outward passage crew was needed aboard. Ahead of a mission, the actual four-man operational crew took over, and afterwards a return passage crew replaced them while the midget submarine was being towed to safety.

X-Craft were deployed for numerous tasks, such as cutting underwater telephone lines in the Far East, landing personnel ashore on intelligence-gathering missions ahead of D-Day, and guiding assault forces towards their beaches during the actual Normandy landings. However, their primary function 'was to make their way into a protected enemy anchorage and either lay themselves alongside the target and drop large explosive charges underneath, fused to explode' later on, or to 'attack by means of attaching limpet charges to the bottom of the target'.[57] In this case the diver needed to exit the submarine by the escape hatch, lay the charges and re-enter it via the escape hatch while it remained submerged waiting for him. Likewise, divers had an important role to play in cutting a way through the steel mesh netting that protected some harbours, and ensuring it did not foul the submarine's propeller or hinder it in any other way.

Lieutenant Ian Fraser, an X-Craft skipper, was awarded the Victoria Cross, together with his diver, Leading Seaman James Magennis, for an attack on the

Japanese warship *Takao*. As he explained, there were two tanks or side cargoes on either side of an X-Craft, which contained high explosive, and it was these which could be dropped as indicated above. Alternatively, they might be employed to carry limpet mines, each of which contained around 200lbs of high explosive, and had the timers pre-set before being attached to a ship's bottom with magnets. Potentially a combination of high explosive and limpet mines could be carried, depending on the task to be accomplished.

On 22 September 1943 X-Craft conducted a daring and effective attack against *Tirpitz*, while she was anchored in Kaafjord in North Norway.[58] This paved the way for further attacks, notably Operation Struggle, when the 10,000-ton cruiser *Takao* was targeted in the Strait of Johor, Singapore, on 31 July 1945 by midget submarine XE-3 under the command of Lieutenant Fraser, having been towed from Borneo by HMS/S *Stygian*. Years later he recalled the tension and challenges his crew faced during the operation, when, fuelled by Benzedrine tablets, they spent 19–20 hours submerged, during which the air supply became increasingly stale:

> We made the passage of the Straits of Singapore ... Now this cruiser which we'd been detailed to attack was lying in the Admiralty dockyard in the north side of the island, and it meant going 12 miles up a channel [the Johor Strait] ... and we navigated our way up the channel until we saw the *Takao* ... lying very close in shore and heavily camouflaged ... We ran in and went underneath it, settled on the bottom, opened the door, put the diver out.[59]

It then took Magennis considerable time to scrape off the barnacles from underneath *Takao* in order to be able to securely attach six limpet mines. Once he was safely back on board, XE-3 flooded down. Then, much to her crew's horror, they discovered she was stuck in a hole under the Japanese ship, and the tide was going out.

> It took about 20 minutes. I was really quite frightened, going full ahead, full astern, blowing tanks, just trying to nudge a hole in the seabed so that we could climb out. And eventually we did come out, went up a bank and onto the seabed proper, where we found that one of our side cargoes hadn't come off and it was stuck [leaving the submarine lopsided to starboard]. Diver had to go out again and lever this thing off, which he did about 50 yards away from this cruiser, ... [although] his diving suit was leaking and sending bubbles to the surface [risking detection] ... eventually ... we made our way back out of the Johor Strait. The gate [of the boom] was still open and we got out through the gate and out to sea ...[60]

Anti-Submarine Warfare (ASW)

During the inter-war period there was considerable complacency and a general lack of preparedness and training within the navy regarding counter-ing the threat posed by enemy submarines. This was despite the Germans establishing a potentially potent U-boat arm by 1935. Partly this was due to the harsh economic conditions of the time that precluded development of anti-submarine weaponry, and ensured the navy was to be short of the neces-sary destroyers and other escort vessels to counter enemy submarines in any future war.

Another reason for not taking the submarine threat seriously, was that it was assumed that submarines would only employ submerged attacks, even though during the First World War German U-boats had made numerous successful surface attacks against Allied merchantmen. Blind faith was there-fore put in Asdic, a device for detecting enemy submarines underwater. In 1937 the outgoing First Lord of the Admiralty, Sir Samuel Hoare, even opined that 'the submarine is no longer a danger to the security of the British Empire'.[61] Better known by the American term sonar, Asdic took its name from the initials of the Allied Submarine Detection Investigation Committee established during the First World War, and entailed transmitting an under-water sound beam. As Captain Bob Whinney, who commanded the destroyer HMS *Wanderer*, explained: 'The beam was actuated – pushed out – by an oscillator ... a heavy disc, around 2 feet in diameter, containing built-up layers of quartz crystal.' These 'had the property that if high voltage, low amperage current of a frequency to match the thickness of the layers was applied, the layers of quartz would vibrate', creating 'a physical sound wave which took the form of a cigar-shaped pulse or transmission'. When this con-tacted anything underwater it sent back an echo, and the oscillator 'could be directed to point at a target' and 'lived inside a dome under the ship's bottom which an electric motor would raise inside the hull or lower to protrude during an operation'.[62]

Ronald Walsh served aboard a number of ships, including as an Asdic operator on HMS *Bulldog*, a B class destroyer launched by Swan Hunter at Wallsend in December 1930. She saw significant action, notably as an escort in the Atlantic during 1940–1941, where Walsh spent many hours on duty with his earphones on in the Asdic Cabinet, discreetly jotting down poetry in calmer moments to help ease the monotony, as the equipment would transmit automatically, so that there was a danger of falling asleep. The Asdic Cabinet:

> was situated right on the bottom of the ship, just above the oscillator, which sent out the electronic beams that picked up the submarine or any

other echo. So I was more or less on the bottom of the ship over the top of the oscillator. And then I would do four-hour watches down there all the time we were at sea. There were two or three of us and I would always be down in there till I was relieved. After four hours down there, night or day, it didn't matter which, I would come up into the mess, sling the hammock and get into that or remain on the mess deck ... That was my sole job, listening for contacts.

The safety of the ship depended on you, and you had to sweep whatever area you were told to sweep and if there was a submarine there you had to pick it up, the echo. And if you missed it, well that was it ... And as soon as you got an echo you reported it to the bridge ... They would then decide whether it was worth bothering about or not.[63]

According to one naval officer, who served successively with the 8th Escort Group and B1 Escort Group: 'You could hear the "pings" [of the Asdic equipment] through a loud speaker on the bridge, and some things just obviously aren't a submarine but a submarine gives a really solid echo, a real "ping". So you'd scout around a bit more and if necessary shake it up with a depth charge or hedgehog [a type of anti-submarine mortar] and see what's there. You can get a "ping" off a shoal of fish, and from porpoises and whales but you can hear them sing underwater.'[64] This simply did not happen with a U-boat contact. As Captain Whinney recounted, an integral part of the equipment was a range recorder, which measured the length of time between the transmission and the echo, and, since the speed of sound through the sea was known, it was possible to calculate the range or 'the distance of the echo from the ship in yards'. Consequently, a genuine submarine contact could be identified by 'the pitch of the echo', as if it were approaching this 'would be higher than the pitch of the transmission, and conversely, if it were retiring, the pitch of the echo would be lower'.[65]

Yet despite the faith the Royal Navy had in Asdic, there were numerous flaws with the system. These were highlighted by Alan Burn, who served under the legendary Captain Frederic Walker, one of the most determined, inspirational and successful anti-submarine officers involved in the war. Its range was limited to 1,500–2,000 yards under favourable sea conditions, plus its range reduced as the speed of a ship increased. Some submerged objects, such as wrecks, could send back an echo that confused operators looking for a U-boat. Water conditions, such as layers of water at different temperatures, could equally impair its performance. The system required skilful operators, especially to contend with the Doppler effect highlighted above, and Asdic had not been fully tested in conjunction with the convoy system prior to the outbreak of war. Another significant drawback was that Asdic 'lost contact with a deep U-boat at a range of about 750 yards, or a shallow U-boat at about 150 yards'. This loss of contact was dubbed the 'Blind Period', when an attacking ship had no way 'of knowing what evasive action the U-boat might be taking'.[66] Another naval officer noted how U-boats would often 'dive ahead of the convoy; before they could hear you, they could see your smoke, and [would] stay under until the convoy came over, and come up in the middle and torpedo one or two ships on each side of them. And all the water would be turbulent and therefore they were very difficult to locate by Asdic.'[67]

Despite these drawbacks, there were successes with Asdic during the early phases of the war at sea. On 21 November 1940 the corvette HMS *Rhodo-dendron* was assigned to protect Convoy OB 224, and had rendezvoused with it off the Mull of Kintyre before taking up a position astern as the rescue vessel. Early in the morning two merchantmen were torpedoed in quick succession. *Rhododendron*'s captain, Sir Robert Atkinson, explained what occurred next:

> Later, about six in the morning, trailing behind the convoy, again to our astonishment, at first light we saw a U-boat trailing the convoy. We at this time were returning to the convoy, having fallen behind picking up survivors. He hadn't seen us and we came up on him, we didn't open gunfire. It was almost dark and when he did see us he dived and we were on him fairly rapidly and got a really good Asdic contact. I think we made one or two attacks and finally it was clear he was sunk. Huge grunts, huge bubbles, vast quantities of oil on the surface of the water, and we had sunk him, U-104.[68]

Similarly, on 29 June 1941 U-651 was detected and sunk by the ageing Scott class destroyer HMS *Malcolm* of the 8th Escort Group, while employing her Asdic equipment. At the time Captain Charles Fetherston-Dilke was serving as her navigation officer, and takes up the story:

> We got an Asdic contact and we attacked a number of times, we and another destroyer called HMS *Scimitar*. Eventually we lost contact with her. And I remember this was in daylight and we had the doctor on the bridge and he suddenly sighted a puff of smoke on the horizon, and we put up our binoculars and there by God was a surfaced submarine. And this smoke was her starting up her diesels, and so we sped along at about 31 knots which was all the *Malcolm* would do and eventually we saw this submarine sink, and there was the most enormous thing, like a lilo, a great air cushion, I suppose about 30 feet by 30 feet, and on it were all

these Germans who'd abandoned ship. They couldn't dive, was the answer, they'd surfaced and there was some defect which prevented them from diving. Anyway we picked them all up, the entire crew from captain downwards. There were no casualties and we had them on board until we got back to Londonderry, where we disembarked them.[69]

As indicated, one of the disadvantages of Asdic was that its beam was fixed in elevation and it lacked range. Invariably a ship going into attack, particularly against a deeply submerged submarine, lost contact early on in its run-in to drop depth charges. By 1943 refinements in the technology had occurred, including the Asdic Q Attachment, which overcame this problem by allowing contact to be maintained with a deeply submerged U-boat. This led to the development of the Type 147B Asdic that could measure a submarine's depth below the surface. Consequently, as the Battle of the Atlantic reached its peak in mid-1943, it became possible for escorts with this equipment to discern the depth, range and direction of travel of U-boats.

Other forms of detection and tracking entailed direction finding or monitoring wireless/radio signals from U-boats. Lieutenant Commander Peter Kemp noted how the 'bearings of all U-boat signals received [from direction-finding stations in the UK and abroad] were passed to the U-boat tracking room in the Admiralty where they were plotted and the positions obtained signalled out to the relevant units at sea'.[70] While it was not often possible to gain the exact location of a U-boat, the technology, which was refined as the war continued, often enabled the British to get within 25 miles and so it was possible to warn convoys and naval units in the area. Likewise, as the war progressed, warships were fitted out with High Frequency Direction Finding (HFDF) or 'Huff Duff' equipment. This included HMS *Hurricane*, a destroyer earmarked for the Brazilian Navy but taken over by the Royal Navy during the war. According to one of her officers, HFDF was:

capable of intercepting the wireless transmissions from U-boats. In fact we had an officer on board whose sole job it was to deal with 'Huff Duff'. And if you got what was called a ground wave signal that meant that the submarine was extremely close, within 30 miles of you, a sky wave and it might have been 100 miles from you. It was a tremendous asset because if you got one of these ground wave signals it was worth turning around onto the bearing of the signal, and speeding down it at 30 knots, and as likely as not you'd see this chap still on the surface if you were lucky. And of course he'd dive without wasting time and you'd pick him up. It was a tremendous advantage.[71]

Denis Logan, an HO signaller aboard Captain Frederic Walker's HMS *Star-ling*, which led the 2nd Support Group in the North Atlantic during 1943–1945, remembered his skipper's methods, and how HFDF was harnessed against U-boats:

> They would get an HFDF contact ... the two radios would pick up the signal from ships wide apart and beam onto it and perhaps go 100 miles, and he [Walker] would find that U-boat then start attacking that U-boat. He would lose it after a couple of attacks and the ships would go round in circles. Then he'd walk up and look at the chart and look at the compass and tell the Officer of the Watch to steer so and so. And it would go in that direction and there it would be. They just could not get away from him, it was most uncanny.[72]

Radar had also a role in locating submarines, albeit one officer reckoned the set on his ship was of limited value for surface use because it was designed as an air warning set. As he put it, 'at least it was something and it would some-times pick up small things like a conning tower, especially if you had a very good operator'.[73] At the start of the war radar was still in its relative infancy, and yet by late 1940 the Admiralty Signal Establishment had laid the founda-tions for a set of sufficient quality, known as the Type 281, that worked on a 3-metre wave band and had surface and air detection capability. Simul-taneously, a 50-centimetre set (Type 284) was issued, and both these ship-borne sets proved useful for range-finding in their surface capacity rather than being employed for search and warning. Later the Type 291 was introduced, which worked on a 1 ¼-metre wavelength, and was equipped with a revolving aerial so as to provide an all-round search capability.

However, to successfully detect a small target, such as a partially sub-merged or surfaced U-boat, a much shorter wavelength was required. British scientists developed the idea of what was termed the resonant cavity mag-netron, and in March 1941 this led to the introduction of a shipborne set that could detect a surfaced submarine at 5,000 yards, a partially submerged submarine at 2,800 yards, and even a periscope at around 1,300 yards. As Lieutenant Commander Peter Kemp expounded, this was a significant breakthrough:

> It carried with it a double advantage: it gave to Allied escort vessels an accurate means of locating surfaced U-boats at night and in thick weather; and it operated on a wavelength that was inaudible to the radar search receivers, operating on 1.5 metres, with which the U-boats were fitted. With the centimetric radar fitted in aircraft as well as escort

vessels, any U-boat located could be attacked from the sea or from the air without any prior warning of attack.[74]

A related and important innovation was the Plan Position Indicator, consisting of a cathode ray tube attached to the rotating antenna of a radar set. This provided the operator with a visual picture of the surrounding sea, and could reveal objects such as a surfaced U-boat. It had a useful application in convoy warfare where it enabled escorts to maintain accurate screening, and could be employed to rapidly help identify friend from foe. Similarly, in late 1943 the sonobuoy was introduced; this could detect a submerged submarine by picking up its propeller noises on a submerged hydrophone attached to a radio transmitter which sent the result to warships. Another invention in detection was the Magnetic Airborne Detector (MAD), where 'the magnetic field of a steel-hulled submarine was used to provide a response in an airborne magnetometer', although this did not see concerted use until 1944, when the Germans had introduced the schnorkel which gave U-boats greater capacity to remain submerged.[75]

Illumination at night was another challenge, and had received scant attention before the war; this was a significant drawback given the penchant of many U-boat commanders to choose surface attacks by night as their main tactic. In mid-1941 British scientists had developed 'Snowflake', a flare that overcame the problem and lit up a convoy long enough to give escorts time to properly engage the enemy. Developments in radar ultimately made this technology virtually redundant.

The introduction of newer and better ships was also a boost to the navy in its efforts to counter enemy submarines. This included the Castle class corvettes, an improvement on the earlier famous Flower class; the new corvettes were larger, had less cramped living accommodation and greater range. One such was HMS *Leeds Castle*, built by W. Pickersgill & Sons of Sunderland and launched in late 1943. An officer who joined her as she was commissioned recounted that the Castle class were 'a new concept altogether. They were slightly bigger than the Flower class and they carried 90 men. They had good Asdics, the anti-submarine equipment ...'[76] Similarly, River class frigates, with a maximum speed of 20 knots, were capable of countering surfaced U-boats that were not as fast. The use of prefabricated building technology also witnessed the introduction of the Loch and Bay class frigates that proved popular with many sailors. By 1943 with ships like these, plus sloops, notably of the Black Swan class that were highly seaworthy, it became possible to form dedicated support groups, trained and equipped for anti-submarine warfare, without stripping escort groups of the resources they needed to protect convoys. As Denis Logan from the 2nd Support Group outlined: 'Our job was to get between the wolf packs and the convoy routes and to break them up ... For example, RAF Coastal Command used to fly the Sunderlands [flying boats] out and if they made sightings they used to send us after them ... The system was the moment they [U-boats] broke the surface, the guns opened up because they could fire off torpedoes. It was unfortunate for them that they had no ways of showing surrender.'[77]

Having better ships and improved methods of detecting U-boats, and good training in their use, was clearly all-important. However, the navy also required the weaponry necessary to effectively tackle submarines once they had been located. Sir Robert Atkinson commanded a number of corvettes in the Atlantic during 1940–1943, and recounted that if a U-boat was spotted on the surface:

> you'd immediately report it to the commanding officer and attack it ... If it were underwater you'd report your contact and you'd hold him for 200 yards or so and keep watching his position because early in the war you had to pass over them before you could drop depth charges, which meant water was in turbulence.[78]

As indicated above, initially depth charges offered the primary means of attacking a U-boat. According to Captain Charles Fetherston-Dilke, 'You rolled them over the stern or fired them out of mortars called depth charge throwers which threw out to the sides. Thus if you had both the mortars and the ones going over the stern, that constituted a pattern of depth charges. The maximum we could do was fourteen – that was a big bang.'[79]

The depth charge had evolved little from those deployed during the First World War, and had to explode close to a submarine to do any real damage. A standard attack pattern comprised five depth charges launched in the manner indicated above, and these took time to sink before exploding, so as to allow the attacking ship to clear off. Early in the Second World War it was found difficult to set depth charges to explode deep enough to damage submarines that were capable of diving to greater depths. Consequently, a new type was developed that could be set to explode as far down as 500 feet. The naval depth charge was also adapted with Torpex explosive and a new firing mechanism, so that by 1943 aircraft could employ these with lethal effect against submarines. However, as Christopher Collis, a sub-lieutenant aboard HMS *Leeds Castle*, discovered, depth charges still had their limitations:

> When you attacked a submarine, having picked it up when it has dived, and you've got it on the Paching the submarine you lose contact, the

contact's too close, and thus you lose contact as you go over the submarine. And its slightly guess and by God as to where you drop your depth charges, and what depth you set them off at because each depth charge has a pressure gauge on it which you can turn to resist certain pressures, and go off at that depth, a certain depth, you see.[80]

Sometimes depth charges would not actually destroy a U-boat but instead force it to the surface where it could be finished off or even captured. Notably this occurred with U-110, which when boarded during 1941 yielded invaluable intelligence material, including various German naval documents, code books and a complete Enigma machine, all of which were later analysed by government code-breakers at Bletchley Park. Commander David Balme vividly remembered the events leading to the capture of U-110, when as a young sub-lieutenant he was serving with HMS *Bulldog* from the 3rd Escort Group. The convoy had turned 45 degrees away from where they expected the U-boat to be, with HMS *Bulldog* in the centre of the escort group as leader, and ahead of the convoy:

> The *Aubrietia* [a Flower class corvette] on that side of the convoy immediately got contact and fired depth charges ... We were just about arriving on the scene then when she fired her second pattern of depth charges and it pushed the U-boat to the surface, which was the dream of all escort vessels. You could see the U-boat coming to the surface, and you really knew you'd got her ... We immediately opened fire and so did all the other escort vessels onto the conning tower with every gun we had ... The noise inside that submarine must have been desperate as the shells and bullets rattled onto the hull.[81]

Subsequently, the badly shaken U-boat crew abandoned ship and were seen tumbling into the water. As U-110 did not immediately sink, Captain Joe Baker-Cresswell of HMS *Bulldog* sent across a boarding party led by Balme, an action for which he was later awarded the Distinguished Service Cross.

However, the standard method of Asdic contact and depth charge attack was not sufficient, especially when U-boats employed surface attacks by night. According to Lieutenant Commander Peter Kemp, a weapon was needed that could engage a submarine whilst it was held in the Asdic beam of the attacking ship. 'This obviously meant a forward-firing weapon of sufficient range to avoid the inevitable loss of Asdic contact as the attacker closed on the submarine before releasing depth charges.'[82] The Hedgehog, a multi-spigot mortar that launched twenty-four contact-fused projectiles a distance of around 250–300 yards in front of the firing ship, was devised to meet this requirement, and started being fitted to vessels in 1941. An officer aboard HMS *Hurricane* explained how the Hedgehog:

> was mounted in the position of the forward gun, 'A' gun. Again it was a mortar and it fired twenty-four projectiles each containing 30lbs of explosive, and it fired about 300 yards ahead of the ship. And when they came down in the water, if one of those hit the submarine and detonated then the whole pattern counter-mined and went off together, so that was a good big bang. The great advantage of the Hedgehog was that you could maintain contact with the Asdic right up to the moment of firing, whereas with depth charges you lost contact because you had to go over the submarine in order to drop the depth charges. So that was a considerable advance, you could creep up quite slowly and fire this thing ahead of you and it wouldn't damage the ship but hopefully would damage the submarine.[83]

Although it was a dramatic improvement, the Hedgehog was still difficult to direct accurately, particularly against a deeply submerged U-boat, plus it required a direct hit to be effective.

A further improvement that emerged during 1944 was the Squid. Again this was an ahead-throwing weapon that fired three time-fused projectiles that sank rapidly. It had the great advantage that, unlike the Hedgehog, its projectiles did not actually have to hit the submarine before detonating, so could inflict damage even if they were not within lethal range on explosion. Again, like the Hedgehog, 'you still had contact, and it became much more accurate to sink a submarine. Mind you, if the bombs were going off at a shallow depth you knew all about it ... you were steaming into a quite large explosion.'[84]

Countering U-boats was fraught with tension and fear, even if sailors did their best to hide it. By mid-1944 the Germans were not only using the schnorkel, but were also deploying newer, improved models of U-boat, plus they had introduced the acoustic torpedo which homed in on a ship's propeller noises. Aboard HMS *Tintagel Castle*, one of the new Castle class corvettes, during April 1944 her captain Sir Robert Atkinson and his crew endured a gruelling engagement that resulted in the sinking of U-878. The submarine was spotted in Home Waters lurking near a convoy, and *Tintagel Castle* was ordered to search for it. Fortunately she soon obtained Asdic contact and by that stage in the war had a very experienced crew:

> The submarine made the mistake of going very deep and remaining almost stationary. About 500 feet deep ... and the pressure on its hull was simply enormous. We had this latest Squid equipment and we

obtained contact, calm sea, stationary U-boat ... He was extremely skilful, turning away just before every attack, turning his turbulent water towards us ... Many attacks were absolutely aborted at the last moment because of the turbulence resulting from his manoeuvring. It took about 28 seconds for a Squid pattern to sink and explode at say 700 feet, which he now was.

We hunted that boat all night from about half-past five at night until five in the morning, seeking, waiting, being cruel. Once or twice I held back from an attack. It would unnerve him. He'd wonder what was happening. We would try to attack at what we thought would be the change of watch time, so we gave him no peace. I think we had about six to ten attacks during the night with depth charges. Finally we got him with a huge underwater explosion, which shook the *Tintagel Castle* and put all our lights out ... It was very different from the early days when you were armed with a 4-inch gun and ninety depth charges ... it all could be over in 30 minutes like with U-104.[85]

The destroyer HMS *Petard* achieved the rare distinction during the war of sinking a U-boat, an Italian submarine and a Japanese submarine. During October 1942 U-559 was spotted by an aircraft in the Mediterranean, and promptly dived so as to evade the destroyers sent to hunt her. Petty Officer Reg Crang aboard HMS *Petard* recounted how U-559 'was always trying to creep away into deeper water and we did lose contact from time to time, but the attack on it by the four destroyers went on for about 10 hours, with all four destroyers dropping depth charges in turn. So they had a really traumatic time in that U-boat but their captain and crew were superb and they stuck it out until late at night.' Eventually, after being subjected to such a prolonged attack, U-559 surfaced close to HMS *Petard*, providing her crew with their first glimpse of the enemy: 'we could see its emblem painted on the conning tower ... a white donkey. And the German crew had been so traumatised I think by their experience, having been depth charged for so long, that they couldn't get off that U-boat quickly enough and they were slithering down the casing and swimming over towards the destroyers.' One of the destroyers had to leave and the remainder 'opened fire on the conning tower of the U-boat when it appeared, when it was caught in the searchlights, and the Germans were desperately trying to reach some kind of safety via the destroyers. We put down scrambling nets so they could climb to safety and be taken prisoner.'[86]

Orders had been issued that in cases like this, U-boats were to be captured, if possible, rather than sunk, because as with U-110, this type of incident could yield invaluable intelligence material. A seaman aboard HMS *Petard* recalled how he had been instructed as a member of the boarding party to throw a chain over the conning tower, so that 'if there was any chance they [the U-boat crew] might want to shut the conning tower and go down again they could not do it because the chain was over the top and they couldn't shut the watertight doors to go down, so that was the idea from the officer'.[87] Famously, three men – Anthony Fasson, an officer, Colin Grazier, a naval rating, and Tommy Brown, the NAAFI canteen boy from HMS *Petard* – swam across to U-559. With help from a boarding party that arrived in a whaler, these three recovered numerous documents, including code books that the U-boat crew had failed to destroy, and crucially these helped Bletchley Park once again crack the German Enigma code. However, U-559 had been badly damaged and started to sink rapidly, tragically before Fasson and Grazier were able to get clear. They received posthumous George Crosses, while Tommy Brown, who survived the incident, only to die later in the war attempting to rescue his sister from a house fire, was awarded the George Medal.

Six weeks later HMS *Petard* was responsible, along with a Greek destroyer, for tackling the Italian submarine *Uarsciek* in the Mediterranean. After being attacked with depth charges, the 'submarine gave in pretty quickly', and according to Petty Officer Crang it 'surfaced at night and it was caught in our two searchlights, and of course we opened small arms fire, but it was obviously surrendering very quickly'. With some trepidation a boarding party was again organised. Fortunately the submarine remained afloat for a con-siderable time, enabling the boarding party to obtain 'code books and also maps of minefields, which proved to be of great relevance at the time because the navy was planning an invasion of Sicily' and subsequently Italy, so 'that saved an awful lot of casualties because those mines were swept up before invasion'. It was decided to take the *Uarsciek* under tow, but it sank en route to Malta. Nevertheless, all the Italian prisoners were aboard the *Petard*, plus the captain 'had retrieved ... a ceremonial flag, which was an enormous flag like a big carpet really, and we went into Malta waving – he was waving it from the bridge himself in triumph, and the Maltese had flocked to the docks because they had word somehow of the Italian submarine being sunk'.[88]

On 12 February 1944 HMS *Petard* went on to sink the Japanese submarine I-27 in the Indian Ocean. Together with her sister ship *Paladin* and the cruiser HMS *Hawkins*, she was escorting a convoy from Aden to Columbo when the troopship *Khedive Ismail* was torpedoed, causing great loss of life. For the crew of *Petard* this was 'a frightening sight because it was so un-expected. We didn't expect a submarine to get in, right in amongst us, and the *Khedive Ismail* went down within two minutes.' The convoy scattered, leaving the two destroyers to deal with the submarine, presenting them with the 'agonising decision as to whether to depth charge' given that it 'was so close to the group of survivors'.[89]

Stanley Reynolds, a seaman aboard HMS *Petard*, recorded what happened as the destroyers opened fire on the large Japanese I-class submarine which had surfaced after being depth-charged. 'I was up on the upper deck watching these shells being fired, but it didn't seem to make a lot of impact. And the other destroyer that was with us, the *Paladin*, it decided to go in close and was going to ram the submarine but our captain gave orders not to.'[90] Despite being the more junior ship, *Paladin* did ram the submarine and suffered serious damage, and nearly sank as a result. Consequently, HMS *Petard* went in

> close and used throwers for depth charges, they weren't dropped, they were fired from the side, close so that they would be near the submarine, and try to blow it up from there. There was no action from the Japanese submarine but it was still moving about 8 knots, so it was still moving away or in a direction, wherever it was going it wouldn't stop. So eventually we decided to lay off and fire torpedoes at it. Well, whether the settings were wrong, there were seven sent off from our destroyer to sink it and not one of the seven could have hit. There was no explosion, nothing, and the Japanese submarine was still moving, there was nobody on the conning tower or anything. So obviously you couldn't make out what was going on, really ... the last resort was one torpedo left ... and that last one they say was fired, was the one that sunk the Japanese submarine ... I don't think it was the torpedo ... I think they must have set charges on the submarine and just blew it up.[91]

Air power was another significant tool in the Allies' anti-submarine armoury, and it is impossible to overstate its impact against U-boats, most of which were submersibles, not true submarines. This ensured that they had to spend periods on the surface to replenish their air and recharge their batteries, making them vulnerable to attack, even if they dived. Similarly, when U-boats employed anti-aircraft guns to fight it out on the surface, they were potentially vulnerable. Alongside RAF Coastal Command, Fleet Air Arm aircrew were also engaged in the anti-submarine effort, especially once escort carriers were provided in sufficient numbers to provide convoys with adequate air cover.

Initially bombs were employed by aircraft against submarines, but as the war progressed depth charges and 3-inch rockets proved more effective. According to one FAA pilot, rockets were better than depth charges

'... because you could fire these things at 1,000 yards ... They were extremely easy to launch. You had to be at more or less a right angle, which is pretty steep in the first place, in order to get the 90 degrees you want on the side of the target ... You aimed at the conning tower and pressed the tit.'[92] Alternatively, pilots were trained to look out for the conspicuous swirl left by a diving U-boat and to use that as an aiming point for dropping depth charges.

Another form of tackling a surfaced U-boat in daylight was termed a combined attack. This was outlined by a Swordfish pilot from 813 Squadron FAA, although he never experienced it in action. An aircraft that sighted a U-boat was to remain out of range of its anti-aircraft guns, and radio for help. Typically, this would constitute 'one further Swordfish and a fighter [a Wildcat] and the leading Swordfish would be armed with rockets, the second Swordfish with depth charges preferably, and the fighter with its front guns'.[93] The idea was that the leading aircraft would give the signal, then the fighter would strafe the U-boat, making its gunners keep their heads down, then the leading Swordfish would fire its rockets from around 800 yards, swiftly followed up by the other Swordfish dropping its depth charges.

A vivid impression of the value of aircraft in countering submarines can be gleaned from the experiences of Commander Maurice Henley. He flew the Swordfish Mk III, with all the latest anti-submarine warfare equipment, including Air-to-Surface Vessel (ASV) Mk X radar. While serving with the escort carrier HMS *Campania* during 1944–1945, he was engaged on Arctic convoy duty. On 13 December 1944 he sank U-365, albeit he was not credited with this kill until after the war. Returning from an air patrol, the lead aircraft picked up a contact that turned out to be a surfaced U-boat. However, they were in the awkward situation of having one aircraft with depth charges and no working radar, while the accompanying aircraft had radar but no depth charges. This aircraft therefore had to home in and drop flares, while Henley mounted an attack using depth charges:

There was this U-boat going flat out looking much bigger than I'd seen before with this most tremendous wake, enormously long, broad wake. So I carried on my turn and the observer suddenly said 'He's diving ...' So I turned round and headed back towards the target and got to him about 60 degrees on the bow and tracking him just forward of the conning tower. And just before it went under the nose I pressed the release button on the throttle and felt the effect on the aircraft as the depth charges came off. They were dropped on a distributer set so they would drop 30 feet apart ... And we used to drop in a dive to keep the Swordfish speed up to

130 knots and pulled up and started to turn to starboard ... Apparently, I got a dead straddle ... There was this enormous column of water in the air, and I could see the wake of the U-boat going right into the middle of this ... The next thing we saw was the rear third of the U-boat sticking out of the water at about 45 degrees.[94]

Chapter Four

The Experience of Convoy Work

Within hours of the outbreak of war on 3 September 1939, the torpedoing of the British liner *Athenia* off the north-west coast of Ireland compelled the Admiralty to introduce a convoy system in the Western Approaches. Eventually this was expanded to incorporate most of the main shipping routes in the Atlantic. Ironically, Kapitänleutnant F.J. Lemp, the commander of U-30, which sank the *Athenia*, had exceeded his orders. In doing so he helped initiate the Battle of the Atlantic, 'the first of the two great battles fought during the Second World War upon which the future of Europe depended'.[1] The sinking provided the perfect justification for the British Admiralty, with the belligerent Winston Churchill at its helm, to assume a highly aggressive stance almost immediately the war started, albeit numerous challenges had to be overcome, including instituting effective convoys.

Despite the reservations of many senior naval officers, the convoy system had proved its worth during 1917–1918 by reducing casualties to merchantmen when unrestricted U-boat warfare threatened to sever Britain's trade routes. Consequently, many of those tasked with implementing a convoy system during 1939 had this positive earlier experience to fall back on. While many convoys were vital in transporting goods and supplies of war materials to Britain, others were needed to transfer men and equipment to war zones, particularly in North Africa, the Middle East and the Far East. 'By 1943 Atlantic convoy routes formed a huge interlocking pattern, and linked to it was the convoy route in the Indian Ocean, from the Cape of Good Hope to the Red Sea and Persian Gulf.'[2] Petty Officer Robert Crick was serving aboard the Kent class cruiser HMS *Cornwall* when war was declared, and recalled:

> We spent the next two years running convoys from Freetown [Sierra Leone] and escorting them round the Cape as far as Durban or sometimes we'd pick up ships at Durban or Cape Town carrying troops that had come from England and run them up to Aden. We'd go into Aden to refuel and they'd go through the Suez Canal to get to North Africa ... We spent a lot of time doing that. And on the way back we'd be on our own and doing a search of the Indian Ocean for raiders.[3]

However, merchant ships traversing the Indian Ocean and the Pacific were frequently expected to do so without any form of naval escort. Although it ceased to function once Singapore had fallen to the Japanese in 1942, it is important to appreciate that early in the war another significant convoy route was that between Bombay (Mumbai) and that island fortress, which at the time was widely assumed to be impregnable against attack. Other notable convoys included those in the Mediterranean, especially to the beleaguered island of Malta while it was besieged by the Germans and Italians. Equally, convoys in British waters on the east and south coasts gained a degree of notoriety amongst sailors from the Royal Navy and merchant seamen, not least owing to the presence of mines and the relative ease with which they could be attacked by enemy aircraft or ships. As the war progressed, numerous Arctic or Russian convoys embarked on hazardous journeys in northern latitudes, in order to ferry arms and supplies to the Soviet Union to support that country after it had been invaded by Nazi Germany. In doing so they put a strain on naval resources that were already hard pressed.

A signaller who served aboard the destroyers HMS *Hursley* in the Mediterranean during 1942 and HMS *Oribi* in the Arctic during 1944–1945, recounted that:

> from Alexandria to Malta taking the convoys through was pretty hairy, I must say. There was a lot of loss of ships, not at all a nice time ... I am not sure whether the Malta convoys were the worst or not because I was also in the Russian convoys. With the Malta convoys the weather was fine, of course, and pleasant, which meant there was more action, whereas in the Russian convoys the weather was foul and one thing and another, and the submarines and aircraft couldn't operate in the same way.[4]

A notable innovation was the Defensively Equipped Merchant Ship (DEMS). These carried Royal Navy gunners or even soldiers detailed to protect merchant shipping, many of whom eventually transferred from their parent units to specialist Maritime Anti-Aircraft Regiments of the Royal Artillery. According to Albert Johns, a naval rating who served as a DEMS gunner, the term was an 'overstatement' because 'we had very little in the way of armaments with which to defend ourselves' and soon 'realised the Merchant Navy was a front-line target and we jokingly called it "Death Early My Sons"', but this turned out to be too true to be funny'.[5]

The Royal Navy also committed armed merchant cruisers (AMCs) to protect some convoys, including *Jervis Bay* and *Rawalpindi*, both of which were sunk in epic confrontations with German battlecruisers. AMCs were small passenger liners modified as stop-gap warships, equipped with obsolete guns and manned mainly by naval personnel. By 1943 most of the surviving AMCs were released from the Royal Navy and returned to their former owners, who ran them as troopships, because they had proved 'too weakly armed to stand up even to a German disguised raider, and they were always extremely vulnerable to U-boat attack'.[6]

During the war the numbers of escort vessels made available was increased but, as indicated above, the situation initially was often dire, especially in the Atlantic. One former Merchant Navy officer recounted how in 1940 the protection to convoys offered by the Royal Navy was minimal:

> It was very sparse indeed. One also had the understanding that the navy were involved with the wretchedness of Dunkirk and other commitments, including the Mediterranean, so that North Atlantic escorts were very limited in numbers. And again one takes one's hat off to the small ships of the Royal Navy, such as the corvettes, the armed trawlers and of course the primitive type of destroyers which were supplied. The heavy weather, how some of these small ships managed to survive at all in the North Atlantic gales is still quite a mystery to me, and it must have been hell to have been on a small ship during those days.[7]

As the war continued, the Royal Navy started employing newer ships on escort duty, and the Flower class corvettes proved particularly useful. These relatively small ships were derived from the design for a civilian whale-catcher, had limited armament and were slower than most marks of U-boat. Even so, despite their tendency to roll prodigiously and the uncomfortable living conditions aboard, many wartime sailors considered that 'they were splendid little ships. Their main advantages stemmed from the initial simplicity and seaworthiness of the overall design, driven by extremely reliable engines.'[8] Additionally, they were comparatively cheap to build, could be mass produced, and were readily modified so as to meet operational requirements and the introduction of new technologies and equipment.

During 1940–1943 Sir Robert Atkinson commanded four successive corvettes during the Battle of the Atlantic: HMS *Rhododendron*, HMS *Azalea*, HMS *Anemone* and HMS *Pink*:

> Early corvettes had an open forecastle, not very good, very cramped and the crew were right forward, very cramped indeed, flooded in the foredeck most of the time. An open bridge in the North Atlantic was pretty severe. You went through the crest of a wave. You went through the trough of a wave. You thought you were never coming up again but we did. Later they modified the design to what they called an enlarged

forecastle, the whole of the foredeck was extended towards the bridge, which meant that the crew could come fore and aft without being swept away or totally soaked every time they went forward.[9]

Convoy Organisation

A former wartime naval intelligence officer reflected that the experience of convoys proved an integral component in the overall war at sea. 'It was to be a race between the German U-boat building programme and the time when it would be possible to bring into operation a fully integrated system of end-to-end surface and air escort of convoys. Once that was in operation, the defeat of the U-boats was certain.'[10] Yet it would take the Allies a considerable time to achieve this enviable position and many lives and ships would be lost along the way.

Crucial to the conduct of convoys was their organisation. Merchant shipping was chartered or requisitioned by the Ministry of War Transport, which arranged cargoes and destinations, although the formal ownership of ships did not alter. At the various ports of departure a system of Naval Control of Shipping officers was introduced, one of their main functions being to allocate individual ships to specific convoys. The actual make-up of convoys depended on many factors, not least the speed, characteristics and destination of individual merchantmen. As Rear Admiral Sir Kenelm Creighton stated, 'It was patently no good placing a 6-knot freighter in a 9-knot convoy; nor would any purpose be served by assigning a ship with a cargo for Canada to a convoy going to Gibraltar. Equally useless would be to put down a ship which could not finish loading till Saturday for a convoy due to sail the Tuesday before.'[11] This might sound like common sense, but the requirement for secrecy and the pressure of operating under the confusion and tension of wartime conditions could make such fundamental issues more complex than they might otherwise have been.

Broadly speaking, there were four types of merchant ship: passenger liners, most of which operated to a timetable, had some of their running costs covered by mail contracts, and could carry limited amounts of cargo. Cargo liners were designed to carry specific cargoes and operate in particular regions. Tramp-ships sailed wherever there were cargoes to be carried, picking these up in one port and taking them to another. Finally coasters operated around the British and Irish coasts and off the coast of the continent, running scheduled services or were hired for specific voyages. With the outbreak of war two other types emerged: 'blockade runners consisted of a small fleet of large, high-speed and well-armed motor launches operating from Hull to small ports in Sweden' where they loaded up with ball bearings. By contrast, rescue ships 'were mainly ex-coastal passenger ships specially converted and equipped for their work of picking up survivors from ships sunk in convoy'. By 1943 there were enough rescue ships 'for one to be allocated to every fourth North Atlantic convoy' and some also did sterling work supporting Arctic convoys. Although under Royal Navy control, they were operated by their original crews.[12]

With the exception of convoys between Britain and Gibraltar, where slower ships were included, initially convoys comprised merchant vessels supposedly able to steam at between 9 and 14.9 knots, although in actuality the slowest speed was often below the 9 knot threshold. Ships that were faster or slower than this were routed independently, despite this potentially putting them at substantial risk, given that a surfaced U-boat was reckoned to be capable of 15 to 17 knots.

During the war various refinements to convoys occurred or were experimented with. In the autumn of 1940, for example, 'the upper speed limit was reduced to 13 knots in an attempt to speed up imports by faster passages from ships capable of that speed'. This system only lasted nine months because 'heavy losses among the slower of the independently routed "fast" ships had resulted in an overall reduction of imports'.[13] Likewise, evasive routing was employed, whereby convoy routes were adjusted according to information about enemy attacks, the monitoring of U-boat wireless activity and later the code-breaking efforts of Bletchley Park, the Government Code and Cipher School that crucially proved able to read German Enigma naval codes.

Changes to convoy routes were also made with reference to new methods of protection and the altering circumstances of the war, such as when the capitulation of France in June 1940 forced the routing of London-bound vessels around Scotland rather than via the English Channel. Similarly, in 1943 the German defeat in North Africa, coupled with the Italian surrender, 'simultaneously reopened the Spanish Mediterranean ports and created a new transatlantic supply route to service the armies fighting their way northward through Italy as well as a semi-permanent pool of ships running supplies between North African and Italian ports'.[14]

According to the novelist and naval historian Richard Woodman, one of the chief reasons why so many convoys in 1939 could only travel at 8 knots was because the harsh inter-war economic situation had not encouraged investment in new ships, especially those of the tramp-ship class. These 'were back-breaking, coal-burning relics, just capable of hauling their bulk cargoes of grain, iron ore and coal about the watery wastes of the world ... sparsely fitted, and riddled with cockroaches and rats'. Vessels built as standard war-tonnage merchantmen during the First World War had also by 1939 'deteriorated with age and neglect'.[15]

At the outbreak of war Henry Fellingham was Third Mate aboard the Cardiff tramp-steamer SS *Trefusis*, half-way between Panama and Australia with a cargo of sulphur from Galveston, Texas, bound for Australia:

> We'd had a zig-zag clock put on board, a clock by which you did certain patterns of zig-zagging … and we were ordered by the Admiralty to start zig-zagging and we also dimmed our navigation lights. At that time we just had Coco tins that we pierced and put over our lights, although we were very far from any land or even the sea lanes, because we were in complete isolation out in the Pacific.
>
> … the *Trefusis* was a very low powered ship. She was actually the slowest ship in most convoys we were in because she was an old ship [1914–1918 vintage] and being a coal-fired steamer you had the problem of pulling the fires at the end of each watch. The firemen used to pull the fires and the steam used to drop and your speed used to drop. You then had to ask them to put the revs on and revs on, and you were falling back onto the ship astern of you, and you had this big problem.[16]

Similarly, SS *Lautaro* of the Pacific Steam Navigation Company was an ageing ship. According to her Radio Officer, George Monk, she 'suffered from a lot of problems'. On one voyage in February 1943 they departed 'Liverpool, joined up with convoy. Then half-way across the Atlantic bad weather flooded our forecastle and we had to put into Reykjavik, Iceland. We spent two weeks there undergoing repairs.'[17] Earlier in his service Monk had sailed aboard MV *Empire Confidence*: 'A motor vessel of around 5,000 tons, and had a very unusual background as this ship was built in 1935 for the Nord Deutsche Lloyds service between Bremen and the west coast of South America … she was designed for some 20–24 passengers, a single screw motor vessel. She was captured by HMS *Despatch* and then taken over by the Ministry of War Transport and run under the Royal Mail Lines.'[18]

Typically, ships in convoy were arranged into columns to form a rectangle, broader than it was long, with columns around 600 yards apart, and with each ship approximately 400 yards behind the one in front. A major naval lesson learned from the First World War was, as Rear Admiral Creighton explained, was the value of deploying 'the Battle Fleet on a broad front to present the least possible target to an attacking U-boat'. During the Second World War that same principle was applied to convoys, especially in the North Atlantic. 'So with a fourteen-ship convoy there would be seven columns of two, for the idea is to have never more than two ships in column.'[19] Yet opinions differed over the merits of convoy among the crews of merchantman. Henry Felling-ham, a veteran of several convoys, recounted how:

> Convoy gave you a sense of protection, no doubt about that. It also gave you a wonderment as to why you are a better target in a way as many ships. I mean a submarine has only got to fire a torpedo into a convoy and the chances are that it will hit something, whereas, if you are on your own the submarine has got to get into position and fire at you exactly. But I think it proved during the First World War and the Second World War that convoy was the best form of protection. So we accepted convoy but convoys are a very difficult kind of thing to bear because you were on constant watch. Your job on the bridge of a ship in convoy was a complete power of concentration because you had so many things to contend with.[20]

Particularly vulnerable ships, such as those carrying passengers or those with valuable cargoes such as tankers, tended to be placed in the centre of a convoy so as to provide them with increased protection from U-boat attack. A further indication of the importance of the convoy system in protecting ships can be gleaned from the experience of Commander Maurice Henley. As a young pilot with 813 Squadron, Fleet Air Arm, he flew Swordfish Mk III aircraft from the escort carrier HMS *Campania*. During 1944–1945 she undertook Arctic convoy escort duty, by which time the tide of the war had turned dramatically against the Axis powers, and the provision of both escort vessels and air cover for most convoys had vastly improved. On Convoy RA62, returning from Russia to Britain, the layout was as follows:

> The convoy organisation was such that the centre columns of ships were shortened a bit and so those ships in the outer columns were longer and formed a sort of three sided box, and the carriers used to operate as far as they could inside the box, so in fact the merchant ships were protecting the carriers which in turn were protecting them.[21]

Given the formations deployed, clearly convoys in all theatres could occupy a significant amount of space at sea. This was something that Eric Hills found difficult to comprehend, when as an inexperienced young stoker aboard the cruiser HMS *Manchester*, he took part in Operation Substance, one of the famous Malta-bound convoys. On leaving Gibraltar his 'first reaction was that it was too far spread out in the lovely, bright blue Mediterranean. I thought a convoy was tightly packed around a few ships ... it was so far out ... but this was my first convoy.'[22]

Initially it was thought impracticable to control more than thirty to forty ships in a single convoy. However, over time and with experience much larger convoys were formed. One of the biggest ever recorded was HX300 of July–August 1944, which comprised an impressive array of 166 ships. As indicated, the various convoys in the different theatres were all designated specific code numbers, and for security reasons these sometimes altered during the war. Ultimately over 500 different convoy codes were employed, ranging from AB to ZT. For some the name of a home port was employed, so that convoys from Halifax were prefixed with HX or HXF in the case of fast convoys. Likewise, convoys with an SC designation referred to Sydney Cove in Nova Scotia where they had formed up, rather than meaning a slow convoy. The famous PQ series of Arctic convoys were given their name after the initials of a naval staff officer, although later their designation was changed to JW. Another well-known convoy route was that which shipped troops to the Middle East, and was given a WS designation, leading them to be dubbed 'Winston's Specials' after the Prime Minister.

Convoy routes had their own operational cycles. Typically, the HX series worked on a four day cycle, although in 1942 New York replaced Halifax as the departure/end point on the western side. By the middle of the war it was possible to employ an interlocking convoy system which incorporated the entire American coast down towards the Caribbean.

Among the earliest convoys to be established were those running up and down the east coast of Britain between London, the River Tyne and the Firth of Forth. As wartime naval officer Alan Burn explained, 'east coast convoys were coded FN northwards, and FS southward. They ran on a two-day cycle in each direction, starting with FN1 and FS1, progressing to FN100 and FS100 and then restarting time after time as the war rolled on. They were escorted by the destroyers, sloops and A/S [anti-submarine] trawlers of the Rosyth Escort Force ...'[23]

Economically these east coast convoys were essential, even if they lacked recognition when compared with the better known Atlantic and Arctic routes. The merchant crews had to be of a high standard, and differed from ocean-going crews because they had signed home trade articles specifically allowing them to work closer to home. The cycle for an individual ship would entail two days sailing up the coast, two days loading up, followed by a two day return voyage. George Monk experienced a number of these convoys during the war:

They were all civilian ships, these colliers belonging to civilian com-panies. And they would do one trip a week, north- and south-bound. And yet the whole war effort hinged on these colliers because you wouldn't have had any transport, electricity/power, gas, industry in the southern part of England to back up the invasion [D-Day] if no colliers ran.[24]

In contrast, most Arctic convoys, like those to Malta, tended to be massive naval operations, or, as one naval Fighter Direction Officer put it, 'a very serious programme in naval warfare'. During PQ18 he served aboard *Empire Morn*, a catapult-armed merchantman (or CAM ship), equipped with a Hurricane fighter that could be launched for one sortie only, the pilot then having to ditch in the sea or fly to the nearest friendly airfield if he had enough fuel:

> that was quite an interesting trip. We sailed from Loch Ewe and joined up with the American contingent, and we were forty ships strong, merchant ships and a massive escort, close escort. And apparently although we never saw them a massive Fleet escort in case of capital ship engagements elsewhere, we knew not where and we had our course to take to Archangel.[25]

Like convoys in the North Atlantic, those in the Arctic tended to entail the assembled merchant ships steaming 'in a formation of short columns on a wide front to frustrate U-boat attack'.[26] When the first PQ convoys were mounted in the autumn of 1941, the original intention was for convoys to run on a continuous cycle, with one leaving Iceland bound for Murmansk every ten days. Between 1941 and 1945 a total of forty convoys were run to north Russia, ferrying a variety of armaments, equipment, tanks, aircraft, raw materials, food, medical and other supplies, eventually amounting to more than £420 millions' worth of goods from Britain alone.[27]

To command the merchant ships, a convoy commodore was selected, usually a retired senior Royal Navy officer, who had voluntarily reduced his rank to Commodore Royal Navy Reserve (RNR). This included Vice Admiral Sir Malcolm Goldsmith, a veteran of the Battle of Jutland in 1916, when he had commanded a division of the 9th Destroyer Flotilla, and who later became the King's Harbour Master in Malta, before being put on the retired list in 1931. 'He was back as an ocean commodore on 4 September 1939, taking his first convoy out on 7 September 1939, and completing thirty-eight convoys, plus a number of military convoys, before the end of the war.'[28]

The commodore would position himself in the leading ship of the central column, together with his staff. Typically, each commodore had a requirement 'for a minimum of five staff: a Yeoman, a Petty Officer Telegraphist, a Leading Signalman and two Signalmen'. The last three ratings were often engaged for hostilities only, although initially 'there was a serious shortage' of personnel to perform these functions.[29] While the commodore oversaw the merchant shipping, ultimately command and control of convoys rested with the senior Royal Navy officer commanding the escort, albeit he was typically younger and held lower rank than the commodore. Rear Admiral Creighton served as a 'Commodore of Convoy' and described what it entailed. The idea was to:

> sail aboard one of the merchant ships and control the navigation, zig-zags and stationing of vessels in convoy. It was to him that the masters would signal their troubles, the commodore acting as their interpreter to the escort commander, who would probably have little knowledge of the vagaries of merchant ships and the difficulties of trying to manoeuvre them in company. Within the convoy the commodore passed all the orders.[30]

With an admirable degree of foresight, training/instruction was instituted before the war on subjects such as convoy tactics for former flag officers, including Creighton and Goldsmith, who went on to become convoy commodores. This involved courses at Greenwich College, the Royal Navy's university, to prepare such men once more for sea-going duties, and to update them on contemporary practices and technologies.

Before most convoys set out there was a conference which acted as a form of briefing, and could vary in complexity depending on the size and nature of the specific convoy involved, and where the ships were anchored prior to forming up. Usually up-to-date meteorological information would be provided, and warnings given over the dangers of making smoke and straggling, i.e. allowing a merchant ship to fall behind the convoy. Details would be provided on matters such as 'the intended route, steaming order, convoy speed and special signals ... expected submarine concentrations would be explained and the location of "friendly" minefields disclosed ... composition of the escort and various rendezvous and refuelling points for the warships'.[31] Likewise, 'each master was given a sealed envelope. Inside was a plan of the route to be followed, his destination and his ship's position relative to the rest of the convoy on the commodore's order to form up'.[32]

Control over all convoys was also exerted from ashore, and this had particular resonance in the Atlantic. With the closing of the Port of London to ocean-going convoys in early 1940, Liverpool assumed great importance, and in the Operations Room at Derby House, Western Approaches Command HQ, plots were maintained that charted the Battle of the Atlantic and the situation in Home Waters. Notably, Western Approaches Command centralised and galvanised operational control of convoys and anti-U-boat efforts under one man. Its foundations were laid during the late 1930s by Admiral Sir Martin Dunbar-Nasmith, who had been awarded the Victoria Cross as a submarine commander during the First World War. These foundations were successfully built upon by Admiral Sir Percy Noble, invariably considered a dapper and charming commander-in-chief. In November 1942 he was succeeded by Admiral Sir Max Horton, described by a Royal Navy officer who knew him during the war as having 'a flair for picking the right men' and 'more personal charm than any man I have ever met, but he could be unbelievably cruel to those who fell by the wayside' and did not meet his expectations.[33]

Crucial to this land-based effort in support of those at sea was the work done at Derby House, and other facilities, by women from the Women's Royal Naval Service (Wrens). During 1942–1945 Ida Stedman served as a plotter at a Coastal Forces base in Dartmouth, predominantly acquiring the necessary skills on the job, while under the supervision of more senior, experienced personnel:

> We had a great big table with a graph and all the shipping routes and ports and places. As you got a plot it was in numbers of the squares. You got it into the Plotting Room from the radar station. One person would be sitting listening to the plots, and writing them down and the other one would be putting them on the plot, and another one would be putting it up on the wall on the board. So always three on duty and a duty staff officer ...
>
> You had to identify whether it was a convoy, an E-boat, or whatever it might have been. With the plots the track it went on [assisted with this]. An E-boat would have been coming from the south, but sometimes Gannets were mistaken for E-boats, they seemed to make a thing on the radar, and we used to make plots of them ... Our own convoys we knew what course they were going on and at what time they should be at a certain place.[34]

Similarly, Audrey Roche worked as a rather isolated cypher officer stationed in Southend-on-Sea during 1941–1942. This was where:

> all the merchant ships for the east coast convoys gathered, off the end of Southend Pier. And so it was entirely convoys, there were no escort vessels, they used to come but we didn't have any sort of dealings with them much, or the merchant ships much, which were mainly colliers or green [new/inexperienced] ships over from America.
>
> Again, you didn't know what was going on anywhere else. Occasionally you would see signals which gave you a bit of idea what was going on

because of course another thing that they had there were MTBs [motor torpedo boats]. And you'd get signals in about the battles between E-boats [German MTBs] and the MTBs. And we'd get the signals about attacks on the convoys, and that sort of thing, but it was a very restricted view of the war ... You heard what happened, and heard that convoy such and such had arrived safely ... The tele-printer was always plain language but you had to use cyphers when dealing with ships.[35]

Conditions and Challenges

One of George Monk's earliest Atlantic convoy experiences was as the radio officer aboard SS *Beaverbrae* of the Canadian Pacific Line. It was of around 10,000 tons gross, with a twin screw turbine and capable of 14 knots. During July 1940, crucially before the Germans had consolidated their U-boat and air bases in France:

We sailed from London, coastal convoys southbound, that's down the English Channel, convoy for about four days out from the West Coast, then on our own to the St Lawrence and Montreal. We did not export cargo in this ship. We had a turn round in about four or five days, then we were fully loaded and returned from Montreal to Halifax to await convoy. We were in Halifax about three days, convoy left, we were vice commodore of Convoy HX59, and we had no problems crossing the Atlantic, no attacks. We did have fog, as is usual in parts, which is normal in the North Atlantic at that time of year. And then we were diverted to the north about route, which meant we had to go north of Ireland up through the Minches, around Scotland and down the east Scottish coast to Methill on the Firth of Forth, where we joined an east coast convoy to London. We weren't attacked, even on that part, from what I remember.[36]

Other merchant seamen were not so fortunate. Recounting one of his first wartime voyages, Neil Hulse described how his convoy was pounced upon in the North Atlantic by U-boats as it laboriously ploughed homewards from Halifax. The experience had a certain unreal quality to it because his own ship was not targeted:

In the long distance the first ship was torpedoed, then another and another. Out of forty ships, I think roughly thirteen ships were lost on that particular voyage. That was my first encounter with war at sea.

It was to me personally a long distance affair because I was never very close to a ship to see the misery or the screaming of the people being burnt. It was always about three columns away from me at that time ...

The Oerlikon 20mm anti-aircraft cannon was a reliable and much-valued weapon. Its rate of fire was 650 rounds per minute, with a magazine capacity of 60-round drums. (*David Smith*)

Designed to replace the Swordfish, the Fairey Albacore was more powerful and had an enclosed cockpit, although it was still outclassed by its predecessor. (*David Smith*)

Fairey Barracudas with their wings folded on the deck of HMS *Formidable*. This was a three-seat torpedo/dive-bomber flown by the RN, including against the *Tirpitz*. (*David Smith*)

Built by Chance Vought, the Corsair was a large and powerful naval fighter dubbed the 'bent-wing bastard from Connecticut'. (*David Smith*)

The Grumman F4F Wildcat (*aka* the Martlet in British service) was, according to Captain Eric 'Winkle' Brown, 'blunt-nosed, square-tipped, and looked like an angry bee'. (*David Smith*)

This aerial view of HMS *Formidable* provides an impression of the challenges pilots faced when taking off or deck landing. (*David Smith*)

HMS *Formidable* at Malta. An Illustrious class carrier, she served in the Mediterranean until the autumn of 1944 when she joined the British Pacific Fleet. (*David Smith*)

On 4 May 1945 HMS *Formidable* was hit by a Kamikaze off Sakishima Gunto. (*David Smith*)

HMS *Eagle* was lost in the Mediterranean. As can be seen here, she was a conversion of a Chilean warship. (*David Smith*)

Queen Elizabeth class battleship, HMS *Barham*, was torpedoed by U-331 off Sollum in November 1941. (*David Smith*)

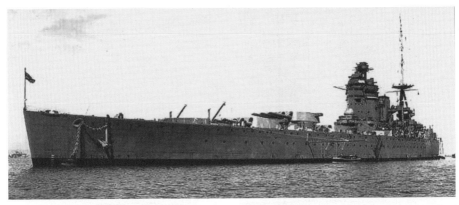

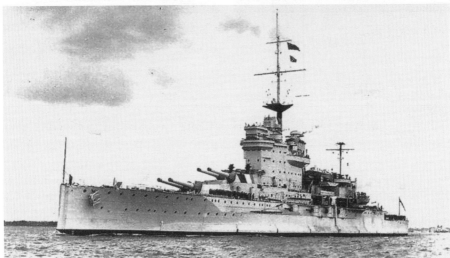

(*Top*) The battleship HMS *Nelson* served with the Home Fleet and Force H before undergoing a refit and joining the East Indies fleet in 1945. (*David Smith*)

(*Middle*) HMS *Warspite* saw action with the Home and Eastern Fleets, and with Force H, notably supporting amphibious operations in Italy and Normandy. (*David Smith*)

(*Bottom*) HMS *Edinburgh*, a Southampton class cruiser, was lost in the Barents Sea during April 1942. (*David Smith*)

Colin Kitching at his action station, one of the gun positions on HMS *Edinburgh*, wearing his anti-flash gear. (*SWWEC*)

Join the Navy and see the world! George Trevett served in the Caribbean, Far East, Mediterranean and Britain. He is pictured here on a visit to Cairo. (*Jess Trevett*)

George Albert Trevett enlisted in late 1940 and trained as an observer with the Fleet Air Arm. (*Jess Trevett*)

George Smith worked as a coder, and is seen here relaxing at Nuwara Eliya, Ceylon (Sri Lanka), at the shore establishment HMS *Gould*, June 1946. (*David Smith*)

Many ex-liners, including *Worcestershire* (pictured here), were fitted with obsolete guns and commissioned as armed merchant cruisers in an effort to counter German raiders. (*David Smith*)

Other merchantmen, including RMS *Otranto*, were pressed into service as troopships. (*David Smith*)

HMS *Jersey*, a J class destroyer launched in 1938, was mined off Malta in 1941. C.B. Blackmore was a cartridge man on A gun, the turret on the forecastle. (*David Smith*)

(*Top*) Lieutenant Commander C.H. Knollys experienced intensive action in the Far East in 1945 on HMS *Saumarez*, an S class destroyer launched in 1942. (*David Smith*)

(*Middle*) Flower class corvettes, such as HMS *Anemone* pictured here, were instrumental in winning the Battle of the Atlantic. (*David Smith*)

(*Bottom*) Black Swan class escort sloops, such as HMS *Starling* shown here, were similarly vital in countering U-boats. (*David Smith*)

HMS *Serene* at Malta in 1946. She was an Algerine class minesweeper, a type that proved most efficient. (*David Smith*)

HMS *Tyne*, a depot and repair ship that served with the Home Fleet until 1944 when she was transferred to the British Pacific Fleet. (*David Smith*)

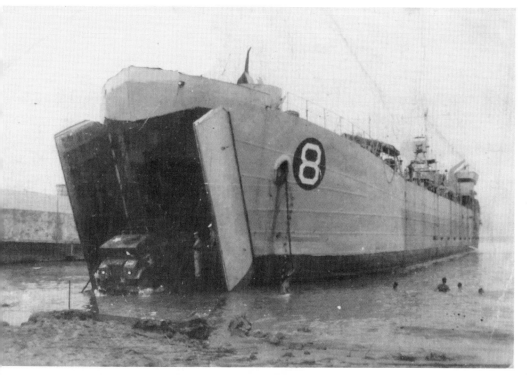

Landing Ship Tanks, like LST 8, were an essential ingredient in amphibious warfare, especially in bringing armour and heavy loads ashore. (*George Henderson*)

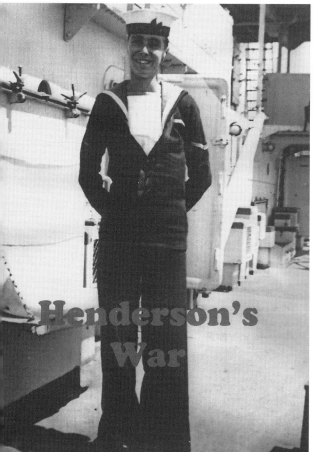

Henderson's War

George Henderson pictured as a leading rating returning home on a Loch class frigate. He served on LST 8 in the Mediterranean and Normandy before retraining as a torpedoman and seeing action with a submarine depot ship in the Far East. (*George Henderson*)

LCP (L) were of wooden construction and built in the USA and supplied to the Royal Navy under Lend-Lease. This photograph shows part of Colin Kitching's flotilla in action. (*SWWEC*)

Coastal Forces was a glamorous, if dangerous, branch of the Royal Navy. Crews engaged in nerve-wracking and exciting operations in the English Channel and elsewhere. (*David Smith*)

MTBs like these near their base at HMS *Hornet* were integral to Coastal Forces, and in many cases were maintained by scores of Wrens. (*David Smith*)

Boxing, like football, rugby and deck-hockey, was a popular sport in the navy. (*David Smith*)

Sailors tried to keep clean, even under harsh conditions. Here a group are dhobying or washing clothes. (*David Smith*)

Holystoning (scrubbing) wooden decks, traditionally with brittle sandstone, was still a routine activity on some warships at the outbreak of war. (*David Smith*)

Issuing the rum ration aboard HMS *Royal Oak* in 1939. (*David Smith*)

Sailors enjoying a tickler, a hand-rolled cigarette using ship-issue tobacco. (*David Smith*)

Seahorse, one of the numerous S class submarines that saw extensive war service. She was lost in January 1940 when attacked by German minesweepers in Heligoland Bight. (*David Smith*)

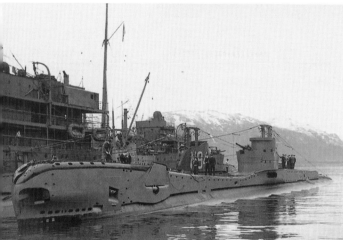

The T class submarine *Tigris* alongside the submarine depot ship HMS *Titania*. She was subsequently lost in the Mediterranean, cause unknown. (*David Smith*)

The control room aboard a submarine clearly illustrating the cramped and claustrophobic conditions that typified a submariner's working and living environment. (*David Smith*)

At the end of the war, an important task facing the Royal Navy was helping to repatriate former prisoners of war. Here Australian ex-POWs are seen playing cricket on HMS *Formidable* en route to Sydney. (*David Smith*)

A wartime romance: George Smith with his then girlfriend Nancy (later his wife) at Saltwell Park, Gateshead, July 1944. (*David Smith*)

As a young man, one had the optimism that it would never be you and nothing would happen to your own ship.[37]

While organisation and command and control were important, at sea warships and merchantmen in convoy still faced numerous potential obstacles, even if they did not encounter the enemy. According to an official wartime booklet, initially it could be difficult to persuade the Admiralty that merchantmen did not 'always combine the discipline and precision of warships' and that 'some merchant crews and ships were a source of worry, straggling in convoy, belching smoke, throwing too much garbage overboard and showing lights'. Similarly, having to place 'fast and slow, new and old ships in the same convoy harassed both Admiralty and merchantmen', and it proved difficult for the Ministry of War Transport 'to find an escort for every ship as soon as she was ready to sail' and to deal with delays caused by 'suspected mine-laying in channels'.[38]

Moreover, convoys had traits that were anathema to the majority of merchant seamen, conditioned by their peacetime experience to giving other vessels a wide berth. Consequently, many did not 'relish having to sail in close proximity by day and by night without lights and with a crowd of other ships', plus having to deal with constant changes of course due to the zig-zag was 'hair-raising'.[39] Further tension arose from the need to cooperate with the Royal Navy, an inescapable requirement of working in convoy. According to Merchant Navy officer Neil Hulse in 1939:

> We never had any experience of the dramas of close convoy work. This really was a shock when we had to do zig-zagging at night blacked out and in bad weather with ships of varying standards and speeds. Some were very poor steering ships, and so before enemy action ever started, it was the drama of convoy work which alerted us to the hazards yet to come.[40]

Among some of the most awkward convoys were those in British waters, either along the east coast or in the English Channel. Having been barred from ocean-going service on medical grounds, George Monk obtained the relevant certificate to serve as a radio officer on coastal craft. As part of the crew of SS *Bowcombe*, a typical east coast collier, he made several voyages during 1944. Just as earlier in the war, 'the U-boat menace, air attacks and mines' were still a potential threat. Coupled to this was 'the American Air Force ... If they'd been on a raid over Germany and couldn't drop everything, they held them until they got to the coast and decided to drop them in the sea before they got on land. It's amazing how near they came to sinking some of the east coast convoys.' Late in the war another danger to coastal shipping was Hitler's 'V' or vengeance weapons. 'In London we had some very near misses in the river with the V-1s because they were coming over that way.'[41]

Another challenge with east coast convoys throughout the war was navigation. As George Monk remembered, this centred on the principle of what merchant seamen knew as

> keeping within the tramlines because it was essential for convoys which were only two columns each. The east coast was marked with buoys and you had to go from buoy to buoy to buoy. And as such on one side you faced the shore and on the other side you faced minefields. So it was essential to keep within these tramlines as they called them.[42]

Similarly, a Merchant Navy officer with significant experience of Atlantic convoys considered that:

> The most difficult convoys I was in during the war were on the east coast, running between Methill, the Tyne and Southend because these were in two lanes. The width of the channel, which was a swept channel for mines, was not much greater than for two ships abreast. And so you had very tight limits into which you could steer, and then the types of ships, some little coasters. I always remember one ship called the *Brastead*, and you can guess what we used to call her. But she used to be our next ahead and she used to do this thing about the fireman. You'd be watching her, she'd be about two cables ahead, and all of a sudden she's right on top of you almost stopped, and you'd have to go right out almost as far you dare because of the minefields. And she used to drop back three or four ships behind, and then a new fireman came along and stoked up the fires again, and she'd go steaming off with her 'bone in her teeth', as we called it and get in front of you again. And she used to do this day and night. And really we were more scared of her than we were of E-boats and mines.[43]

The east coast was tough for the Royal Nay too, especially early in the war when the Luftwaffe posed a serious threat. During 1940 Alexander Downing served as a signaller aboard HMS *Curacoa* with the 1st Anti-Aircraft Squadron in the North Sea, and recalled that 'the whole of the east coast was a sort of bomb alley, yes, it was pretty rough all down the east coast'.[44] HMS *Curacoa* was later sunk in a collision with *Queen Mary* off the coast of Donegal. As Downing recalled, she was

> a 4,000-ton cruiser [Ceres class] and we were based on Scapa Flow, and they were very, very noisy those east coast convoys at that time because

they were under constant air attacks ... And we were one of the main anti-aircraft ships. I think we could empty our magazines if we fired continuously for half an hour. That was the sort of gunnery we had on it. We were bristling with guns, 4.7s, Oerlikons and much smaller guns. We really were a noisy, noisy ship. We were getting attacked by aircraft which we understood came from Stavanger in Norway. And as I say, the 4.7s, Pom-Poms, .5 machine guns, Maxims made us a very noisy companion. In the time I was with her, we steamed 30,000 miles up the east coast, so I was told by the navigation officer.[45]

Likewise, Henry Fellingham noted the sorts of conditions facing merchant shipping in the English Channel during 1940, and the desperate measures that were sometimes taken in order to provide protection against enemy aircraft. On 3 July his ship left Southend as part of Convoy OA178, about the same time as HMS *Foylebank*, an auxiliary anti-aircraft vessel, was bombed in Portland harbour, during an action in which Leading Seaman Jack Mantle was awarded a posthumous Victoria Cross for standing by his gun despite being mortally wounded.

The Germans were starting to use the French airfields, and we had a terrible pasting in the Dover Strait and right down as far as Portland. We lost fourteen ships out of the fifty or sixty we set sail with. I'll always remember the Australian gunner when these Junkers dive bombers were coming in he'd put the Ross rifle on the corner of the wheel house, and would take his aim at the dive bomber. This was all we could do. We had no anti-aircraft armament whatsoever.[46]

Mines were another constant threat, and the fear that these indiscriminate weapons generated resonates throughout the accounts of many wartime seafarers. According to Henry Fellingham, they were one of the things that 'scared me almost more than anything because there was no forewarning of any kind. They just suddenly went up, and it was one of the times when we used to sleep in life jackets on the east coast because of the mine problem.'[47] Floating or moored mines laid by enemy aircraft, U-boats or ships 'floated' up to the correct depth, having been dropped on the sea bed where they remained anchored, and detonated if a ship made contact with one of their horns. If they were spotted they could be countered by merchant seamen using the Ross rifle, which was thought to have good penetration, with 'the hope of "holing" the mine and leaving the seawater to sink it'.[48] Magnetic mines were even more frightening, as 'when a ship passed over a mine lying on the bottom [of the sea] a needle was deflected by her magnetic field' and

'this deflection of the needle "made" a contact which exploded the mine'.[49]
A form of protection against magnetic mines that was developed during the
war was degaussing, whereby shipyard workers fitted what Master Mariner
Sir David Bone described as an 'insulated belt around the hull' of a vessel 'on
the level of the main-deckline' so that 'she was said to be immunised'.[50]
Essentially, passing an electric current around a ship in the manner outlined
above reduced the ship's magnetic field, making her less susceptible to these
mines. Magnetic mines for a period were considered to be Hitler's secret
weapon, such was their impact on both merchant seamen and the Royal Navy.

During June 1941 George Monk was assigned to SS *Auditor* of the
Harrison Company, and when a ship in his convoy hit a mine, there were
unexpected and somewhat humorous consequences, despite the gravity of
the situation:

> She was a steam ship of some 5,000 tons. She was loading and was bound
> for Cape Town and India. Again we travelled up the east coast to
> Scotland. A strange thing happened near Flamborough Head, the ship
> ahead of us, one Ellerman's City Lines was a motor ship and she set off a
> mine, and this went off underneath us so we got a severe shaking. It was
> very hard to stand on deck. [At this time] all ships on the east coast were
> fitted with anti-aircraft kites [akin to small barrage balloons to deter
> low-flying enemy aircraft, especially dive bombers]. And by the severe
> shaking it released the winch controls which held the reel of the wire for
> the kite, and it wasn't until later that we realised the kite had gone up to
> the full length of the wire ... The convoy commodore signalled: 'Why
> are you playing with your kite?' It was just one of those unfortunate
> things where the winch had let it out, so we had to reel it in to the proper
> height of 200–300 feet.[51]

For merchant seamen and the Royal Navy the weather in the Atlantic was a
major issue, regardless of whether convoys were engaged by the enemy or
not. According to one naval officer who experienced numerous convoys in
corvettes, Atlantic weather was simply:

> dreadful. I think during the war I crossed the Atlantic 104 times in differ-
> ent convoys ... wind, mostly rough seas, on average you have a gale every
> four days. So you pitched and rolled all the time, and slept if you could.
> The crew of course slung hammocks so they were free to move about.
> The officers had bunks and you wedged yourself in as best you could.[52]

Even in good weather life could be stressful, because, according to one
merchant seaman, 'that heterogeneous collection of ships of all sizes, types

and speeds called a convoy requires that each individual shall make constant adjustment to course and speed to maintain position relative to the next-ahead and next-astern so that the convoy can always act as a unit in an emergency'.[53] This required discipline and immense powers of concentration, and could become nightmarish when encountering fog. For convoys, foggy conditions ensured that the crew of each ship were constantly 'peering, listening, tensed to take immediate action to avoid collision'.[54]

When collisions did occur, they could inflict severe damage on the vessels involved. Ronald Walsh spent part of his war as an Asdic operator aboard the ageing W class destroyer HMS *Windsor*, on patrol in the North Sea and protecting east coast convoys between Harwich and Immingham:

> We went out and picked up the convoy and we were about an hour or two out of Harwich, half a day out, and it had been a mucky day to start with but a sort of a fog dropped, really foggy, came down just like that in a couple of hours. Then we found we were in the middle of the fog with the convoy and visibility was down to a couple of hundred yards ... We were going along and we got a couple of scares for E-boats that didn't materialise. And we were going along nice and steady.
>
> All of a sudden I was slung off my mess stool and fell on the floor. I got up and there was a lot of shouting in the fog ... and it seemed a screeching noise of some kind, I couldn't make it out. And I thought I'll go and have a look and see what's happening. I didn't think we'd been hit by a torpedo because there was no real explosion ... I got down to the quarter deck and ran into this wall, a metal wall, and I looked up and it was one of these Liberty Ships [a type of merchant ship specially mass produced in America] ... She'd steamed into us and we had a nasty gash, mainly it seemed above water level ... The ships parted and we lowered collision mats [large heavy woven mats] over the side and secured them ... So we then made our way back to Harwich. When we got there, they had a look at us and stuck a plate over our outside temporarily. Then we made our way up to Immingham, so we could have it repaired properly in dock up there.[55]

One solution for dealing with fog was for each ship, except those at the tail of each column, to tow a fog-buoy to make navigation easier for the ship astern. Merchant Navy officer Henry Fellingham used these in the Atlantic:

> These were a piece of wood in the form of a cross and on the cross piece there was a scoop, and when it was being towed along by the ship, the scoop used to scoop up the water and produce a column of water of

about 3 to 4 feet high, and that was what you had to use to steer by. The idea was to keep it as near to your bow so you could see it from the bridge.[56]

Using a fog-buoy in the above manner could ensure that each ship remained at the regulation distance of at least two cables length, as the spout of water they created acted as a warning to the ship astern. However, keeping on station was still a huge challenge, as in fog, the 'flat, uncertain half-light of drifting grey vapour there was neither shape nor colour', so at times 'even the fog-buoys were almost invisible'.[57] Similarly, night-time posed a significant challenge, especially for merchantmen in an era before radar was widely available:

> you had the problem that you couldn't tell the man at the wheel to follow the ship ahead which you could in daytime. You had to give him compass courses to steer, and he'd wander off and you'd find yourself wandering off the line of the column of the convoy. You had to continually bring it back into line.[58]

On Arctic convoys the weather was an inescapable feature of life aboard merchantmen and warships alike, and could be savagely cold. To give an indication of this, the quartermaster aboard HMS *Venomous*, an ancient modified W class destroyer, recounted: 'I remember the captain asking for a cup of tea, coffee or cocoa, and by the time it was made and you got up to him it was ice.'[59] Owing to the smaller nature of their vessels, the crews of warships often had an especially awkward experience. Having served as a teenage deckhand on tugs, Sidney Taylor from Hull enlisted in the Royal Navy during 1942, and after completing his training was posted to HMS *Seagull*, a relatively small Halcyon class minesweeper of 835 tons employed in the English Channel and the Arctic. He recalled escorting one Arctic convoy:

> The weather got a little bit bad, about Force 7, and we finally arrived off Iceland and passed close to the cliffs, and the blast from those cliffs, it was very, very icy. One of the crew was called Jenkinson and he had this disease where he didn't have a hair on his body, head or anywhere else. So obviously he had to wrap himself up, and his fur cap blew off and we had to take him below because he was really hurting, he was screaming ... it got right to his head, it was that keen, that frost.[60]

Another seaman, George Burridge, worked as a radar operator aboard the cruiser HMS *Belfast* in Home Waters, the Arctic and off Normandy during

1942–1944. During convoy protection duty in February 1943 he vividly remembered steaming

> straight up to Iceland, and it was then that we ran into what professionals called the worst storm they'd ever seen, 80 foot waves and that's quite a lot of waves. And the *Norfolk* which was part of the 10th Cruiser Squadron had the top of A turret, about 1–2½ inches of steel ripped off. We ourselves lost what was called a 6-inch loader, which was practice equipment for the gunners to practise without actually loading the guns. This was an enormous thing about 10 feet high and 8 feet wide, bolted to the deck. This was partially ripped out of the deck and then lashed up to try to save the thing, but the storm went on and it went overboard and took the guard rails with it. Several of the lifeboats were damaged as well.
>
> It was hopeless working in such conditions because the ship did roll quite badly to about 40 degrees, and you were waiting for it to come back, and it would go further still, and you'd think for heaven's sake is it going to come back again, quite frightening. It had a nasty habit of doing that, it was very uncomfortable, and getting around ship in those conditions, of course everything was wet, slippery, metal ladders, dangerous, very uncomfortable.
>
> To get to your place of work, there were safety ropes all along the low waist of the ship, which you had to clip onto and run along otherwise there was a strong risk of being swept overboard. That was compulsory, and of course in those waters, we were told quite clearly that if you were washed overboard, if you couldn't be picked up within three minutes, then they didn't bother because you'd be dead anyway. Hypothermia would set in and that would be it, so look after yourself was the order of the day.
>
> Arctic weather was very, very cold. It was made quite clear when you went on the upper deck that unless you had gloves on you were likely to lose skin if you touched bare metal ... [Sailors were also employed] chipping ice off the upper deck again because if it takes on too much weight, there's a distinct risk it could capsize. So chipping ice off the guns and the upper deck was a fairly routine job for people, if you were not wanted for watch keeping.[61]

Tensions between the Royal Navy and Merchant Navy formed a further strand of convoy experience, especially when the latter witnessed naval personnel in apparently comfortable shore postings taking advantage of their position, while they risked all in the Atlantic or elsewhere, with only limited recognition. In Belfast, for example, one tanker crew were understandably upset by the antics of the local degaussing officer, a navy lieutenant commander, who asked their captain 'if he could send a bunch of his squaddies as he called them to get some petrol for his car because he only had enough for official business and he would like to use some for other purposes'. Not knowing how to react, the captain felt he had best acquiesce to this demand.[62]

At sea there could often be a love/hate relationship between merchant seamen and the Royal Navy. As one experienced merchant seaman recalled:

one of the problems we found at sea in the convoys was that they [the RN] were very much our bosses. We used to chug along like a lot of sheep. Very frequently we'd get an alteration of course as much as 90 degrees, not knowing why or where we were going or what was the reason. We just turned 90 degrees and steamed completely away from our destination for sometimes days. The RN escort were darting round like a lot of snappy sheep dogs, and we were the sheep with our tails between our legs. We got that kind of resentment I think. In those days it was the merchant ships that used to catch the worst of the enemy action because the destroyers were far faster and lighter draft, had depth charges and other armament, so they were far less vulnerable to enemy action than we were.[63]

Likewise, a senior naval officer bemoaned that the peacetime relationship between the two services was poor, and this transcended into wartime. 'For years we [the RN] had turned up our snobbish noses and maintained that the Merchant Navy was something to be seen and not heard. Apart from their officers and seamen doing periodical training in warships, and many of us travelling to and from foreign stations in liners, there was lamentably little mixing. It was entirely our fault that they thought that we thought we were some superior form of sea life.'[64]

Unlike their naval colleagues, merchant seamen were not necessarily geared up for combat either, despite the introduction of DEMS and the issuing of armaments to merchant ships. In contrast, sailors in the Royal Navy expected to see action and were generally operating vessels designed with that in mind. As Robert Craddock, who saw action on destroyers during Malta and Arctic convoys expressed, with regard to being bombed: 'I was up on deck most of the time and it didn't worry me because being active servicemen we got trained for that kind of thing and we knew what we was doing.'[65]

Another issue was that the strain of continual convoy work took its toll on ships as well as men. If they were not actually sunk through enemy action, then near-misses, rough seas and bad weather could all hinder warships and merchantmen alike. The aircraft carrier HMS *Eagle* joined Force H in the

Mediterranean as a replacement for HMS *Ark Royal* in March 1942. An air mechanic who served aboard her described how:

> Our job was to supply the island of Malta with aircraft, and in the first month we was there, the month of March, we did three trips up the Med. Each trip was a full blown naval operation, battleships, cruisers, destroyers, submarines, a real big escort to take us down … And each of those trips we got to within 500 miles of Malta and flew off the aircraft and then we turned back. The aircraft made the last bit themselves but each of those three trips was in itself a naval battle because we were up against the might of the Italian Navy and the German Fliegerkorps. Now by the time we'd done the third one, the *Eagle* was so battered around with concussions underwater, bomb explosions and high speed manoeuvring that she literally was unseaworthy.[66]

Clearly convoys in all theatres potentially faced the threat of encountering the enemy. In this respect U-boats, aircraft, surface vessels and raiders were a distinct challenge. By October 1940 the Germans had at least six raiders at sea, armed merchantmen that employed clever tactics and regular changes in disguise to successfully prey on Allied merchant shipping. Likewise, forays by warships against Atlantic trade routes were a significant concern. As Third Mate aboard SS *Trefusis*, Henry Fellingham was involved in the epic convoy HX 84, when the armed merchant cruiser HMS *Jervis Bay*, escorting the convoy, famously took on the German pocket-battleship *Admiral Scheer*:

> it's a time-honoured tradition in the Merchant Navy that the Third Mate relieves the First Mate at five o'clock, two bells, for his tea. And I went up on the bridge at five o'clock and this was Guy Fawkes Night. 5 November 1940 … After the Mate had gone down I noticed that the ship ahead of us had a flag signal flying. I can't remember the exact flags but translated I read the code book … and it said attention is drawn to the bearing indicated and the bearing indicated was 330 if I remember rightly, which means you must look at compass bearing 330. So the convoy was completely as normal up to then. I got my telescope out and put my telescope to the awning spar and looked at bearing 330 and I saw there a ship, which was a battleship … She was almost hull down which means she would be about 10–15 miles away and I saw some lights coming from the side, and I thought at first that she was signalling, and I thought it must be one of ours and she's signalling to us. The next thing we heard the howl of the 11-inch shells flying over us. The first salvo landed about 100 yards to one side of the *Jervis Bay* which then started to put on speed

and pull ahead because she was in the middle of the convoy almost, to pull ahead of the convoy to get at the *Admiral Scheer* but the second salvo hit her and she was on fire in no time at all. And every salvo hit her then. As far as I could tell, if the *Jervis Bay* fired a shot, it didn't get anywhere near the *Admiral Scheer* ...

We were the rear ship of the third column. The commodore was the head ship of the fourth column and the *Jervis Bay* was between the third and the fourth, always tried to keep abreast of number two in the column ... Smoke shot up from her and then a pall of smoke came over her. Within a very short time you could see flames ... I think that the first salvo hit abaft the bridge, more above the engine room. Later the second salvo killed Captain Fegen, who got the VC posthumously for this action.

The convoy scattered. In our instructions that you get from convoy conferences, you are told how to scatter and you have books on it. In no way could anybody call this a scatter as required by the book because everybody was dropping smoke floats for a start, and some ships were even firing their 4-inch guns in the direction of *Admiral Scheer*. And it was just bedlam. You were passing through smoke and coming across another ship at very close quarters, and you had to go hard over and stop your engines and so on like that to avoid hitting her.

The thing which saved the convoy was the darkness. For some reason the *Admiral Scheer* chose to attack the convoy about half an hour before dusk, at five o'clock in the evening and this was November. Within half an hour of her opening fire it was almost fully dark. And consequently she didn't have the chance to pursue as many ships as she might have done because she was using her searchlight by then. And what we did in the *Trefusis* and what everyone else was doing as soon as they saw the flash of her guns or searchlight, you put your stern to that position and steamed as fast as you could.[67]

According to the official history, out of the thirty-seven ships of convoy HX 84, all but five were saved by Captain Fegen's action in *Jervis Bay* by challenging 'her redoubtable adversary to a most unequal duel'.[68] While serving as a seaman aboard the AMC HMS *Comorin*, Thomas Jones heard about the fate of *Jervis Bay*, the ship with which they had alternately been escorting convoys. This was especially moving as many of the crew of *Jervis Bay* were RNR lads from the north of Scotland, and were good mates with the sailors from *Comorin*.

One ship would leave Bermuda with a convoy and the other would leave Halifax, Nova Scotia, with another convoy. And they would come across the Atlantic. I always remember they said to 20 degrees west. And then, the local shall we say, Western Approaches convoy would take over which was mainly destroyers and escort vessels. We hadn't got Asdic or anything and in those days Jerry hadn't got to the Western Atlantic, but unknown to us on this particular convoy we handed the convoy over of about forty ships to the *Jervis Bay* ... and it was our turn then to go back to Bermuda. Then we left the ships close to the *Jervis Bay* and about four or five o'clock in the afternoon it was noticeable that we turned round and we were going flat out back in the direction that we'd left. And the skipper came over the intercom and said the *Jervis Bay* and the convoy were being attacked, and we were going back to give assistance.

Then we'd only got back on the way for about two hours and we turned round again, and was told to get as far away from the situation as possible, as this raider had more or less annihilated the convoy and the *Jervis Bay*. And with this we didn't know what to think, then, whether we were cowards in doing this or sensible.[69]

Numerous merchantmen, including SS *Auditor*, were victims of U-boats during the war, and in proportional terms merchant seamen actually suffered greater casualties than the Armed Forces. One of *Auditor*'s radio officers outlined what occurred the moment she was torpedoed by U-123 in the Atlantic on 4 July 1941, and the emergency measures that were taken in the radio room:

I was asleep at the time of the explosion which occurred at about 1.00pm ship's time ... thrown out of my bunk because the explosion opened up the port side of the ship and in doing so this acted like a rudder and the ship heeled right over. I scrambled into my clothes, grabbed my hammer bag, that was a bag in which I kept a few bits and pieces, ... pay book, handkerchief, one or two things you might need in a lifeboat. Ran along the deck to the Radio Room, all the lights had gone out because the main engines had stopped after the explosion. My Chief was in the Radio Room with the Third Radio Officer [many ships now carried three] ... who'd been on watch and was severely shaken because the explosion occurred virtually below that point of the ship.

The Radio Office was a complete shambles but fortunately our emergency lighting was working, so we could see what we were doing and the Chief was now sending out his position ... The Deck Officers supplied the Radio Room with the ship's estimated position for the next four hours in half hourly positions, so that in an emergency the Radio Officer on watch when instructed to transmit his SSSS message [the

signal notifying that a merchantman been attacked by an enemy sub-
marine] had the information in front of him. He didn't have to check
with anybody and this made it much easier to get your position away
quickly. Because let's face it, the sole purpose of a Radio Officer here was
to transmit and warn other ships and to send back to the Admiralty that
we'd been sunk/destroyed by enemy action.[70]

Nor were warships immune from being torpedoed in convoys. During
Operation Pedestal in August 1942 a lavish naval escort was laid on to support
merchant ships bringing relief to Malta. Among the warships involved were
four aircraft carriers, including HMS *Eagle*, sunk north of Algiers early on in
the operation by U-73, which had been lying in wait in the Mediterranean.
George Amyes, an air mechanic from the Fleet Air Arm, who was serving
aboard her at the time, vividly recalled what happened:

The first thing I knew was there were four distinct detonations and the
ship lurched. And I didn't realise then that we had been torpedoed.
Funnily enough what went through my mind was that we'd hit a school
of whales, and I thought where are the whales coming from in this area
at this time of year, and then the ship started to list. Then I saw a pair of
sea boots hurtling through the air followed by other debris, and as the
ship listed a bit further I thought 'aye-aye we're in trouble here, what's
going on?'

The list started to develop quite rapidly and my feet started to slide
from underneath me but fortunately I was on the upper deck under one of
the 6-inch guns and then people started to hurl themselves up from the
lower decks. The marines who were on the upper deck, they started to
jump regardless of orders or anything else. I saw two of them go over the
side and hit the rising torpedo blister [the anti-torpedo bulge integral to
the design of many warships of the period] as it came out of the water and
their legs came straight through their torsos and they smashed themselves into jelly and slithered off into the water. And I thought 'we really
are in trouble here because if that's the kind of thing that's going on ...'

By now other people were sliding down over the side of the ship. And
when I went down over the side of the ship there were two other sailors
there who were clinging to each other in despair, they couldn't swim.
A ship's officer came down, I don't know who he was, but he just grabbed
one of these sailors in each arm and I heard him say 'now's your chance
to learn' and he dived over the side with these two. And the ship's keel
was coming up and up. And I thought 'if I don't get off here quick I am
going to be smacked in the face by the keel when it comes up, I am going

over as well.' I half blew up my lifejacket and more or less slithered, jumped, scrambled and went into the water.

By that time there were bodies all the way round and rubbish and oil. The ship had slewed completely out of line and the force of the ship moving actually pushed me away from the ship, and I went down about 20 feet I should imagine ... and looked around floundering and was more or less on my own. I started to paddle away in any direction to try and get my bearings and looked round to see the ship and I just had time to see the last smudge of it as it disappeared.[71]

Equally, attacks by aircraft, especially dive or torpedo bombers, could prove devastating against ships. The crew of SS *Empire Lawrence*, many of whom were from the Merseyside area, experienced this at first hand as part of PQ16, a Russian/Arctic convoy in May 1942. She was a freighter of around 8,000 tons, and served as a CAM ship, and was equipped with radar (RDF) that crucially provided the convoy with early warning of air attack, provided it could be kept working. According to one of her naval ratings, air raids became 'fairly constant' after three days out from Iceland, but like many wartime servicemen he was 'pretty inured' to bombing, having lived through the London Blitz and worked in war-torn Birmingham prior to enlistment.[72] Merchant seaman Neil Hulse joined her in Birkenhead as Second Officer, prior to the convoy, and recorded the events that led up to her sinking:

We were No. 11 ship, that's the extreme left of the front line of the convoy, when three planes dived low at us again and whilst we did our best and opened fire almost point-blank, I remember two bombs whistling over the wheel house and they hit No. 1 and 2 hatch. This holed the vessel on the port side in No. 1 hatch, and you could tell by the list that she had that she was making water. The Captain then ordered that it was time ... to abandon ship for no doubt we were going to roll over in half an hour ... So the Captain with the First Officer took the confidential books from the Chart Room and they went down to the galley to get these books fired in the oven. Then the lifeboats on the port side, one lifeboat was launched without any problem, and on the starboard side I was directed by the Captain to go and take command of the starboard lifeboat ... I hastened the crew to get down and I even had my sextant and my chart ...[73]

Others had an even more dramatic experience. As a young rating and radar operator, Commander William Grenfell had only recently finished bravely climbing the main mast of *Empire Lawrence* with the radio mechanic in order to repair damaged cables. Then, on 27 May, there were prolonged and heavy air attacks, and at 2.00pm he'd just left the Radar Office for his turn off duty, and climbed up onto the upper deck to watch what was happening when

> we heard the roar of aircraft and we looked at the stern ... and there was a Ju 88 dive bomber coming straight at us, and you wouldn't believe it but I actually saw the head of the pilot in the cockpit with his goggles and everything. And he came down at us, machine-gunning all the way, machine-gun bullets were hitting the bulkheads, the sides of the ship and so on. They didn't hit us, there were about three or four of us, and we all went down in a heap on the deck and just lay there. And seconds after-wards there was this tremendous bang, and he dropped a bomb and it hit No. 2 hold which was just ahead of the bridge ... and there was ammunition in the hold and this exploded. The ship just lifted up and sank back into the sea, then wavered and slowly went down by the bow but we didn't sink ... The Captain then signalled abandon ship because we were sinking. We took to the boats and I went to a boat on the starboard side ...
>
> And the boat was being lowered and we hit the water when there was the roar of aircraft and down came around five aircraft, and there was the most unearthly explosion ... All I can remember is flying through the air. It was probably only seconds but felt a long time. And I could see huge shapes flying through the air with me, chunks of metal, and there was one shape that looked like the funnel of the ship ... And the next thing I knew, I was in the water and it was freezing.[74]

He was then pulled downwards by the sinking ship, only to pop to the surface like a cork once her boilers burst, and spent twenty minutes desperately clinging to wreckage before being rescued. Although suffering from exposure, he was fortunate to survive; many of his crew mates died.

Escort Duty

Initially the ocean-going escort system was underdeveloped, with perhaps only one escort vessel allocated to every two convoys in the Atlantic. How-ever, by 1940–1941, with the situation becoming more serious, the Royal Navy made more ships available, so that an average of two ships per convoy acted as escorts. These came from an assortment of AMCs, ageing destroyers, sloops, trawlers and early corvettes, because the modern destroyers were held back for battle fleets. However, in time newer models of corvette and more destroyers became available, so that an average of at least six ships per convoy served as escorts. As the King's Regulations made clear, it was their job to stay with a convoy and protect it; hunting U-boats or other enemy craft was very much a secondary priority. Crews were often a mixture of experienced seaman and those HOs who had never been to sea, leading one officer to comment 'what limp shadows we were then of Escort Groups to come'.[75]

In contrast, convoys in the Mediterranean and Arctic tended to be major naval operations in their own right, often with significant escort and covering forces being provided. During 1940–1943, in the operations to relieve Malta, the Royal Navy alone lost one battleship, two aircraft carriers, four cruisers, a fast minelayer, plus a host of smaller destroyers, minesweepers and forty submarines, not to mention the damage incurred by many ships and the losses to minor vessels.[76]

According to a sailor who served aboard a number of ships, including the destroyer HMS *Aldenham* in the Mediterranean during 1942–1944, certain escort work entailed a mixture of routine and boredom, sometimes punctuated by the excitement of contact with the enemy:

> It could be among the most tedious work of the whole war, day after day watching and waiting, sleepless nights and maybe never seeing or hearing a thing. Then suddenly, out of the blue, all action, guns blasting away at enemy aircraft, depth charges tearing the sea apart in search of some elusive U-boat, and perhaps in the convoy, a torpedoed merchant vessel shuddering and disintegrating in her death plunge into the ocean.[77]

A further sense of the routine nature of escort work can be gleaned from the experienced ex-submariner Captain Jack Broome, who spent part of his war commanding the destroyer HMS *Keppel* and was often Senior Officer Escort in convoys:

> The cycle ran: convoy conference, off to sea with a new flock, shed it and collect a homeward-bound flock; on arrival in Londonderry: repairs, maintenance, training, a couple of days' exercising at sea, convoy conference and so on.[78]

Similarly, an officer aboard the destroyer HMS *Bulldog*, who saw considerable action in the Atlantic in 1941 with the 3rd Escort Group, explained that:

> We were escorting convoys from the UK. A convoy would consist of about forty merchant ships and they would come, some from Liverpool, some from the Clyde where we were, and some would come up the east coast and join us off the north-west tip of Scotland ... As you set off into the Atlantic you had your whole convoy of forty ships and our escort group would consist of about three destroyers, three or four corvettes,

and a couple of armed trawlers and a rescue boat ... The object being that no escort vessel could afford to pick up survivors of ships torpedoed.

And we used to take this convoy across to a position south of Iceland and then we'd go into Iceland to refuel. And another escort group would come out of Iceland and take the convoy on for another four days. And so then that second escort group would pick up another convoy coming from America to the British Isles, and they'd stay with them for about four days. Then we'd come out of Iceland, having refuelled, and take it back home. So the whole cycle worked and a destroyer could only stay at sea for about seven days without refuelling ... So you were always having to refuel, and that's a terrific use Iceland was. It meant we could get the convoys well north in the Atlantic as far as possible from U-boat bases.[79]

Yet beyond the routine, close convoy escort was a demanding task, especially for the Officers of the Watch in each warship, who 'had to ensure that the correct zig-zag was made at the right time ... keep exact station on the guide of the Fleet: ... watch the escorts next to him on the radar screen in case they made a mistake' and 'watch for unwieldy merchant ships veering out of position and for sudden breakdowns'. All this was set against a backdrop of his Asdic potentially performing poorly owing to 'numerous underwater sounds all around, and sometimes by interference from other ships' transmissions", plus the cluttered nature of his radar set owing to having several ships in close proximity and the 'spurious echoes' these created. Ultimately, all such 'extraneous distractions' could prevent escorts from effectively forming a screen to prevent U-boats from sailing underneath a convoy or, worse, surfacing in the middle between two columns where they could inflict serious damage.[80]

The importance of having an escort can perhaps best be illustrated by what occurred to the ill-fated Russian-bound Convoy PQ17. In January 1942 the Germans sent *Tirpitz* to Norway, and this battleship potentially posed a huge threat to Allied operations in northern waters, along with other surface vessels, including *Admiral Hipper*. Against a convoy, where the shipping was concentrated, such surface raiders could do immense damage, and yet if a convoy was to disperse or scatter it could become a much easier target for U-boats and aircraft. When PQ17 was launched in July 1942 aerial reconnaissance indicated that *Tirpitz* and *Admiral Hipper* had vacated their moorings in Trondheim, leading the Admiralty to surmise that the convoy was in grave danger of being intercepted. Consequently, on 5 July it was ordered to scatter, and the majority of the escort left the merchantmen, believing it was to block the approach of the German ships. In fact both *Tirpitz* and *Admiral Hipper* were returning to harbour in Norway, and so U-boats and the Luftwaffe were able to take advantage of the situation and decimate the exposed merchantmen. Of the thirty-six vessels that started the voyage, two had been forced to turn back, ten were sunk by U-boats, and thirteen more, plus one rescue ship, were destroyed by aircraft. These ships now lie at the bottom of the Barents Sea, and took with them over 99,000 tons of valuable supplies and equipment intended to help the Russians. In the immediate aftermath at least 300 men were thought killed, missing or taken prisoner, and other survivors were seriously injured, some of whom would die as a result of their ordeal.[81]

As Vice Admiral B.B. Schofield outlined: 'The difference in meaning between "disperse" and "scatter" is important. Ships in convoy ordered to disperse would merely cease to keep formation, and each ship would proceed at her best speed to her destination. [In PQ17] all ships were bound for the same port, Archangel, they would obviously remain in fairly close company with each other for some hours. On the other hand, ships ordered to scatter immediately ... proceed in accordance with a plan laid down on courses which will separate them from each other as quickly as possible.'[82]

The impact of the infamous 'scatter' order has reverberated down the years. As the official history has indicated, the First Sea Lord, Admiral Sir Dudley Pound, had a reputation for interfering in lower-level operational matters from London, and may well also have been suffering from the effects of an arthritic hip and a brain tumour that was to kill him a year later. According to a sailor aboard the auxiliary anti-aircraft vessel HMS *Pozarica* that formed part of the close escort:

> when they said you are going to scatter, then the convoy ... had no defences because they scattered in all directions, and the submarines and aircraft were just picking them off. We got together with the *Palomares*, the other anti-aircraft ship, escort trawlers and we carried on right the way through to Novaya Zemlya, and we were in there about two days and then around the ice pack to Ekonomiya which was just off the coast of Russia and into Archangel ...
>
> The order was really, really wrong because why they scattered [was] because they were frightened of the German battleships coming out to knock the convoy to bits. But they were still in harbour. All the orders for this came from England. They were miles away and didn't know what was happening.[83]

Another seaman, who worked in *Pozarica*'s Transmitter Room recounted:

> We left Belfast on 23 June 1942. Prior to leaving Belfast the crew were issued with tropical clothing, so they naturally thought they were

heading for the Med ... But it didn't turn out that way because we eventually headed north towards Iceland and we anchored just off the port of Seidisfiord and stayed there ... while waiting for the convoy to come across from America, across the Atlantic. And we joined up with the convoy shortly after that date ...

And we took up station near the centre of the convoy, being an ack-ack [anti-aircraft] ship ... And for the first few days everything was quiet ... The first sight we saw of the enemy was a Blohm und Voss BV138 [reconnaissance flying-boat] and that circled the convoy day and night, going round in different directions, clockwise then anti-clockwise. The Blohm und Voss stayed the whole journey, not the same plane because they did change. But the enemy knew exactly what the position was, and how many ships, through these planes. And just a day or so later of course we were then attacked by dive bombers ... and they just seemed to pick off the ships and one of the first ships to be torpedoed was a Russian tanker, and that just went up in flames ... And I remember coming off watch at midnight and went into my hammock for the four hours I was off, in the night, and then came up in the early morning again. When I went down there were four ships off the starboard bow, one off the port bow, same at the stern. They were there when I went down and I came back up the following morning watch they'd disappeared, just gone. That's how it was most of the trip. We did have trawlers and destroyer escorts and they were right out on the horizon, plus there were some heavy cruisers coming up astern of the convoy.

After about a week to nine days, the Captain cleared the lower deck of the *Pozarica*, and informed the crew about what was going on ... And he said he'd just had a signal that the convoy would have to scatter and each ship would have to make port independently and the heavy cruisers coming astern of the convoy and all the destroyers would have to report back to Scapa Flow. And the ships were just picked off one by one because some didn't have any escorts. And the *Pozarica* she sailed north ... and we actually ran into an ice field for a couple of days.[84]

A significant development, particularly in ultimately winning the Battle of the Atlantic, was the deployment of designated naval support groups as opposed to escort groups. These tended to be more uniform than escort groups, were equipped with faster vessels, usually of the same type, and would hurry to assist any convoy that had run into difficulties, chiefly by hunting down and destroying packs of U-boats that were lurking in the vicinity, leaving the escorts free to shepherd the merchantmen to safety. As Commander

D.A. Rayner recalled, his group consisted of new Hunt class destroyers, 'and would go everywhere very fast and in close order, carrying out manoeuvres that could not be carried out by the escort groups, because of the wide differences of speed and turning circle between their individual ships'.[85]

In Rayner's case he rapidly found that this saw his group escorting fast convoys of troopships ferrying over American soldiers from training camps in Iceland to Britain ahead of D-Day. They were not attacked, but 'a surfaced attack on a 15-knot convoy was not very likely. If a surfaced U-boat came in from before the beam he would be detected by the radar of one of our escorts, while if he came in abaft the beam his own maximum speed was so little in excess of the convoy's that he would certainly "lose bearing" (i.e. drop behind) his target and never get into a firing position.' Likewise, with large ocean convoys of around sixty to a hundred merchant ships he reckoned that 'our closely packed little party, carrying out a permanent zig-zag, would have deterred any but the most determined of U-boat commanders'.[86]

Alan Burn served under Captain Frederic Walker, one of the greatest support group commanders of the war, and observed that by 1943 experience, particularly in the Atlantic, demonstrated that the synergy 'of continuous air support with adequate surface escorts could fight a convoy through a concentration of U-boats with limited losses to the merchant ships and unacceptable losses to the U-boats and their air support'. Consequently, every convoy required 'a close escort, a support group in the deep field, an aircraft carrier and aircraft to keep the U-boats submerged and drive off German shadowers' or reconnaissance aircraft.[87] This incorporated the efforts of RAF Coastal Command, whose flying boat crews attempted to escort convoys when in range. Crucially the handful of Very Long Range (VLR) Liberator bombers operated by Coastal Command would also appear miles out from the British Isles, and this did much 'to lift the morale of the dog-weary crews' of ships in convoys.[88]

Similarly, the role performed by the Fleet Air Arm in flying maritime aircraft from escort carriers, including HMS *Campania*, was vital in providing convoys with adequate air cover, and something that took time to establish effectively. Commander Henley, who served aboard her late in the war on Arctic convoy duty, outlined how: 'The usual air patrols we flew were known as Cobra 20s ... it was a circular patrol 20 miles radius from the commodore, round and round the convoy. It was a slow spiral as the convoy moved ahead, two aircraft at a time, one would head off from the carrier in one direction and one more or less in the other direction ... two and a half hour patrols, anything longer and the crew's efficiency would suffer owing to the cold and poor weather, etc.'[89]

Chapter Five

Amphibious Warfare

Historically Britain's position as a leading naval and maritime power gave her control of the sea. Potentially this enabled force to be projected from the sea against an enemy's coastline, almost at will. During wars and campaigns preceding the Second World War, amphibious operations have therefore featured. Yet during the inter-war period, like many important aspects of naval warfare, the British neglected amphibious operations. Partly this was because there was little central organisation of defence after the First World War, and the three armed services acted as rivals competing for dwindling resources. Inter-service rivalry similarly affected the level of cooperation between the armed services, an issue fuelled by the response to the outbreak of war in September 1939. Initially it proved practicable to divide the conflict into three distinct, self-contained spheres, echoing First World War experience. The army would again be landed on friendly French territory, forming a British Expeditionary Force (BEF), and be prepared to mount offensive operations on the continent. The Royal Navy would blockade Germany, hopefully forcing the Nazi regime into submission. Simultaneously, the RAF, the youngest of the services, would drop propaganda leaflets and prepare to launch a devastating aerial blow against the enemy's homeland via a strategic bombing offensive.

The disastrous campaign in Norway, during which the RN played a major role, and the fall of France in May/June 1940 changed the situation. Shortly after the evacuation from Dunkirk, a Combined Operations organisation was established, which embraced all three armed services. According to an official wartime booklet: 'Its primary function is to provide training for amphibious warfare, which comprises all kinds of offensive action from small raids to large assault landings,' plus Combined Operations was expected 'to plan and execute raids on the coasts of the enemy'.[1] All such work rested heavily on the navy, which 'had to provide hundreds of ships to designs that were virtually unknown before the war and were of no use for anything else', plus it had to man them, largely by relying upon 'hastily trained conscripts who learnt how to operate these vessels, but little else about the navy'.[2] In contrast, during large-scale amphibious assaults the army essentially fought as normal once ashore. Likewise, the RAF was involved with many tasks that its aircraft could do normally, such as bombing enemy strongpoints and lines of communication, dropping paratroopers, aerial reconnaissance and spotting, and providing air cover for invasion forces.

Numerous commando raids were mounted by Combined Operations during the early 1940s. However, despite the undoubted bravery and determination of those involved, and their effect on enemy morale, 'tip-and-run'-type raids were not a war-winning strategy on their own. If the Allies were serious about returning to the continent, large-scale opposed amphibious landings would have to be considered. Few in the early phases of the war were perhaps fully aware of just how important these operations would become or the extent of the complexities they would necessarily entail. Advances in weapons technology, particularly artillery, ensured that many advantages lay with the defender. Consequently, the attacker required significant fire support to stand a chance of being successful, not just from their own organic artillery but also from warships and the air. In any major seaborne assault, attacking troops were liable to require armoured and transport vehicles to be landed, plus significant amounts of fuel and supplies had to be built up to support offensive action. This logistical burden fell heavily on both the Royal and Merchant Navies. Simultaneously, the conditions had to be created to enable material to be safely landed. Ultimately, a bewildering array of landing craft and landing ships were required to support any beachhead, most of which had not even existed prior to 1939. Large-scale amphibious landings similarly relied on the warships, submarines and smaller craft of the RN to perform various tasks, including protecting landing areas, escorting convoys, minesweeping and bombarding targets ashore. Another important area, highlighted by this chapter, was the need for effective staff work and planning, without which any landing risked descending into chaos.

Equipment and Training

Key to the activities of Combined Operations were landing ships and landing craft. Originally the distinction between the two was that landing ships were 'capable of making a sea passage on their own bottoms', while landing craft 'would have to be transported to the invasion area and put into the sea'. As landing craft increased in size, this distinction blurred because 'many were able to make passages on the open sea'. Additionally, the majority of 'landing craft were designed to beach', whereas landing ships did not do so, apart from those intended to bring equipment ashore.[3] Essentially, both had to be capable of carrying troops and equipment, but there were other vessels intended to carry smaller landing craft, and those employed for specialist support or logistical roles. During the voyage to Normandy on 5 June 1944 a junior RNVR officer aboard a motor minesweeper (MMS) was astonished to encounter a landing barge kitchen (LBK). Crewed by thirteen cooks, nine seamen and three stokers, these ungainly vessels provided hot meals daily for hundreds of men serving on the landing craft supporting the Normandy beaches. 'The kitchen craft closely resembled an overgrown caboose set on a barge, and its many smoking stove-pipes made this unseaworthy Noah's Ark look most out of place battling it out in the mean sea toward Normandy.'[4]

In contrast, the Landing Craft Assault (LCA), as the name implied, was intended to bring troops ashore, particularly in an opposed landing. An experienced rating who operated the type described them as being akin to 'a shoe box, 40 feet long and 8 feet wide and 3 feet high ... They were very crude and basic and they carried thirty-five assault troops, and were powered by two Ford petrol engines. They said that the petrol tanks were self-sealing but I was never sure about that.'[5]

The Landing Craft Infantry (Large) or LCI (L) was an ocean-going assault ship developed by the Americans at the behest of the British. It had a displacement of 250 tons, was 153 feet long and 22 feet in the beam, and could land around 200 troops from the deck, ideally dry shod, via two ramps on either side of the bow. They were functional but luxurious by British standards. Sub-Lieutenant John Hilton (RNVR) collected one from America, and recalled that he 'was overcome to find that I had my own cabin, with fitted wardrobe, filing cabinet, desk, safe, and interior spring bunk complete with reading light. There were showers both for officers and ratings, and the ratings had a very spacious mess deck, quite apart from their sleeping quarters, where every man had his own bunk. The galley was beautifully equipped, with an enormous cold storage room and refrigerator adjoining.' Likewise, 'quarters for the troops were almost equally good'.[6] Another RNVR officer noted they 'were admirable in many ways, not desperately uncomfortable' but cautioned that 'their landing ramps for troops were far from satisfactory', plus with a draft of only 4 feet at the bow and 6 feet at the stern they appeared to be 'alarmingly shallow for crossing the Atlantic'.[7] In contrast, the Landing Craft Infantry (Small) or LCI (S) had a displacement of 110 tons, and looked a little like an MTB. 'It could carry 100 men and had a crew of 17 ... a wooden hull and upper works, with large, unprotected tanks containing high-octane fuel.' Troops 'landed down gangplanks pushed over the bows on rollers'.[8] Even when the craft grounded on a beach, this could be precarious as the swell lifted the stern, making the gangplanks unstable, and threatened to tip men off into the sea. Consequently, they were better suited as raiding craft for commandos than as landing craft in seaborne assaults, but even then their characteristics were a challenge.

There were several marks of Landing Craft Mechanised (LCM) that could land a tank or other vehicle such as a jeep. One of the most numerous was the LCM (3), which was mass-produced in America and supplied to the RN under Lend-Lease. The 'after end of the tank deck was plated over and the cox'n placed there in a small, bullet-proof shelter where his all-round vision was greatly increased', but unlike earlier models these craft could not be hoisted when loaded with a tank.[9] A development of the LCM was the Landing Craft Tank (LCT), again numerous marks of which were manufactured. The basic idea was that whereas LCMs had to be 'transported to the beach area and could only carry a single tank', LCTs could 'make an open sea passage and carry three of the heaviest tanks (40 tons) then contemplated'.[10] After enlisting in 1942, Brian Carter spent most of his naval service on landing craft. He recounted:

> The LCT Mk IVs were just over 200 foot long by 38 foot wide, tapering slightly at the bows and stern, which were cut off square. A huge ramp door formed the bows, which could be lowered for beaching purposes so that tanks and other vehicles could be driven off, the same as in most other landing craft. There was a large anchor at the stern, and a small kedge anchor at the bow.[11]

Additionally, there was a bridge on top of the wheel house, a mess deck, a small galley, an engine room with two 500 horsepower diesel engines, and two 15 kilowatt generators. The tank deck 'was large and uncluttered, and an excellent place for recreational purposes' when not carrying loads, and a small covered area aft 'termed the troop space' served as a cabin for the petty officer motor mechanic.[12] However, conditions for troops were pretty basic and with 'little undercover accommodation ... they had to camp as best they could under the canvas sheets that covered their tanks" while toilet facilities consisted of 'two "bucket and chuck it" thunderboxes positioned on the open deck'.[13]

Crucially LCT crews had to learn how to deliver their loads and then extricate themselves from a beach. As an officer with the 45th LCT Flotilla expounded:

> You really want to know the gradient of the beach that you're going into. You go in, it depends on the sea, you don't go in fast or it would be a hell of a job getting off again ... You go in and drop your ramp once you've got there, with your kedge anchor out astern. Then with your ramp

down you unload your vehicles/tanks ... Then you do it the other way around, lift your ramp and kedge off.[14]

Likewise, a boy seaman signaller with the 103rd LCT Flotilla explained that when the kedge was dropped, it was 'like an anchor, and that pulls you off the beach. If you go onto the beach there's no way you can get off the beach without the kedge. Your engines won't pull you off. That's why a lot of the craft never went right onto the beach ... You've got to find a hold for your kedge, no use dragging it behind you otherwise it can't pull you off.'[15]

Some landing craft were used for specialist adaptations, such as the Landing Craft Support (Medium) (LCS (M)). These were based on the LCA, armed with a 4-inch smoke mortar and machine guns, and had armoured plate as protection. Hugh Irwin joined Combined Operations as a regular RN officer in 1942, and took command of a flotilla equipped with these craft. He explained that the LCS (M) were:

Landing craft with twin .5 machine guns, a 4-inch smoke mortar, and chloro-sulphonic acid for making a smoke screen. They carried a crew of six to eight Royal Marines, and two or three naval ratings, and these craft were lifted by a derrick into a liner [a Landing Ship Infantry (LSI), a converted merchantman] like a lifeboat. The object was to support the landing craft that went into the attack, and these LCS would machine gun any position that opposed the landing craft ... HMS *Ulster Monarch* [an LSI able to carry 580 troops and six LCAs] would anchor then the landing craft would be lowered. They would go in line astern, two columns, and then at a specific moment they would go line abreast, and almost charge the beach ... We would be on the port or starboard side of the lot, not middle, so we could oppose any gun that was going to shell or enfilade the craft.[16]

Another adaptation was the LCA (HR) or Hedgerow. According to one RNVR officer, these 'each fired twelve spigot mortars on to the beach with the idea of detonating or unearthing landmines [and clearing a path through beach obstacles] for tanks and infantry. We trained at Studland Bay, Dorset, working from Poole Harbour. Each Hedgerow carried a refill of twelve mortar bombs. The 80lb bombs had an 18-inch fuse rod on the nose that detonated on the surface. They were fired by a ripple switch; the operator turned the handle and the bombs went away in pairs in rapid succession.'[17] These were among the smallest landing craft involved in D-Day and were towed across the Channel; tragically several were lost in bad weather due to being 'towed under' because their towing cables were too taut.[18]

Likewise, the LCT lent itself to various conversions, including the Landing Craft Tank (Rocket) or LCT (R), capable of plastering a beach with up to 1,064 RP-3 60 lb rocket projectiles. Another variant was the Landing Craft Gun (Large) or LCG (L), equipped with two 4.7-inch guns and two to four 20mm Oerlikon anti-aircraft cannon. These helped to bridge a gap in naval bombardment. While the heavy calibre weapons on warships were extremely valuable to troops ashore, shells could not be landed too close to friendly forces for fear of inaccuracies and the spread of the blast. Invariably warships could not get close enough inshore to tackle beach defence positions adequately, and if they tried they were vulnerable to enemy artillery from the shore. By contrast, LCGs could get in close to the shore to engage fixed defences, and presented a relatively small target to the enemy.

Another adaptation of the LCT was the Landing Craft Flak (LCF), speci-ally designed as an anti-aircraft vessel to provide cover for landings. Howard Dowell, a signaller with the Royal Marines, joined LCF 32 ahead of D-Day, and remembered that she was bristling with pom poms [2-pounder guns] and Oerlikons set in emplacements. His first impression on boarding her in Southampton was that she was 'ghastly, the shape very much like a coffin. And I was expecting something a little more sleek than that. It was an awkward-looking vessel. It hit every wave, and this sent shudders through the whole ship, being blunt at the front. You were seasick at first but got used to it.'[19]

Likewise, a wide variety of ships were employed by Combined Operations as the organisation expanded. The various LSI 'remained under the Red Ensign and with their masters in command. In addition to mercantile crews, each carried a substantial contingent of naval officers and men whose duties were to control beach-head operations and man the LCA with which the ships were equipped.'[20] Other types included the Landing Ship Dock (LSD), essentially a self-propelled floating dock that proved useful as carriers for landing craft; Landing Ship Headquarters (LSH), vital in maintaining com-munications with the large number of units involved in major amphibious landings; and Landing Ship Fighter Direction (LSF), used to provide coordi-nation of air assets in an invasion area.[21]

Another important type was the American-built Landing Ship Tank (LST), regarded as marvellous by many who served on them, and well suited to delivering tanks and heavy loads during landings. This was despite being 'notoriously difficult to keep to a steady course' at sea, something that initially ensured LST 'signalmen were overworked making signals regarding station keeping', and routinely the 'signal of two black balls (I am not under control)' had to be kept 'ready to hoist'.[22] Petty Officer Sydney Hook of LST 403 described how on Convoy ATLC 10 out in the Atlantic, the 'ship was only doing 3 knots, and rolled something terrible'. However, provided you did not suffer from seasickness, conditions aboard were good. 'Everybody had a bunk' – not necessarily the case on all British ships. There was a 'hanging locker each, good galley. Everything was built like a conveyor system, feeding 200–300 troops. We had good grub when there was good grub around.'[23]

The design evolved from a British requirement for a large seaworthy vessel capable of transporting at least twenty tanks on ocean voyages, and landing them on beaches around the world. This presented a challenge, as a shallow draft was required to access beaches, but this ensured LSTs had awkward sea-going characteristics. The LST (2), the most numerous, had a displacement of 3,800 tons fully loaded, was nearly 328 feet long with a beam of just over 50 feet, and had a maximum speed of 11.5 knots, leading servicemen to dub them 'Large Slow Targets'. Effectively a cross between a cargo ship and a flat-bottomed landing craft, they had large bow doors that could be opened to let down a ramp from the tank deck. By the manipulation of thousands of gallons of ballast that could be pumped to or from tanks near the bows, they could be sailed onto or off enemy-held beaches, or just as easily use existing harbour facilities. Alternatively, by 1944 a Rhino ferry, basically a flat-topped pontoon with outboard motors, could be employed to carry cargo from an LST to the shore.[24]

A major lesson that emerged during the war was that in an amphibious landing the various ships involved had to be tactically loaded. 'The rule "last in first out" must be strictly adhered to and the stowage of tanks, guns, transport, stores etc.' must be strictly in accordance with the tactical requirements of the landing, plus loads had to be evenly distributed throughout the force, so that the loss of a ship did not hinder the whole operation.[25]

Another challenge was the inexperience of personnel in Combined Operations, given that many were Hostilities Only, including many conscripts. Londoner Victor Longhurst, who joined the 103rd LCT Flotilla, recounted:

> [I had] never been on board a ship. I found it very difficult to adjust, but the Flotilla Officer, I was his personal signalman ... and one day he said to me I think it would do you good if you spent time on one of the craft that was ferrying stuff from Portsmouth to Southampton and other places. So I spent about ten days on one of the landing craft and got to know a bit about the signalling, had a bit of practical experience, then went back into the office [ashore].[26]

Related to this was the dynamic between the different sailors who served on landing craft. For example, LCTs had a commanding officer, first lieutenant and six seamen, including gunners, a wireman (electrician) and motor mechanic. Importantly there was also a coxswain, although they often lacked experience, and from 1941 the RN 'determined that all coxswains should be at least leading seamen', although it 'was reluctant to reduce standards far enough to allow sufficient men to be promoted', and many were selected from the best coxswains of minor landing craft.[27]

A former holiday camp near Portsmouth became HMS *Northney* in 1941, and spawned several other camps for training landing craft crews. Likewise, Inveraray on Loch Fyne, Scotland, proved useful, owing to the beaches in the area and the scope for live firing, and became home of the Combined Training Centre (CTC) HMS *Quebec*. As the war progressed, other sites were employed in an effort to give all branches of the navy who were employed with Combined Operations the appropriate training.[28] Rating cadets, for example, underwent officer training at HMS *King Alfred* in Hove, before going on to HMS *Lochailot* in Scotland, where divisional officers greeted them along the lines of: 'I can bite as well as bark. I shall expect you to work hard and play hard, this is going to be no rest cure. There will be PT – lots of PT – and worse things beside ... I don't like failures.'[29]

Thomas Sutton volunteered for Combined Operations because, having previously served as a seaman on the battleship HMS *Howe*, he 'wanted something smaller', as *Howe* was 'too big and too regimental, and on a smaller ship I thought I'd be my own master'.[30] Subsequently, he was commissioned and served on LCTs in Normandy and north-west Europe. Ahead of D-Day there was a lengthy period of training:

> You're practising all the time, loading vehicles and off-loading vehicles, so that as a crew you can lower the door ramp in order to let the vehicles off as quickly as possible. And you are going through all the exercises, like the evolutions on a battleship, that may fit you for a particular occasion, whether it being towing, navigation, all manner of exercises, no different really to any other ship but specifically with the idea of carrying tanks ... And maintaining a training efficiency for a particular occasion which you didn't know when it was going to happen. You've got to be quite sure that there's enough water, it's not too deep, firing guns, etc.[31]

This might all sound straightforward but, as another LCT officer stated, landing troops, equipment and vehicles/tanks on a beach in relatively shallow water 'was by no means an easy exercise'.[32]

Raiding Experiences

Under Admiral of the Fleet Lord Keynes, and his successor as Director of Combined Operations, Lord Louis Mountbatten, part of the remit of the organisation was to mount commando raids. Ironically the commandos came from the army during the first years of the war, as the Royal Marines – although part of the navy – were not able to raise commandos until later, and these played a significant part in operations during 1943–1945. The navy had to assemble the necessary shipping for any commando raids, and provide support to these endeavours.

During 1941 two raids were launched on the Lofoten Islands, deep within Nazi-occupied Norway. One of them, Operation Claymore on 4 March, was to destroy herring and cod oil factories, which were useful to the German war effort in the manufacture of explosives; take prisoners; bring back recruits for the Norwegian forces; and sink any enemy shipping that was encountered. The broadcaster/writer Ludovic Kennedy took part as a young naval officer aboard the Tribal class destroyer HMS *Tartar*, one of five destroyers assigned to escort the raiders. 'It was a bold plan and one that assumed that neither enemy warships nor planes would be at hand to offer resistance.'[33] The navigation of the Royal Navy proved superb and 'four landings were made, No. 3 Commando going ashore at Stamsund and Henningsvaer, and No. 4 Commando at Svolvaer and Brettesnes'.[34] Little opposition was encountered, and a good deal of fraternisation with the locals occurred, 315 Norwegians eventually volunteering to go to Britain. 'It had been resoundingly successful. We had remained unmolested in enemy waters for nearly twelve hours, done considerable damage to German shipping and installations, and brought back with us 200 German prisoners ... all without a single casualty. The press gave the operation widespread coverage and praise', which was significant from a morale perspective given that Britain still stood alone against Hitler.[35]

Another sailor recalled what the operation was like from the perspective of the crew of HMS *Edinburgh*, one of the cruisers detached from the Home Fleet to provide close support to the operation.

> There was every possibility that the ship might be in action, and might even be sunk. So that was a strange feeling. Very cold, ice and snow. We were the covering force, so didn't see much of the landing ships, which were two cross-Channel steamers [converted to carry landing craft]. We were with them all the time. Then when we got to the Norwegian coast they dropped small boats and we didn't see them at all. The small boats went in, and we heard a lot of the battle of course, and there were one or two German planes. These came out but never attacked us because they could see we were far too powerful.[36]

Operation Archery, launched in late December 1941, again targeted Nazi-occupied Norway, this time at Vaagsö. However, the idea was to raid a defended port, which, according to Lord Mountbatten, who addressed the raiders beforehand, would be a 'test pilot run ... For nobody knows quite what is going to happen and you are the ones who are going to find out.'[37] This was an ambitious plan, and the overall aim, as well as 'harassing the German defences on the coast of south-west Norway', was to 'attack and destroy a number of military and economic targets in the town of South Vaagsö and on the nearby island of Maaloy, and to capture/sink any shipping in Ulvesund'.[38] No. 3 Commando from the army was to conduct the raid, together with personnel from the Royal Engineers, Royal Army Medical Corps, plus intelligence officers and a press unit. Troops were landed at five separate sites by the RN and supported by the RAF. It has been regarded as an example of a 'classic fighting raid' owing to the commando landings and the street battles that followed, and may have fostered Hitler's obsession with Norway, as further German troops and resources were sent there that might have been better employed elsewhere.[39]

An officer aboard HMS *Kenya*, a 6-inch cruiser that supported the raid, commented:

> It was a very eerie sensation entering the fjord in absolute silence and very slowly. I wondered what was going to happen for it seemed that the ship had lost her proper element, she was no longer a ship at sea. Occasionally I saw a little hut with a light burning in it and I wondered whether that light would be suddenly switched off, which would mean the enemy had spotted us, or whether it would continue to burn as some Norwegian fisherman got out of bed, stretched himself and went off to his nets.[40]

One of his fellow officers noted how, as the moment of the raid approached, 'it was most disturbing that there was so little left to do because everything had been done beforehand. We noted the time, exactly one minute late, that the landing craft were lowered and could just be seen through glasses, black beetles crawling in the shadow of the mountains up the black waters of the fjord. We heard our aircraft overhead and saw their welcome of heavy, familiar tracer fire rising quite slowly from the surrounding slopes.' Subsequently, the crew of HMS *Kenya* waited nervously as they eased around the headland, and at any moment expected to be ordered to engage an enemy battery that they knew would be there. 'The naval bombardment opened at 8.48am, the *Kenya* firing a salvo of star shell which lit up the island of Maaloy,' thus indicating the target to naval gunners and where RAF bombers were to drop smoke bombs. This was followed by salvoes of 6-inch shells, and destroyers joined in the bombardment, so that between 400 and 500 '6-inch shells fell upon a space not more than 250 yards square'.[41]

Operation Chariot, the famous raid on St Nazaire in March 1942, was another classic combined operation, heavily reliant on its naval component. Its purpose was to deny the German warship *Tirpitz* use of the massive Forme Ecluse or *Normandie* dock, which could have enabled her to mount forays against Allied convoys in the Atlantic. This was achieved, although at significant cost. Of 611 men who entered the Loire, 169 were killed (105 naval personnel and 64 commandos), mainly during the various river battles that occurred. Integral to the operation was the destruction of the lock gates of the Forme Ecluse, a feat that was achieved by ramming them with the aged destroyer HMS *Campbeltown*, packed with explosives using a delayed action fuse. Additionally, the raid was to destroy 'the smaller South Lock gates and their installation', plus 'key points such as pumping machinery for the Bassin', and finally 'any U-boats and shipping were to be subsidiary objects in that order of priority'.[42] As well as *Campbeltown*, the naval forces comprised two escorting Hunt class destroyers, HMS *Atherstone* and HMS *Tynedale*, while a number of MGBs, MTBs and motor launches (MLs) provided protection and carried commandos, plus the submarine HMS *Sturgeon* assisted in navigating the force successfully to the mouth of the Loire.[43]

Operation Jubilee, a reconnaissance in force, was launched against Dieppe on 19 August 1942, and was likened by one veteran to 'a naval version of the charge of the Light Brigade'.[44] As the official historian cautioned, Dieppe was far from an ideal target for a raid: 'It was heavily defended on both sides of the harbour, and there were high cliffs from which the sea approaches were easily commanded. Except at the town itself openings in the cliffs were few and small, the beaches were narrow, and rocky ledges restricted the state of the tide at which landing craft could approach', plus there was a formidable sea wall that effectively defended the town.[45] Casualties were heavy; around 68 per cent of the Canadian troops landed were killed or wounded, as were 247 of the 1,057 commandos deployed. The navy lost a destroyer and thirty-three landing craft, suffering 550 casualties in the process, while the RAF took 190 casualties. Lord Mountbatten, Chief of Combined Operations at the time, maintained that Dieppe provided lessons which proved invaluable later, plus convinced the Germans that the Allies might again try to storm a Channel port, when this was not the case. Another lesson was that permanent naval assault forces were needed that possessed 'a coherence comparable to that of any other first line formation' instead of the RN collecting together ships and vessels from a multitude of sources for any combined operation.[46] There was also a need for specialised armour and 'intimate fire support right up to the last moment while troops crossed the waterline (the most dangerous place on the beach) and closed with their objectives'. Yet as Major General Julian Thompson succinctly remarks, 'it did not need a debacle like Dieppe to learn all this and more'.[47]

Having volunteered for the navy, Colin Kitching trained at HMS *Raleigh* before later being posted to HMS *Edinburgh* as an ordinary seaman and commissioned warrant candidate (CW). In 1942 he was accepted for a commission and underwent officer training at HMS *King Alfred* before being posted to Combined Operations. Subsequently, as a Sub-Lieutenant RNVR, he commanded an R boat or LCP (L) – Landing Craft, Personnel, (Large) – at Dieppe. These were a 'mere 37 feet long; made of seven-ply wood with no armour protection' and ideally suited to 'hit-and-run'-type raiding, whereas, 'the full scale assault landing was not really our scene'.[48] However, they had to take part as at this stage there were too few more suitable landing craft available in Home Waters, given that the build-up to Operation Torch happened simultaneously. Kitching's flotilla was tasked with carrying a floating reserve of French Canadian troops, but had little idea of where these might be landed.

Under heavy shellfire the twenty-six boats of two flotillas performed an elaborate manoeuvre which got us into perfect line abreast. I had by then taken over the wheel of my LCP, having stationed the coxswain on the bridge with the stripped Lewis gun, our only defensive weapon. We were soon engulfed in the enormous cloud of smoke. Suddenly we emerged to find ourselves close to – of all places – Dieppe's central promenade beach. The gunfire intensified: apart from shells from the headlands we now had mortar bombs, together with machine-gunning from the hotels at the back of the promenade.

The sheer din was unbelievable, added to by my coxswain, who was enjoying himself on the Lewis gun right above my head. Our line abreast formation held magnificently; by now the soldiers crouching on the decks of the LCPs, ready for the touch-down [were] beginning to suffer casualties ... at this point a mortar bomb exploded to port, alongside my boat. As I held the wheel a metal fragment cut through the strap of my wrist watch, grazed the back of my left hand and buried itself in the woodwork around the window screen.

At the end of our line the touch-down went well, though the 5th Flotilla ran out of beach under the cliffs and could not land everyone dry shod. My soldiers hit the shingle beach quickly, led by their lieutenant who, I was sad to see, crumpled up no more than a dozen strides away. The general scene on the beach was appalling. A couple of LCTs were lying broadside, burning fiercely. Tanks were stranded on the shingle, motionless. Dead, and wounded Canadians ... lay everywhere. Others, still in action, were sheltering as best they could under the sea wall.

Once my boat was free of troops I backed it off the shingle. In spite of the mayhem my crew and I had survived. Exactly what our naval casualties were at this stage was unclear. But what was only too obvious was that if landing the troops had been hazardous, picking them up again – a much longer job – would be suicidal.

A couple of miles out to sea, the 4th and 5th Flotillas regrouped and checked damage and casualties. We had lost five LCPs: out of 104 officers and ratings manning the boats, 21 were dead, 9 wounded. Considering the terrific weight of fire the losses were fewer than I had feared. I suspect our tiny craft, well spaced, were too small a target for really accurate fire. As for the unusually high proportion of killed to wounded, a direct shell hit on a flimsy LCP loaded with high octane petrol resulted in the boat being blown apart.

Time passed. The sun continued to shine. The RAF and the Luftwaffe maintained their private quarrel above. Shells from the shore kept the LCPs constantly on the move. The crews ate corned beef sandwiches, rather dry by now, and drank tea from large Thermoses known as safari jars. Occupying our thoughts was the question of the withdrawal: it would take at least ten minutes to re-embark tired and wounded soldiers – how could LCPs survive so long on that beach?

At about ten o'clock we began to form up again in a coherent flotilla order, preparatory to going in again. Just as we were bracing ourselves for the lethal and impossible task, the naval commander (Captain J. Hughes-Hallett RN) cancelled our mission. He, too, realised that not only would the use of LCPs be suicidal but it would also not achieve the object of rescuing as many soldiers as possible. Instead he sent in armoured landing craft ...[49]

Large-Scale Amphibious Landings

There could be prolonged periods of relative inactivity for those serving with Combined Operations, when the onus was on training and practising amphibious techniques prior to the next operation. However, during the course of the war the RN, Royal Marines (RM) and Merchant Navy were involved in several large-scale amphibious landings. Dubbed 'the Dakar fiasco' by Evelyn Waugh, who took part with the RM, Operation Menace was called off at a late stage.[50] It was an attempt to install General de Gaulle's Free

French movement in Dakar, Senegal, during September 1940, as from a British perspective 'the possibility of the Germans filtering into the French West African colonies bordering our route to the Cape was alarming'.[51]

A brigade HQ and four battalions of RM, together with specialist small units, totalling 4,200 men, plus 2,700 Free French troops embarked on transports in Liverpool. The RN allotted several ships from the Home Fleet to escort the expedition, collectively termed Force M. It comprised two battleships, HMS *Barham* and *Resolution*, the aircraft carrier HMS *Ark Royal*, the cruisers HMS *Devonshire* and *Fiji* (later torpedoed and replaced by HMS *Australia*) and *Cumberland*, plus ten destroyers and smaller craft. Unfortunately in planning the operation, the extent of support for the Free French in West Africa had been miscalculated, and there was a risk that it might provoke war with Vichy France, which had sent warships to Dakar. Moreover, the force failed to achieve an element of surprise and Vichy resistance was tougher than expected, and the assault force was soon withdrawn to the safety of Freetown, Sierra Leone. According to the official historian, inevitable difficulties occurred in 'conducting a combined operation at a great distance from home bases', which were 'enhanced by the international character of the enterprise, with all the problems of personality and language which that involved'. At least 'the ability of the Navy safely to convey large expeditions overseas had again been demonstrated'.[52]

Subsequently, an amphibious assault on Madagascar (Operation Ironclad) was planned, again far from home. It was launched owing to the strategic importance of that island. Captain Stephen Roskill (RN) explained: 'As the tide of Japanese success swept south and west in the early months of 1942, it was natural that Allied eyes should be anxiously turned towards Madagascar. Not only did its geographic position command much of the southern Indian Ocean, but from its excellent harbour of Diego Suarez enemy warships and submarines could menace our Middle East convoy route most dangerously.'[53] The situation was exacerbated as the French authorities on Madagascar owed allegiance to Vichy France, which had already proved submissive towards the Japanese over the French colony of Indo-China (modern-day Vietnam).

Off Madagascar Lieutenant Commander C.H. Knollys was serving as one of the officers aboard the battleship HMS *Ramillies* that supported the landings. He recorded the events as they unfolded during the operation:

> ... the invasion of Diego Suarez. And that was the reason we were flying the flag of Rear Admiral Syfret, who was in charge of the operation.
>
> Madagascar dominated the Mozambique Channel between itself and Africa, thus posing a potential nuisance to our regular Cape route

convoys should the island fall into hostile or uncooperative hands. And this, it happened, was the case, for the island was controlled by Vichy France, our allies turned foe.

Of greater concern was the port complex of Diego Suarez, at the northern tip of Madagascar. The Japanese must not be permitted to exploit this strategic island. Therefore an amphibious assault force, comprising 9,000 troops, plus support forces, together with naval forces, was directed at Diego Suarez.

At 0415 on 5th May 1942 a channel to beaches on the west side of Madagascar was swept. Transports entered and anchored off the beaches. Aircraft took off from ILLUSTRIOUS and INDOMITABLE and dropped leaflets. Addressed to the Governor of Diego Suarez, these stressed the anti-Japanese nature of the offensive, and encouraged the Vichy French forces to make an honourable surrender. Assuming that the garrison would not surrender without a fight, naval aviation neutralised any Vichy aircraft, and sank the sloop D'ENTRECASTRAUX, which remained, in shallow water, with its deck awash.

At 0552 the troops were ashore, advancing from the west coast towards Diego Suarez, to the north of the harbour, and Antsirane to the south. At 10.53 the Governor states he will not surrender.

On 6th May Diego Suarez was captured, but the other half of the force was held up 3 miles south of Antsirane by strong Vichy defences. General Sturges, the Land Force Commander, came on board and said: 'For God's sake give me some Marines.' So 50 of our Marines, under Captain Martin Price, embarked in the destroyer ANTHONY, and at 2030 went alongside the pier at Antsirane, under heavy fire, and leaped ashore. They had expected No. 5 Commando, consisting of 450 men, to cross the harbour from Diego Suarez and begin mopping up the town in rear so that No. 5 Commando could get past the strongpoint and meet them in the middle. It transpired later that the Commandos had been unable to cross the harbour, having found only one small dinghy.

On 7th May the batteries have not yet surrendered. So we steamed round to the East coast and bombarded with 15-inch. We saw no special results but were told that they surrendered after the seventh salvo. Actually they had surrendered before we started, but the signal did not get through. On completion we entered Diego Suarez. The victorious soldiers on the batteries waved and cheered.

It is a most beautiful harbour, of roughly circular shape, about 4 miles in diameter, with high mountains, rolling hills and fine sandy beaches, crowded with gay-coloured natives.

A beachmaster's assistant, all muddy and bedraggled, slept in my bed last night. The wardroom contains several released Fleet Air Arm pilots who had been shot down and imprisoned. One of them, Everett, said the worst part was being spat at in the street by Vichy French women.

Our Royal Marines returned, bristling with looted French helmets and 'baïonettes'. I saw my Marine servant, Hickman, had a chicken in a basket: 'I liberated it in the town, Sir. ... more use than armoury.'

The only casualty was Marine Hook, who got shot in the groin by another Marine. Captain Price won the DSO. His final signal to General Sturges read: '500 prisoners but no breakfast.'

Colonel Gerboult and Capitaine de Vasseau Martean were tonight brought on board to discuss terms. The latter was Captain of the MOGADOR at Oran and is bitterly anti-British.

The whole operation was a success, the casualties being approximately 105 killed and 280 wounded.[54]

Operation Torch, the Allied invasion of French North Africa in November 1942, was far more ambitious, and designed to achieve control of the region for the Allies. It was made practicable owing to Britain's possession of Gibraltar, and was heavily reliant on naval forces. In essence, around 107,000 troops had to be delivered to their various beaches as part of the initial assault, plus large numbers of follow-up personnel. The operation entailed 'three distinct landing operations separated from one another by hundreds of miles', ensuring that each 'assault had to be in sufficient strength to gain a quick decision'. To this end the forces for each assault were 'organised into all arms groups designated Task Forces – Western for Casablanca, Centre for Oran, Eastern for Algiers'.[55] The idea was that each would be capable of fighting independently without support from the others, and achieve decisive exploitation once ashore.

However, first the navy had to land the troops, as well as protect the convoys carrying them, and shield the landing areas from enemy interference. Vice Admiral Sir Ian McGeogh, then a more junior officer, had only recently been appointed to the submarine P228. Having worked up in Britain, she had been posted to the Mediterranean:

Our patrol at the opening of the landings, which was the beginning of November 1943, was off Toulon originally, because there was a French Fleet there which, at this stage, was thought possibly to be capable of sallying forth under Axis and German command. However, the fleet did not sally forth and the French at least made sure that it didn't, and I was then ordered to continue my patrol eastward along the south coast of

France towards Genoa, and then to go down between Corsica and the mainland and continue my patrol off Naples. And Naples was a major part of the Italian battle fleet. Again there was a prospect that they might sally forth and try to interfere with the North African landings. So the submarines on the Allied side had been positioned so as to try to attack this Italian fleet in that event. I had been told to keep a salvo of torpedoes for the second half of my patrol off Naples for this purpose.[56]

British operational procedures were employed, notably at Oran, where 'a beacon submarine' was used to mark a rendezvous point for the troop transports. MLs then sailed from the transports and 'reported to the beacon to take aboard pilot teams for each beach', before rejoining the flotillas of landing craft. Simultaneously, the submarine moved closer to the shore, and via portable boats landed teams whose job it was to mark the beaches. The piloting parties then led the initial waves of landing craft in, and made contact with these beach teams, so that 'transports [carrying the rest of the assault troops] would move in, through channels swept in any minefields, to anchor about 5½ miles off shore'.[57]

The navigation officer on the destroyer HMS *Opportune* commented how the opening of the operational orders

> gave us the greatest thrill we were to have during all the landings. To see the pages and pages giving the organisation and the carefully planned arrangements, for passing the large convoys through the Straits in darkness; to realise the work, and the hours of study that must have preceded their compilation. And then to examine a mass of charts and maps, and mosaic photographs of the entire French North African coastline, with all military objects shown; to realise then the risks and energy which these must have cost. A 'masterpiece' can be the only description for these, the orders for the greatest sea landing that had until then ever been attempted, with the three simultaneous landings to take Casablanca, Oran and Algiers.[58]

Eric Denton spent much of his naval war with Coastal Forces, and during Operation Torch was one of the officers serving aboard ML 273, tasked with escorting landing craft. Although the operation proved a success overall, with Casablanca, Oran and Algiers all having fallen by 11 November, personnel on the various landing ships and smaller craft could not be certain that all was going to plan:

> The landing craft passed down both sides of the ship and beached ashore and the troops advanced. We didn't hear a single shot fired. We had to

assume that they had landed safely but, of course [we worried] whether they would be walking into a trap a bit later on. War is always a very worrying business.[59]

One upshot of Operation Torch was that it led on to the bloody land campaign against Axis forces in Tunisia, which did not conclude until February 1943. Simultaneously, the British had argued successfully for the invasion of Sicily, as a logical next step. This would provide a springboard to invade mainland Italy, and promised to clear shipping lanes through the Mediterranean, making it possible to use the Suez Canal again and relieve pressure on Malta. The combined Anglo-American invasion of Sicily (Operation Husky) commenced on 9 July 1943, and proved the largest and most complex Allied amphibious operation thus far mounted. It involved an armada of well over 3,000 ships, which, as one RN veteran explained, comprised 'every type from AA cruisers down to minesweepers, assault landing craft of every conceivable design, huge merchantmen, supply ships – their decks piled high with vehicles, oil tankers loaded down in the water below their Plimsoll lines'.[60]

Having joined the Merchant Navy straight from school in the late 1930s, John Cutcliffe had joined a merchantman specially converted to support amphibious operations, while shipping was being gathered on the Clyde for Husky:

the MV *Llangibby Castle* had been converted to an invasion ship, and instead of flak boats on each side she had two fleets of landing craft, [that] came from special davits on each side, swung outboard all the time, and we were part of the fleet going into Cape Passero, which is on the SE corner of Sicily. I remember the commodore's ship was called *Hillary*. It was Admiral Sir Phillip Vian in command. He was a good sportsman. Also in that group was the *Durban Castle*. She was ahead of us, doing the same thing. She'd been converted for the invasion, and we had a reasonably uneventful voyage out to the Mediterranean, slipped through without gaining too much notice, we thought, and as we approached, we went round Cape Bizerte and headed down into the Gulf of Sirte before turning north to go past Malta, and then on towards Cape Passero, and there was one of these sharp little Mediterranean gales blew up, and that was so severe that at one time they were thinking of postponing the whole invasion for 24 hours, which would have been a disastrous thing to have happened. Luckily it died down as quickly as it flared up, and we were able to arrive off the beaches on time, ... very early in the morning, and my job was getting the port-side boats away, loaded and away, and then once those landing craft had gone, we had gun-port doors and ladders on the side of the ship, steep ladders, and the landing ships, LCI landing ships, infantry landing craft, which were much bigger, they came alongside and took off the balance of our soldiers and put them ashore, and once we'd got all that out of the way, which was by about 11 o'clock in the morning, everything went well, there was very little activity ashore that we could see, so we thought we'd relax for a bit, and I went and lay down on my settee in my cabin and the next thing there was an almighty thud and I thought 'Oh God, not again.' And in fact, unbeknown to me, there was a monitor, HMS *Roberts*. She came up alongside, almost alongside, and started shooting off with 15-inch guns at a convoy of vehicles that was coming down a hill, German vehicles, and she was actually shooting over the top of us. Oh dear! Anyway it quietened down after that and we then went back to Oran and picked up German prisoners-of-war and brought them back to this country. And then we went back out to the Mediterranean, and for several months we were running around conveying troops from the North African ports, Algiers, Bizerte, Oran, across to the ports in Italy, mainly up to Taranto, and my 21st birthday was in Taranto.[61]

Planners were presented with countless problems. One of the most vexing was that even with so many ships it was challenging trying to 'satisfy everyone who required a slice of the limited space aboard supply ships and landing craft'. Likewise, disseminating operational orders was a massive headache: 'The typing of the naval orders alone took twenty typists seven days and required the printing of 800 copies.'[62] The final plan was for four divisions and an independent brigade from the British Eighth Army to be landed between Syracuse on the east coast and Pozzallo on the south-east coast, supported by airborne forces, while the American Seventh Army was to assault a 70-mile stretch of coast in the Gulf of Gela in western Sicily. To do this the Americans were supported by the Western Naval Task Force, while the Eighth Army relied on the Eastern Naval Task Force under Admiral Bertram Ramsay RN, a veteran of Operation Torch, and the mastermind behind Operation Dynamo, the successful evacuation from Dunkirk. The Eastern Naval Task Force comprised three assault forces: A (5th and 50th Divisions); B (231st Infantry Brigade and 51st Division); and V (1st Canadian Division), which would sail direct from Britain and join the fleet on the day of the invasion.

Some of the landings entailed 'ship-shore, that is, men and equipment would be carried to points offshore where they were to be transferred to landing craft for the assault'.[63] The beachmaster responsible for landing the

51st Highland Division recalled that the operation went superbly, and was completed in half the time allocated for it, a process assisted by being able to call on Italian POWs as labourers, who filled crevices in the rocky beach with stones, so that 'LSTs could land four abreast, and the stuff could rattle off them ... We found ourselves on the way back to North Africa after two days rather than the four the programme had allowed.'[64] Even so, the scale of the overall operation was challenging, although new technologies, including LSTs and the DUKW, a form of amphibious 3-ton truck, were employed in some cases to deliver men and supplies direct to the beaches, rather than use the ship-shore method.

George Henderson, a chapel lad from Gosforth, Newcastle-upon-Tyne, volunteered for the navy in 1942, and while serving aboard LST 8 experienced action off Sicily. He was surprised how well his LST performed, given they were effectively:

all ballast tanks and weight and big flat-bottomed whales. We were learning as we went along. It's not just a case of charging up on the beach. You must have the right beach and be able to get there and get off, which you could do in the Mediterranean, with it being non-tidal. And ... as fast as you can you go full steam ahead, drop your stern anchor which was a special kedge hook anchor, which was on the stern, and you dropped that and paid out as you went in, then you emptied, opened the bow doors, got all the tanks out and all the stuff off the upper deck, there was a lift that brought down half-tracks, Bren gun carriers, and lighter stuff like wagons [trucks]. Once we got them away, we could heave ourselves off by heaving in on the stern anchor and going astern, manage to pull ourselves back off the beach with it being non-tidal. We could beach in about 4 feet of water, they were remarkable ships, and then we went back for another load.[65]

Another distinct challenge in Sicily (and later Italy) was 'when you made a landing ... trying to keep the Italians off who wanted to surrender. There were thousands of them, and they were ready with their suitcases. We had to put lads on the tank deck with a rifle and bayonet to keep them off. You never got that with the Germans!'[66]

Even more worrying was the absence of Allied air cover, as during much of the fighting in the Mediterranean, including Operation Husky, the Luftwaffe was still potentially formidable. If possible, a comparatively small ship, such as an LST, might seek protection from battleships, cruisers or destroyers in an anchorage. As George Henderson put it, 'all we had were six Oerlikons [20mm cannon] and a 12-pounder mounted aft, which isn't very much protection'. Typically, over the LST's tannoy a warning of air attack would be made, such as 'Enemy aircraft expected 30 minutes from SW', and it could 'feel as if an enemy aircraft had singled you out'. The aircraft would attack from 'whichever way the sun was, and you'd get strapped in your Oerlikon, not that it did that much good, it only had around 1,000 yards range, but it gave you a feeling of security. Then you would see little dots against the sun and they hurtled down, fighter-bombers. Everybody opened up, our aircraft were after them and came into the area of fire from the ships, and the ships never stopped firing. I mean we couldn't tell whose aircraft was who, and just belted stuff up, so I would think some British and American aircraft were shot down by our own ships because you couldn't tell.'[67]

Smaller landing craft, many of which were being employed for the first time, similarly faced numerous challenges. As Vice Admiral Patrick Bayly, a former beachmaster, remembered, there were particular concerns about sand bars on many Sicilian beaches that might have hindered landing craft. The actor Sir Alec Guinness commanded LCI 124. Getting alongside a troopship to embark personnel was a feat in itself, especially in choppy seas. At his rendezvous, 'waves lifted and dropped us a good 6 feet every time they struck' and this dislodged LCI 124's ramps that ran down either side of the bow and were integral to landing soldiers. Necessity dictated that 'instead of being able to walk on board, each soldier had to wait for a wave to lift us sufficiently high and then, with gun and equipment, jump for it'.[68] This slowed the whole process down considerably. Later, at a beach near Cape Passero, LCI 124 'hit Sicily very hard'. They dropped their kedge anchor astern, in case it was required to winch themselves off the beach. Unfortunately, 'another ship, coming too close, managed to sever it' and the craft 'swung round to an unenviable angle'. Coupled with 'immovable' ramps, this ensured the soldiers had to be lowered into the surf via ropes, while the LCI 'lay there at 45 degrees to the shoreline', before being rescued days later.[69]

Despite such mishaps, another member of Combined Operations recounted how he listened to a heartening talk following a news bulletin on 11 July. It was 'on the invasion and particular stress was laid on the craft used to navigate the correct beaches for our lads to land on. It was stated how difficult it was to manoeuvre these craft in heavy seas, the expert seamanship required, etc. I felt quite pleased to think that, at long last, some person recognized the fact that we were doing some valuable work to help the war effort. The speaker was speaking about us.'[70]

Eric Denton and his ML had to form part of an escort for tank landing craft 'which were to beach at Avola at the southern end of the east coast of Sicily', which went well, despite the slow, cumbersome nature of these craft: 'we heard firing from time to time, but there didn't appear to be any violent opposition'. However, when daylight came they were confronted by the disturbing sight of glider troops who had failed to reach their objective and 'were floating on the surface of the sea drowned' owing to the weight of their equipment. They were not able to pick any up for fear of clogging up their decks and becoming inoperable, which 'was very depressing'.[71]

Two aircraft carriers, HMS *Indomitable* and *Formidable*, were earmarked with providing close air support in Sicily, and submarines protected the invasion fleet and helped navigate the naval task forces. A naval support force (Force K) escorted convoys and provided fire support for the landings, and later protected the northern sea flank. An extract from a midshipman's log provides an impression of the intimate, effective support provided by one destroyer, HMS *Eggesford*, during the landings:

Extract from Tuesday 12 July 1943:

0455 Spotted heavy tracer fire from machine-gun nests on 'Hound' firing at and hitting our landing craft. We altered course towards but were now at 8,600 yards range.

0505 Opened fire at 7,400 yards range with rapid salvoes, to 260 degrees, speed 7 knots.

0560 Ceased fire, machine guns silenced.

0512 Spotted another pillbox at 'Bulldog' firing on beach, altered course and increased speed to close beach.

0519 Received signal 'Close and engage opportunity targets on Amber Beach.'

0520 Spotted snipers firing from trees above 'Bulldog' at troops on beaches. Range 5,600 yards. Stopped and turned to fire broadside to port.

0522 Opened fire – rapid salvoes.

0525 Ceased fire. Snipers silenced.

0527 Sighted first planes since landing started – Spitfires.

0530 Beach partly obscured by smoke-screens. We are steaming backward and forwards along the beach 4,000 yards range. Between us and the beach are LCSs firing continually. We are too far off to identify positions and so can't open fire.

0550 Heard heavy machine-gun fire from behind smoke-screen.

0555 Steamed through smoke-screen but firing ceased. Range off foreshore 3,000 yards.

0600 Pillbox opened heavy fire from between 'Bulldog' and 'Hound' onto our troops advancing upbeach.

0605 Range 2,000 yards. Opened fire. First salvo direct hit; when smoke and dust cleared pillbox had disappeared.

0610/0737 Lying offshore watching our troops assault defences and RDF [Radar Direction Finding] station. Could not fire in support for fear of hitting our own men.

At 0737 we sent a signal to Largs [HMS *Largs*, Combined Ops HQ ship]: 'Amber Beach quite peaceful now.'

We spent the rest of the forenoon steaming up and down Amber Beach and adjacent beaches, examining buildings. Closed in to Porto Palo to examine village. Could see our troops capturing stray Italians. Civilians occasionally popped out of the cottages, had a look and popped back in again.

Heavy fighting round Panchino and cruisers and various destroyers bombarding. Monitors lying off Green Beach bombarding heavy defensive positions in hills. 'Asset' Beach attack developing. About three air raids during day.

Joined A/S patrol [anti-submarine patrol] round anchorage during afternoon. Huge convoy now anchored off Red and Green Beaches. LSTs landing tanks and transport on Amber Beach but heavy swell is making things difficult.[72]

Heavier fire support was available from larger warships, including the monitor HMS *Erebus*. Once she was ordered to deal with an enemy gun battery, watched by the crew of HMS *Aldenham*, a Type III Hunt class destroyer. She lumbered inshore, owing to her shallow draft, and eventually 'two great belches of flame and smoke issued from her [two 15-inch] guns, and two projectiles, each weighing nearly a ton, were winging their way inland'. After firing three salvoes, the target was annihilated, and *Erebus* returned to her anchorage.[73] However, *Erebus* did suffer casualties from enemy action during Husky. One sailor explained that they were attacked several times by the Luftwaffe, mainly with anti-personnel bombs, which exploded on impact with the sea:

I remember coming out of the WT [wireless telegraphy] office, which was two decks down, climbing up the ladder, coming up to the combing at the top to step over it with three bodies laid out in various stages of mutilation and the horrible smell of what was, of course, blood. The whole deck was awash. There had been shrapnel that came in one side of the ship and decapitated people and caused tremendous injuries, and went out the other side and, of course, this left an awful lot of blood around, and when we got up from below we found that they were hosing down everything to clear all the mess up.[74]

Success in Sicily paved the way for Operation Baytown on 3 September 1943, an invasion of the Italian mainland. This entailed a relatively straightforward crossing of the Straits of Messina to Calabria by the Eighth Army. A crewman aboard LST 8, part of the invasion fleet, recalled, 'it was just superb – I mean it opened with a 1,000-gun barrage astern of us. 1,000 guns, 1,000 shells in and then it ceased and we were in and that wasn't too bad either.'[75]

As the Eighth Army advanced northwards against German rearguards, an amphibious landing was made on 9 September at Salerno, below Naples, about 200 miles away, that potentially might have shortened the war. Code-named Avalanche, this landing involved the American Fifth Army, comprising the American VI Corps and British X Corps, in tandem with a British airborne landing at Taranto. On the eve of Avalanche, the Italians surrendered, although the Germans were swift to disarm their former allies, including occupying Italian airfields. At Salerno they employed well sited defensive positions, and tanks from the 16th Panzer Division rapidly moved on the coast. The beachmaster responsible for overseeing the landing of the 56th (London) Division recalled how on landing it was discovered 'that what we had assumed were haystacks [it was harvest time] were camouflaged German artillery they'd put behind the beach'.[76]

By nightfall the Allied forces only held four beachheads, none of which had penetrated far inland. Reinforcements were rushed in, and on 13 September the Germans launched a massive counter-attack, which was only halted by naval bombardment.[77] Steve Pooley, a seaman aboard LCL 242, found that they were rather fortunate on going into Salerno. Their 'landing was perhaps 3 or 4 miles off the beach, and the Germans were occupying all that part where we were going in. And we'd heard that day over the radio that Italy had surrendered, so we thought it was going to be easy and didn't realise the Germans were going to be there. But they couldn't get the guns round onto us or we'd have been blown out of the water. Some of them [other landing craft] were hit but we were lucky and they missed us.'[78]

Unlike at Calabria, the landings at Salerno faced determined resistance from the Luftwaffe. Seaman John Lyson, who served aboard the destroyer HMS *Intrepid*, commented in relation to the start of the landings, 'any ideas of a quiet night were soon dispelled – German torpedo planes attacked the fleet, and we seemed to be firing for much of the night'.[79] For George Henderson it was one of the worst operations of his war, 'because we didn't have the air cover, and they used to come and plaster you'. Moreover, 'the troops couldn't get off the beach, and when we landed with the tanks, they were still fighting over the dunes'. Under such conditions sailors did not want to exhibit any signs of fear, or 'let anyone down'. Even so, the pressure was too much for one unfortunate crewman aboard LST 8 who suffered a breakdown. After landing, he was 'like a gibbering idiot on the upper deck. They took him off, and of all places into Salerno, which I thought was a bit much. He'd cracked, and there's no good people saying he's a coward. There's a point at which some can't go beyond and he'd reached it. Never saw him any more.'[80]

Another who felt the pressure at Salerno was a Seafire pilot from 833 Naval Air Squadron, flying from HMS *Stalker*, one of four escort or auxiliary carriers being deployed specifically to provide fighter support. They were issued with Benzedrine on the first day, but 'by the end of the second day, when we had to go out and face a third day, we were all out on our feet … certainly not in a condition to land aircraft with high expertise. So we were mightily relieved when the RAF did get established ashore, and we stood down.'[81]

As author David Wragg noted, Operation Shingle – the Allied landings at Anzio (22 January 1944) – represented an effort 'to bypass resistance' when the Italian front had bogged down.[82] It involved 50,000 American and British troops who were leapfrogged behind enemy lines, in conjunction with a thrust by the Fifth Army south of Cassino. However, as the deadlock continued at Cassino, Operation Shingle transmogrified into a full-scale offensive. Initially the landings met little resistance, but the Germans swiftly rushed reserves from Rome and north Italy, successfully containing the bridgehead. During January–May this resulted in one of the most brutal battles of the Second World War, with the Allies suffering at least 25,000 casualties, out of which 7,000 were dead, while overall German casualties were possibly as high as 40,000. The RN helped put the military forces ashore and provided fire support. However, as the fighting for Anzio unfolded, it also had to mount a shuttle service from Naples in order to keep Anzio resupplied, a role that was not welcomed at a time when shipping was urgently required for the planned invasion of Normandy.[83]

The crew of LST 8 found that this shuttle service was not without dangers. 'Up in the hills, the Germans had a huge [280mm] gun, "Anzio Annie", and she used to open up a few times a day and lob a few shells into Anzio. They were just like an express train coming, and everybody used to dive for cover; we didn't – if it came down on you, it didn't matter whether you dived for cover or not, it would take you and the cover as well. But that didn't weigh on you heavy somehow.'[84] As in any landing, there was the challenge of getting material ashore, but this was aided by vessels such as LSTs being able to use the harbour. 'You could go up against a jetty, bows on, get hawsers ashore and there are always bollards on jetties, and secure them on shore, and get the stuff off.'[85]

If amphibious operations in the Mediterranean were complex, then Operation Neptune, the naval component of D-Day, was even more daunting. On 6 June 1944 over 175,000 troops were landed on five main beaches between the Cotentin Peninsula and Le Havre: Americans at Utah and Omaha, and further to the east British and Canadians at Gold, Juno and Sword. Again naval task forces were assembled: Western Task Force (American) and Eastern Task Force (British). The Royal Navy was extensively involved. Of the 2,468 major landing vessels deployed, only 346 were American, and of the 23 cruisers supporting the landings 17 were from the Royal Navy.[86] A further 1,656 landing craft and other vessels, such as barges, were needed to ferry material from larger ships to the various Normandy beaches. 'When all vessels were taken into account, the total for the operation came to about 7,000 which required to be escorted and brought to the right place at the right time in the right sequence.'[87]

Unsurprisingly, images of the sheer scale of D-Day loom large in the memories of veterans. A Royal Marine NCO aboard LCG 18, remarked how beforehand: 'The Solent was virtually solid with shipping, so much so you felt you could walk from Portsmouth to the Isle of Wight by jumping from ship to ship, a marvellous sight. And of course they've got the [barrage] balloons up as well.'[88] Rear Admiral Edward Gueritz served as a beachmaster at Sword Beach. It was an 'amazing armada, wherever one looked there were craft', while during the bombardment 'the whole horizon seemed to lift up into the air, and I suppose one felt a pang of sympathy for the people who were at the other end'.[89] Similarly, an RM Commando who landed at Sword Beach experienced a heightening of the senses before action, and on 5–6 June:

> Everywhere you looked there were ships of all shapes and sizes. The sky always seemed to be full of our planes with the black and white stripes [these were specially applied invasion stripes for identification purposes] on them. And everything seemed to stand out in technicolour, everything was brighter in my mind than it would have been normally.[90]

The Royal Navy was instrumental in developing the Mulberries (artificial harbours) to be used off the beaches after the landings, and demonstrated that its 'capacity for detailed staff work was greater than often estimated'.[91] Under Admiral Ramsay (Allied Naval Commander, Expeditionary Force), the various Operation Neptune Naval Orders (ON) were formulated. These covered extensive details, including: ON1, the task of the Allied navies in bringing the assault forces ashore, and supporting the build-up phase; ON2, minelaying off enemy ports from the Baltic to the Bay of Biscay; ON3, naval diversions with air support; ON4, assembling the invasion armada; ON5, deployment of naval covering forces; ON6 and ON17, minesweeping, a massive task; ON7, air support; ON8, role of the bombardment forces; ON9, task for assault forces after H-Hour; ON10, follow-up forces; ON11, gaining air superiority; ON12, air defence; ON13, build-up phase; ON14, organising ancillary vessels, e.g. depot and repair ships on D-Day and afterwards; ON16, establishing the Mulberry harbours, another mammoth task; ON17, positions of channels to be swept clear of mines; ON18, extensive navigational and meteorological information; ON19, procedures for captured ports; ON20, movements of the armada from H-24 hours to D+3; and ON21, Force Pluto – the supply of fuel via cross-Channel pipelines.[92]

Related to the above were the Combined Operations' Pilotage Parties (COPPs), around ten men who could be fitted into a submarine, whose primary task was to paddle ashore in collapsible canoes to conduct reconnaissance and survey beaches. Another task using COPP personnel, with crews of X-Craft (miniature submarines) was helping navigate the D-Day armada. The commander of X-23 explained how this was done in relation to Sword Beach, during Operation Gambit:

> We were to leave on the night of Friday, 2 June to cross the 90 miles from Gosport to France and to land at a fixed position off Ouistreham. We actually arrived on the morning of Sunday, 4 June [and] we marked our position through the periscope and sat on the bottom till nightfall. On the Sunday night we surfaced, dropped our anchor so we could stay in the right position, hoisted our radio mast and we got a signal that the invasion had been postponed. [This was due to bad weather. They then retreated to the bottom until the Monday night, surfaced and received a message that the invasion would commence early on Tuesday, so they submerged again and sat it out until D-Day, despite running low on oxygen.] On 6 June we surfaced and put up all our navigational aids: an 18 foot telescopic mast with a light pointed to seaward, a radio beacon and an echo sounder tapping out a message below the surface. This was for the naval MLs to pick up as they brought the invasion force in.[93]

Likewise, the activity of Beach Groups was important in attempting to bring order as troops, equipment and supplies were landed. The military element 'received men and vehicles from landing craft clearing them through to transit areas then to storage depots or the operational front', whereas the naval element, dubbed Beach Commandos, were to 'provide navigational marks to assist in clearance of obstacles below the high water mark; to mark any obstructions ...; and generally to provide incoming landing craft with as much guidance as possible; and to expedite the unloading of their personnel, vehicles or stores, and clear them off the beach as quickly as possible'.[94]

Given the stormy weather in June 1944, seasickness was a significant issue, especially for those in landing craft. A member of the RM Armoured Support Regiment cautioned: 'Never take a trip on a flat-bottomed boat in the middle of a gale. It was awful, even for people that had been to sea and had some idea of the sea. I should think quite a few people would have said "I'd rather go ashore than stay on this thing." Seasickness is a very powerful thing.'[95] Added to this was the fear that landing craft might become swamped or even break up in heavy seas, and several did. Once embarked on an assault, landing craft crews could find that they had effectively reached a point of no return. The skipper of one LCT on D-Day noted that once the anchor was dropped off his beach, it was 'impossible to abort the landing ... for any attempt to stop would have caused chaos and probably the ship would have been blown to pieces'.[96] Thereafter it was confusing and tense for many landing craft crews. Victor Longhurst from Bexleyheath enlisted in the RN as a 17 year old in 1943, trained as a signaller and on D-Day served with the 103rd LCT Flotilla, supporting the Canadians at Juno Beach:

> There were bullets flying all over the place, so it seemed. Well, unluckily enough for me, the bullets hit the wheel house and ricocheted back ... and I got wounded then. But the coxswain who was inside the wheel house got killed because one of the gun ports which was about 9 inches by 3 inches, about the size of a small airbrick ... was left open and a bullet hit him right in the forehead. Now when I got wounded I didn't know I'd been hit. There was a lot of blood, and I said to the gunner, 'Now look, someone has been hit.' And he said: 'It's you, you've been hit,' and there was blood streaming down my arm.[97]

Having already spent three years in the navy by 1944, John Tarbit was an automatic choice for coxswain, especially given so many Combined Operations personnel were inexperienced conscripts. On D-Day his LCA was one of those taking thirty-five American troops into Omaha Beach:

> We set off in line ahead. I was last in the row ... When the dawn broke, I realised there were only five of us [one had been damaged]. Another thing we realised was that the winds and the tide were taking us north towards the British and Canadian beaches, so we had to turn to the right, to starboard, to maintain our position on the church steeple at Vierville ... because we were turning into the waves two of our LCAs were

swamped and sank. The Americans ... were all floating upside down in the water because they had so much equipment ... the only place for their lifebelts was around their waist. And the Americans had these double-barrelled life belts, and they used to inflate them with gas cartridges ... What they should have done is pushed them up under their arms and dropped their other equipment but they hung onto their equipment, so they were top heavy ... so there were 70 backsides floating in the water. The only survivors were our crews of the LCAs.[98]

On hitting the beaches, landing craft crews then had to safely disembark their troops. Acting Leading Seaman Henry Sivelle, coxswain on LCI (L) 169 at Sword Beach, found he 'had to swim ashore with a rope, so if the troops fell down they could pull themselves up because with their heavy packs they'd have a job trying to get up. They were up to their necks in water with guns above their heads.' Until the Mulberry harbour was in place, they had to continuously 'ferry troops to the beach from landing ships'.[99] Similarly, RM Commandos landing on Nan Red Sector, Juno Beach, faced difficulties. An NCO from 2 Section, B Troop, 48 Commando, commented that on exiting their LSI (S)

I was the lead man on the left hand ramp ... Immediately exposed to the machine gun nest, at the far end of the beach. And our progress down the ramp was very, very slow, not like you'd expect from a flat-bottomed boat with the front just dropping down, these ramps were floating about in the heavy seas in as much as the matelots, the seamen, were in the water holding them steady to allow us to get down. We were exposed, as I came down the ramp, two of the fellas behind me were hit by machine gun fire, and we lost a lot of men this way ... Our CO had had the good sense to place our mortar bombs in the bows of the craft, so they did lay down a smoke-screen, and enable us to get onto the beach once we were clear of the water.

The water was neck to chest high, and we had to storm the beach, try to make it across the beach, avoiding the wall where the poor Canadians had caught it, we kept to the left of that, which wasn't in the direct line of fire of the machine guns. There was a lot of chaos on the beach, some wounded lying on the beach, and the Fort Garry Horse tanks were coming in at this time with their hatches down, and a lot of wounded were being badly mauled in the tracks.[100]

John Clegg enlisted in the RM before the war, and on D-Day was serving as an NCO with the RM Armoured Support Regiment, equipped with Centaur tanks armed with 95mm howitzers. He vividly recalled landing on Gold Beach:

> As the landing craft ground onto the sand and the ramp went down, the butterflies started ... you know there's someone on the other side of the beach who wants to kill you ... Whatever angle you come off the LCT, that's the direction the tank drives for the next few minutes otherwise it risked shedding a track if trying to turn in the water ... [Subsequently crews would] press the switch to drop reserve ammunition off. You blow some of the waterproofing off the rear, all done by explosive bolts, and give your tank a better breathing space. Now all that you've learnt in the months previously is brought into being ... If you're in the right place you know where your targets are. Once you've identified somewhere you do the job you've trained for.[101]

Another RM NCO involved in providing fire support was 'Tod' Raven-Hill, who by 1944 had already experienced extensive service in Home Waters, the Arctic and Mediterranean. His vessel, LCG 18, operated off Sword Beach:

> We went in as expected. God knows how many rounds we fired, we were firing the whole time going in with landing craft right up until they landed. And then we went to the flank and started firing ahead of them broadside on according to radio control. And when they'd more or less secured the bridgehead, we sailed towards Le Havre, and anything we saw that could be a gun site we'd open fire on, and if it responded we would get the hell out of it, and let the big ships behind us shell the place.[102]

During Neptune, Colin Kitching was First Lieutenant of an LCP flotilla of twelve of these small boats, now employed on specialist duties. As they had proved too frail as assault craft, 'we were switched to carrying out smoke-laying duties. This was done by way of a highly dangerous substance – chloro-sulphonic acid – pumped under pressure through a jet at the LCP's stern. As soon as the droplets of acid hit the air a huge cloud of white smoke was formed.' On 6 June 'HM LCP Flotilla was part of assault group 321, led by the redoubtable Commander Ryder VC, RN. Our task was to provide smoke-screen cover for the amphibious tanks [Duplex Drive or DD tanks] in the Juno landing area, and for some of the bombarding warships ... [Later] we moved to Sword area on the extreme eastern flank of the bridgehead. The planners had foreseen that for some time the Sword area was likely to be within easy reach of enemy artillery. Reinforcement and supply operations on that beach would be hazardous, and the anchorage at risk: maximum smoke protection would be needed. [Eventually, to support operations in Normandy] the flotilla made smoke every night for nearly five weeks, a very strenuous routine. Operating in the dark was a stressful activity: we had to keep track of where we were going, relative to the wind and to the other LCPs, and constantly be wary of such possible hazards as E-boats [German MTBs], against which we stood no chance.'[103] It may seem strange having to lay smoke-screens at night, but commanders considered that with the congested area off Sword, clouds of smoke in daylight might confuse Allied shipping, and be of more benefit to the enemy than to friendly forces.

Another challenge was the tidal conditions in Normandy, and this had particular resonance for LST crews. George Henderson outlined how:

> With a non-tidal it means that you can land on the beach, and on your way in, the basic idea was to go as hard in as you could go so you could get as far up the beach out of the water or into about 3 to 4 feet, drop your stern anchor which was a kedge hook on the way in, and it would dig into the sand, about 100 yards, a big cable on the stern. And when you were empty you pulled in on your stern anchor and that pulled the ship along into deep water. That's fine in the Mediterranean but in France it's tidal, so by the time we went on and dropped the tanks, and unloaded – because it takes a while to unload as it does to load – and by the time we'd unloaded the tide had gone out. So we're left on the beach about half a mile from the water like stranded whales, you know, all the LSTs.
>
> The LCTs and that would unload and chug back off but by the time we'd unloaded the heavy stuff, the tanks, the tide had gone so we were there until the tide came in. That's not everybody's cup of tea, it's a bit nerve wracking because you can't do anything. You can fire up, but you can't do much else, and you can't help the soldiers. And sometimes we used to carry ammunition. I am talking about hundreds of tons of ammunition, and you're on the beach with nowhere to go, that's when it becomes a bit fraught, but you had to put up with it.[104]

The Royal Navy was also employed in supporting the invasion of Southern France (Operation Dragoon) on 15 August 1944. As Eric Denton recounted, for the crew of his ML, then employed as a minesweeper, 'this was a very hectic period, relieved only by the pleasant view of the South of France from the sea'.[105] The British provided some of the bombardment forces, and did jobs such as escorting convoys. Once, HMS *Aldenham*, with other destroyers, picked-up 'fifty-three identical American Liberty ships, steaming slowly in the direction of the isle of Capri, the Hunts fussing around them, jostling them into position'. During this convoy her crew were surprised to encounter an Admiralty launch flying a massive White Ensign. Aboard was Prime Minister Winston Churchill, 'unconcerned as ever, his sea-going yachting cap clamped down on his head and that inevitable cigar stuck in his mouth, the grand old man himself!'[106]

The operation saw American and French units assault 'in three sectors on a 45-mile stretch of coast to the east of Marseilles', while a fourth force tackled outlying islands thought to be fortified. Only limited resistance was encountered, and although the landings were well organised and executed, according to Captain Roskill it appeared as if 'we took a sledgehammer to crack a nut'. Some 881 warships and 1,370 smaller craft had been allocated to the operation, 65 per cent of which were American and 33 per cent British, a reversal of the situation in Normandy.[107]

As the campaign in north-west Europe unfolded during late 1944, amphibious warfare was again employed to open up the Scheldt and the key port of Antwerp to Allied shipping. This required seizure of the strategically placed island of Walcheren at the mouth of the Scheldt. A seaborne assault was mounted by the RM Special Service Brigade, which since D-Day had been operating as infantry, although trained for amphibious warfare. The landings were made in conjunction with an attack by the Canadians from the landward side. After preparations in the Ostend area, including learning how to operate with newly issued Buffalo and the smaller Weasel, both tracked amphibious vehicles, the assault force was ready. An NCO with 48 Commando explained, 'two Buffaloes each carried a troop, and a landing craft carried two Buffaloes'.[108]

Captain A.F. Pugsley commanded the naval component and on 1 November 'his 181 landing craft started out from Ostend to assault the heavily fortified island, while heavy bombarding ships [including HMS *Warspite* and HMS *Erebus*] came across from England to give their support'. The aerial and seaborne bombardment prior to the attack was hampered by poor weather, and many of the assault craft came under heavy fire; once ashore the Marines often experienced tough fighting. Even so, by 8 November it was clear to its commander that 'the fate of the German garrison was plainly sealed', leading him and 29,000 of his men to surrender.[109]

An officer on an LCT, awarded the DSC during the operation, found it very different from Normandy. 'There wasn't a wide beach, it was very rocky and you had to sort of fight your way in there. We were hit on the way in … a direct hit on one of the vehicles and a couple of the RASC chaps [Royal Army Service Corps drivers] killed. We beached, got rid of them, kedged off, and then the padre stopped on board to see to the casualties.'[110]

Howard Dowell, an RM signaller on the bridge of LCF 32, which was providing fire support, had an equally awkward experience. Having witnessed another landing craft sink ahead of them, they 'went the whole length of the beach towards the lighthouse with all our guns firing. There was no return of fire from the Germans whatsoever. At the end of our run, we turned round and came back, and this was the most frightening period of my life. The German guns raked us for the whole of the run back, although we were firing, and we sustained forty-seven direct hits on that somewhat clumsy craft. The only person who was killed was the PO Motor Mechanic, who came up from the engine room, and stood near the aft port side Oerlikon, and one shell landed and killed him. But we were a lucky ship.'[111]

In contrast, a member of 41 Commando recalled:

We arrived off Walcheren at approximately 6 am, just getting light, 2 miles out, I suppose. And I remember seeing all these twinkling lights ... they were shells coming off the guns that the RAF had supposedly blown out of existence. And the whole island was ringed with guns in emplacements ... As we got closer we could see the light house at Westkapelle, and to our starboard a rocket ship got a direct hit and blew up. There were shells falling all around but we weren't hit ... And we landed about 8.30am, a dry landing, and within three minutes we were inside one of the gun emplacements, where they were having breakfast would you believe, still having coffee. We came in flying with the 'hande hoch' and they did and we had coffee three or four minutes after getting ashore![112]

Clearly there was a vast difference between launching an unopposed landing and one that was opposed. Take the experiences of the 3rd Commando Brigade in the Arakan, Burma, during early 1945. By then the Japanese were in retreat, and XV Corps was tasked with forcing the Japanese 28th Army from the Arakan. To do this, a series of outflanking assaults from the sea were employed, and the terrain was a critical factor. Major General J.I.H. Owen, a veteran of 44 Commando, explained that most of the area was 'tangled jungle-covered hills, only wide enough on top to deploy three or four men in line', and invariably slopes ran down to paddy-fields or mangrove swamps. More-over, the coastal strip and hills were 'intersected by hundreds of tidal creeks (or chaungs)', often very long, unfordable, and with few landing points, while those that did exist were stoutly defended by the Japanese. The lack of beaches ensured that these chaungs offered 'the only means of access to the hinterland'.[113]

The first landing, at Akyab, was unopposed as the enemy had vacated the area. Robert West, an HO, had joined the RM in 1940, and became a junior NCO with 42 Commando. He remembered that at Akyab they still 'had to make sure the villages were clear'.[114] Next it was decided to land the Brigade on the Myebon Peninsula, which entailed blowing a gap in coconut stakes offshore, so that landing craft could access the beaches. According to Robert West, they encountered some opposition:

> Going in, the Japs opened up, and the air force were bombing them ...
> You could see them and you fired, the worst part was the shelling, and
> they're very good at mortars, the Japs, you know. And you used to count
> how many before the first one exploded.[115]

In contrast, it was anticipated by some commandos that Kangaw 'would be a bad one.'[116] It lay east of Myebon, and marked the only route open to the Japanese out of the Arakan, given that the British now held the Myebon Peninsula. 'It was decided to take the long way round, due south from Myebon, and north up into the Daingbon Chaung ... a trip of 18 miles up a waterway whose banks might be held by the enemy.'[117] Subsequently, 1 Commando were to land first and take the key feature Hill 170, then 42 Commando would land and establish a bridgehead, and 5 Commando would pass through this and assist 1 Commando, while 44 Commando would be landed and held as brigade reserve.

> On this operation the Japs did shell, they really did shell. And of course
> they dropped the doors, and once you dropped the doors of the landing
> craft, then there was an opening, and if anyone got a machine gun trained
> on it they could wipe the lot out. What we had to do was once we got out
> we spread out ... We had to take our big haversacks off and drag them as
> it was mud and water up to chest level. We tried to save cigarettes ... We
> got in all right, spread out, took up positions. The next wave coming in,
> some of them hit land mines ... Anyway we consolidated our positions
> after a period of time fighting at a distance.[118]

Chapter Six

Discipline and Morale

There were various reasons why men and women enlisted in the wartime Royal Navy (RN). As historian Glyn Prysor has emphasised, the RN 'was not merely the foremost of Britain's armed forces: it was the most prestigious military organization in the world. Its ships were represented in popular culture as the apogee of national virility.' Warships, especially well known ones such as the battlecruiser HMS *Hood* and aircraft carrier *Ark Royal*, 'were not simply national symbols but physical manifestations of industrial might, of technological advancement and of imperial strength. For British society, the navy was a vital element of national identity.'[1] No doubt the prestige of the navy, along with patriotism, had an influence on many an individual's decision to enlist, but with war on the horizon human concerns came to the fore as well. In July 1939 Bernard Upton was 20 years old, and records that among his contemporaries: 'The general opinion was that it was better to volunteer now for one of the three military services of our choice than to wait to be conscripted into something disagreeable.'[2] Accordingly he volunteered for the RNVR, was trained as a signalman at HMS *Royal Arthur* at Ingold-mells, near Skegness, and later served on a minesweeper as an officer.

Others were swayed by the influence of their father's generation, who had endured the horrors of the trenches during the First World War. Petty Officer Douglas Bruce was given the following practical, if not very patriotic, advice by his father, a veteran of the Somme and Ypres:

Avoid the Air Force – What goes up must come down.
Avoid the Army – You're cannon fodder.
Join the Navy – at least you can rely on three square meals a day and a dry bed, until the ship goes down![3]

Robert Cosh applied to join the Fleet Air Arm (FAA) once the war had started because he found after 'twelve months drilling with a very old .303 rifle in the Home Guard, I knew that the Army was not for me'.[4] By contrast, Lilian Pickering was desperate to join one of the Women's Services. The Wrens seemed the obvious choice, as she had already been 'a Sea Ranger with my Signaller's Badge'. She was eventually asked for interview at Chester, and soon after was 'called up for training in Dundee, Scotland, – as a W/T operator'.[5]

Britain's position as a maritime power and the calling of the sea were also influential factors in motivating men to join the Merchant Navy. As a 16 year old training on HMS *Worcester* on the eve of the Second World War, John Cutcliffe explained how he had 'been attracted to a life at sea by one or two of my friends at school who'd decided to go off and see the world' and came back with tales of their adventures, plus he confessed 'I couldn't envisage myself pushing a pen in a bank or a solicitor's office or anything like that. It had to be an open-air life and I thought the sea gave me the best opportunity.'[6] For Joe Lafferty, another wartime merchant seaman, it was 'in the blood. My father was an ex-seaman, my grandfather an ex-seaman', and 'it was either that or I was coming up for conscription age where I would have been conscripted into the navy or to the army, military, and I wanted to follow in my father's footsteps and my brother's footsteps and so joined the Merchant Navy'.[7]

For the RN, a distinct challenge as the war progressed was that the large influx of Hostilities Only personnel and reservists had to be successfully absorbed by the organisation, even if that led to a dilution of the navy's character. The dynamic between regulars and the different types of reservist was captured in a popular contemporaneous saying, recounted by the FAA pilot Norman Hanson: 'The RN are gentlemen trying to be sailors; the RNR are sailors trying to be gentlemen; the RNVR are neither trying to be both.'[8]

Regardless of their background, both RN personnel and merchant seamen were effectively engaged in an industrialised form of naval warfare during 1939–1945. This embraced such features as 'the nurtured machinery of the engine room; the organized procedures of the wireless telegraphy office' and, depending on the type of ship, 'the drilled routines of the gun, depth-charge or torpedo teams; the choreographed process of the aircraft launch; the bureaucracy of the bridge'.[9] All of which had a factory-like feel to it, and was invariably dependent on the individual working as part of a team to achieve operational efficiency. Behind this lay discipline, fostered by training to inculcate the values of the RN, and ensure that the wartime navy worked both in and out of combat. However, as Petty Officer Bruce cautioned, at an early stage sailors were introduced to the King's Rules and Regulations, plus:

> routines almost like 'Holy Writ' in stone tablets ... If you are wise your best course of action is to adapt to your new surroundings ... stop reasoning, forget logic, forgo common sense, do not question or argue, cease to kick against the pricks and especially those who happen to be running the local operations in which you are now involved! Instead, do what everyone else is doing, think only of your day of release.[10]

Likewise, in the Merchant Navy the discipline necessary for a career at sea was instilled at institutions such as HMS *Worcester*, an old wooden ship moored on the Thames, that was likened by John Cutcliffe to 'a public school afloat'. The onset of war and the risk of bombing saw much of this training moved to Footscray in Kent, but in both cases it was: 'Very strict. Unbelievably strict for someone like myself who'd never come across that before. But you had to learn. You were given a fortnight, sometimes three weeks if they were very generous, to find out what made everything tick, after that you were in trouble if you broke any of the rules.'[11]

Underpinning discipline was morale. What actually comprises morale and makes men fight, and continue to do so, especially in adverse conditions, is a complex subject. One dictionary offers the following definition of morale: it is 'the mental and emotional attitudes of an individual to the function or tasks expected of him with respect to a group: Esprit de Corps'.[12] Certainly this applied to the war at sea during 1939–1945, as esprit de corps was important, with every ship needing to be run as efficiently as possible. Yet numerous personnel served ashore, where discipline and morale were nonetheless important, albeit the context differed from serving at sea. For the purposes of this chapter morale can be said to be not just those factors that engendered a sense of esprit de corps, important though that was, but those that allowed sailors and merchant seamen to cope with the challenges of war and helped them to better perform their duty. This included issues such as comradeship, welfare arrangements, access to medical care, mail, alcohol, tobacco and even sex. Crucially, arrangements for leave had a direct correlation with morale. However, many of these factors were denied to sailors and seamen once they were shipwrecked and/or became a POW. Accordingly, the final section of the chapter considers how personnel coped with losing their ship, effectively their home at sea, and highlights what life was like in captivity.

Conditions at Sea and Ashore

Service aboard a warship or submarine was invariably crowded, wet and cold depending on where it was serving. Even on larger ships space was at a premium, and in the 1940s habitability was not necessarily at the forefront of ship designers' minds. For many sailors the declaration of war led to an immediate feeling of total fatigue compared with peacetime. In September 1939 Rear Admiral Edward Gueritz was a young midshipman aboard the cruiser HMS *Cumberland* in the South Atlantic:

> We were nineteen or twenty year olds, we had a number of boys on board, who were probably sixteen to seventeen, but we were all required

to keep watches. And the degree of readiness dictated whether we were in two watches or four. As two watches were at night, you can imagine there was considerable accumulation of sleep that was missing. And one got into a routine in which things could almost be done automatically. This is the first thing one notices from the change from a peacetime routine to a wartime routine. Although you may go on a peacetime exercise and have the stress and strain, it isn't the same as having it day after day with no foreseeable end. We spent about 109 days out of 118 at sea at the beginning of the war [as] County class cruisers [were] famous for their endurance.[13]

Similarly, combat at sea brought its fair share of strain and disorientation. During the Second Battle of Sirte on 22 March 1942 British warships under Rear Admiral Sir Philip Vian successfully drove off an Italian force threatening a Malta convoy in the Mediterranean by engaging in a long-range gun duel. Subsequently, *Littorio* and three Italian cruisers emerged to the northeast 'and a series of confused fights' occurred, 'with British cruisers and destroyers plunging at high speed through heavy seas, in and out of the smoke-screen which the ships specially detailed for that purpose were still laying'.[14] The battle raged until the evening, and ultimately demonstrated that a smaller disciplined and well trained force could, if handled boldly, hamper a superior enemy, albeit the RN suffered thirty-nine sailors killed and had eight ships damaged or disabled, whereas the Italians suffered damage only to their battleship. A midshipman serving on HMS *Beaufort*, one of the Hunt class destroyers involved, remembered that:

I envied the guns crew who didn't know from one minute to the next what was going to happen next because they were in ignorance but I knew. I knew that we were in an annihilation situation but luckily the *Vittorio Veneto*, I think it was, it might have been her sister ship [Indeed he does in fact mean the battleship *Littorio*] – they were brand new, 35,000-ton battleships, equivalent to the King George V class – there was only one and he turned back just as he was getting the range of the *Breconshire* [one of the merchant ships]. He saw his salvoes fall around the *Breconshire*. None very close but I mean he only fired about four I suppose, three or four. I saw the flashes of his guns but from the bridge they could see the ship but there was so much smoke around I could only see the flashes through the smoke and then he turned round. They did say that he was hit in the last attack but even still he was in such a war-winning situation ...[15]

Friendly fire or accidents could potentially cause casualties as well. One of the worst cases of friendly fire occurred on 27 August 1944 in the wake of the Normandy landings, when Hawker Typhoons from 263 and 266 Squadrons RAF mistakenly attacked a flotilla of minesweepers, sinking two of them and badly damaging a third, resulting in the deaths of 117 officers and ratings and a further 153 wounded. The incident was hushed up for fifty years, and resulted from a failure in communication between the navy and RAF, so when Allied radar spotted five ships sweeping in line abreast they were immediately considered to be German.[16]

Training sought to instil the necessary discipline to cope with the demands of active service, and avoid such incidents. This commenced during basic training, and, as Gordon Wallace observed on joining the FAA, initially this seemed to have little to do with his intended role as an observer. At HMS *St Vincent* his intake spent 'hours in the ablutions scrubbing our collars to give a bleached appearance, ironing our trousers inside out to give the desired figure of eight shape ...'. Subsequently, at the notorious Naval Gunnery School on Whale Island, there was gun drill: 'Standing in line, rigidly to attention, not moving an eyelid until the command rasped out to grasp and turn the appropriate brass knob.'[17]

Notably, at Tobermory on the Isle of Mull, off the west coast of Scotland, Vice Admiral (retd) Gilbert Stephenson was tasked with running courses to work up newly commissioned ship's companies for the Battle of the Atlantic. Known as 'Monkey' Stephenson, he had ASW experience from the First World War, was given the rank of Commodore Second Class, and took an unorthodox approach to training, including insisting that ship's companies conducted close order drill ashore as the first part of any programme. Training was based around 'sustained hard work and relentless attention to detail, in the belief that if a ship's organization and a crew's knowledge of and application of the fundamentals were sound, she would become an efficient fighting unit', although little time was usually spent on anything but the simplest tactics because crews were invariably very raw.[18]

Essential to Stephenson's thinking was 'spirit' or the will to win, followed by discipline, as 'it's no good being the finest men in the world if you are not going to obey orders'. This is why close order drill was valued. Administration was equally important, that is 'making sure the work of a ship was evenly divided; that meals were in the right place at the right time; that the whole organisation of the ship was both stable and elastic'. Finally, he identified the importance of 'technique'. This was defined as 'how to use the equipment' and was deemed worthless 'unless the spirit was right'.[19] Even so, Stephenson was well aware that he was dealing with many sailors who were citizens in uniform doing their war service, and that there was only limited time available to work up ships. Consequently, he turned a blind eye if some naval practices were not observed but he 'came down like a fiery torch' on any 'signs of carelessness or laziness which might lose a ship or drown a crew'.[20]

Something of Stephenson's imaginative approach and character can be gained from the following anecdote. It was common for him to speed over to a ship in his motor boat, board it and fling his cap down on the quarter-deck shouting: 'That's a bomb – what are you going to do about it?' This usually created 'momentary panic' until he tried it on one trawler, where a sailor kicked it overboard. He looked on as his gold-braided cap floated away, and shouted 'Good work', then, not to be out-done, exclaimed: 'Quick, that's a survivor who can't swim – save him!'[21]

Ideally, everyone wanted to serve on a happy ship, which implied one where there was good morale, an effective workman-like ship's company, plus a sense of a fair disciplinary system. Large warships had a commander who could bring contentious issues to the attention of the captain. In contrast, in destroyers, the work-horses of the navy, and in other small vessels it was the first lieutenant, known as the 'Jimmy the One' in naval slang, who acted as executive officer and second in command. The importance of the role was expressed by one experienced officer: 'A good commanding officer may have an efficient ship, but he cannot also have a happy one unless he has a good First Lieutenant.' He supported the captain, especially by offering tactful advice, while simultaneously appreciating the crew, 'whose viewpoint he must learn to understand, and often to represent'.[22] This was in addition to other duties on the ship. Similarly, on landing craft it was the first lieutenant who would ensure that it was ready for sea, and the crew at their designated stations, although disciplinary matters would usually be brought before the skipper in what was known as a defaulter session. The antithesis of this was an unhappy ship, and Captain Bob Whinney explained the phenomenon in relation to the destroyer HMS *Duncan*, which he commanded for a time. On reaching port after being involved in a collision, he noted that the crew:

> were jumpy and lacking in confidence ... This ship had had a poor start to the commission; there had been too many changes among the officers, the Ward Room was not a happy one and there was neither a good feeling throughout the ship nor had there been good accord between officers and men in some branches.[23]

Similarly, a former Royal Marine officer outlined how on his ship:

> We had one commander who was very, very, unpopular. He tried peace-time routines on a, I suppose 60 per cent ... hostilities only crew and this

was very much resented, and the ship's company I must regretfully say found the solution to this was to notice that whenever he went down his hatchway to his quarters aft he hung onto the hatch cover to help himself down, ... somehow the latch holding the cover got loosened and he brought it down on his head one day and we got a new commander. That's the only occasion I remember clearly when we had somebody up with which we could not put.[24]

Conversely, rivalry between the different branches on a ship or with other vessels could have a positive impact. While serving as a Swordfish pilot on a MAC ship in the Atlantic, John Shoebridge and his comrades discovered that they had to work alongside an escort carrier flying the White Ensign of the RN:

they thought they were much better than us, terribly superior they were, we were made to feel the junior partner in a very big way indeed. But they weren't all that wonderful sea boats these escort carriers, whereas, we were. And one day it occurred that they couldn't fly because the weather was too strong, the whole ship was moving up and down that much. And we flew that day. We were very pleased indeed, because we were all RNVR in those days.[25]

Likewise, naval customs could assist ship's companies in coping with conditions at sea, and help regular ratings to inculcate the spirit of the navy in HOs and reservists. The auctioning of dead men's effects was a common practice, with the funds going to their families, and often items might be sold for far greater sums than their actual worth. Another staple, especially on larger ships, was elaborate crossing the line ceremonies when a ship sailed over the Equator, akin to one that occurred on the carrier HMS *Formidable*:

the Court of King Neptune arrived on board ... They summoned the Skipper to appear before them, also the Commander and many Officers, whose crimes were read out and honours bestowed on them. Then the barbers got to work with flour, paste and huge wooden razors on their victims. They seated their victims on ducking stools, poured paste over them and released a catch on the back of the chair. The chair swung backwards and the victims were hurled into a bath of water where bears waited to duck them ...[26]

Naval language also reinforced a sense of identity, and helped build esprit de corps both at sea and ashore. This entailed the use of slang, although naval terminology was equally important. Countless WRNS personnel/Wrens, for instance, on enlisting discovered that rooms were cabins, floors were decks, dining rooms the mess deck, kitchen the galley, and that free time was referred to as Make and Mend, etc.

Wrens did not go to sea because warships were already overcrowded, providing mixed accommodation was thought too difficult, and they were considered too inexperienced to crew ships by themselves. Consequently, most Wrens served ashore, with work ranging from translating German to servicing MTBs. However, some Wrens were employed on harbour craft, even though this might entail bringing crowds of rowdy liberty men back from shore leave. In 1941 Anne Partridge was an officer's steward, 'cleaning shoes, serving meals and working in the wardroom bar' and leapt at the opportunity to volunteer for boat crew, which seemed to offer a more active part in the war. After brief training on knots and signalling, she was soon involved in such tasks as ferrying POWs to shore, usually U-boat crewmen who had been captured by another ship, bringing mail to ships and taking liberty men ashore.[27] Likewise, Angela Mack was one of a select band of Wren cypher officers who worked in wireless offices on Monsters, the codeword for trans-Atlantic liners impressed into service as troopships.

Initially Wrens were mainly recruited from naval families living near ports, and served in a variety of administrative/domestic capacities, the idea being, as a popular recruiting poster stated, to free a man for the fleet. These young women stayed in their own homes and were termed immobile, whereas those who volunteered for service elsewhere were classed as mobile. By the end of the war few naval establishments in Britain could have felt complete without their complement of Wrens. During the course of their war many served overseas, principally in the Middle and Far East. The WRNS reached peak strength in September 1944, 'when there were 74,635 officers and ratings, in 90 categories and 50 branches'.[28]

This included Wrens involved in secret naval communications duties. As P. Bieber (née Furber) found on joining the Y Service:

> our job entailed intercepting messages between German ships, especially between E-boats and MTBs. We were to translate the messages and relay them as quickly as possible by telephone or teleprinter to the relevant naval authority. We were given examples of the kind of messages we might hear and how we should interpret these. It all sounded very exciting and terrifying. At the end of the fortnight we were told that our category was 'Special Duties', we wore no category flashes and nobody knew what we did and we certainly thought ourselves a cut above the others. After signing the Official Secrets Act our importance knew no bounds.[29]

Many Wrens, including the 17½-year-old Barbara Hadden-Scott, worked at Station X, the Government Code and Cypher School at Bletchley Park. They were:

> taken one at a time into the first officer (White) to be asked to sign the Official Secrets Act and to have a really forceful lecture on how it would cost lives and what would happen to us. That we must not talk amongst ourselves. From that day until the 1970s I or my friends did not mention our work to each other. My parents died without having any idea of what I did. They thought that I was a writer [clerk].
>
> ... we were taken to our cabins ... The work was divided into four watches A, B, C, D. We worked for 7 days on each watch, 4pm–12pm then the night watch 12pm–8am, day watch 8am–4pm. Then four much needed days off for watch change. (Stand By) very tired. We lived in huts at the front of the camp. To get to work we went out of the back of the camp and underground. We worked in Bays that had all the machines called 'Bombs' lined up. I worked on one called Stavanger ...[30]

By contrast, J. Dinwoodie was among the first Wren wireless telegraphists drafted overseas to Singapore, where they worked at Royal Naval W/T station Kranji, which was separate from the main naval base. Prior to Japan's entry into the war in December 1941, it was

> a very 'happy ship'. Beside the Wrens there were sailors of the Malayan Navy, Royal Naval sailors, civilian, Army and RAF personnel and we all mixed very happily together, except in the station swimming pool where no mixed bathing was permitted. We were divided into four watches, working roughly naval watches, shorter than we had been used to in the UK. I think all of us would agree that being in the watchroom at Kranje was the hottest time any of us is likely to experience. The heat really had to be experienced to be believed. We were in a concrete building with no windows, no air conditioning (we had been told it had sunk on the way out to the station), constantly manned 24 hours a day so that it was never aired, additional heat from the sets and a haze and smell of smoking that could almost be cut with a knife. No wonder that we went on watch armed with giant flasks of 'aya lima' (lime water) and small towels to wrap round our necks to mop up as much as possible of the constant sweat. The tropical heat of Singapore seemed almost cool by comparison when we emerged from watchkeeping.[31]

Often accommodation for those working ashore was pretty basic. Nissen huts, familiar to countless servicemen and women, were 'flimsy-looking rectangular erections of corrugated iron' and were used on many bases, including at RNAS St Merryn (HMS *Vulture*) in Cornwall.[32] Alternatively, personnel might be billeted in civilian homes, something that was not always satisfactory. A group of Wrens working on a degaussing range at Tilbury, which provided ships with protection against magnetic mines, were quartered in an old vicarage. They were 'always cold' and looked after by the caretaker and his wife who never provided adequate food, so they were compelled 'to go out before breakfast and pick mushrooms to supplement [his] meagre offerings'.[33] Sailors from the RNPS at Lowestoft discovered that many billets were 'filthy, with one lavatory to eighteen men, and infested with fleas which waxed fat on human blood'.[34] By comparison, Lilian Pickering did much better when she served as a Wren W/T operator in Cape Town, South Africa, where she was to help open up the base there for convoys unable to safely use the Mediterranean. She was billeted at the Kommetje Hotel, and Wrens were 'treated as civilian guests', replete 'with an early morning cup of coffee', albeit that did not necessarily 'suit watchkeeping times'.[35]

The so-called stone frigates were another feature of the war ashore, and the term embraced many naval shore establishments, notably those involved with training. Les Roberts underwent basic training at HMS *Raleigh* at Torpoint, before going on an anti-aircraft gunnery course at the infamous Whale Island, where 'your main hope was to survive the discipline' and from there was posted to Coastal Forces. Eventually he was selected for a commission, it having been noted at interview on enlistment that he was potential officer material. Accordingly, he was sent to HMS *King Alfred* at Lancing College, near Worthing, which produced RNVR officers for the wartime navy. This was an intense experience covering 'navigation, seamanship, gunnery, signals, explosives, fleet manoeuvres', as well as providing trainees with 'squarebashing' to instil discipline, plus the course sought to foster leadership qualities.[36]

Having served as a rating aboard the destroyer HMS *Jersey*, C.B. Blackmore was similarly commissioned at HMS *King Alfred*, before volunteering for training as a mine and bomb disposal officer, not fully appreciating what this would entail. After a number of British-based appointments, he was posted to the Mediterranean and saw notable service in Greece, before ending his war in Singapore. This often overlooked work was important and potentially hazardous, as his experience in North Africa demonstrates. Most mines had a metal case, and

> in the centre of that metal case is a cylinder containing 500 pounds of explosive. So that what we used to do was if the mine was sitting on its mechanism plate where all the works were we would blow a little hole –

hopefully – in the casing as far away from the cylinder as we could and then we could place a charge on the actual case, on the actual explosive. And blow the lot. There was one we did [where] it was jammed on. The mechanism plate down on the rocks, and we put the charge in the usual place just a couple of ounces of gelignite and blew it, or at least retired about ten, fifteen foot away behind a little sand dune, and blew the fuse off the charge and the whole lot went up ... all 500 pounds. But fortunately, it was one of those occasions, you know ... we were so close to it that everything, the debris and shrapnel and everything, went right over our heads. It just went straight up and over. We were covered in sand but that was all ... just a little bit of difficulty hearing to begin with. But [that] settled down, no problem.[37]

Numerous Royal Marines served on ships and, as the war progressed, many manned landing craft. However, it was equally possible for RM personnel to experience considerable service ashore. John Clegg provides a case in point. Initially he was drafted to HMS *Nelson*, then he served with the Mobile Naval Base Defence Organisation (MNBDO) in Egypt in 1939 before seeing service in Norway and Britain with 31 RM Howitzer Battery from 1940 to 1942; as an NCO he fought with the RM Armoured Support Regiment in Normandy in 1944, prior to ending his war with an RM amphibious assault unit in India and Java in 1945–1946.

The MNBDO, of which there were two eventually, might have appeared sensible in theory, but had the distinct disadvantage 'of investing manpower and effort in unwieldly, defensive, far from mobile formations which could only lead the RM into a cul-de-sac as far as gainful employment was concerned'. They led a dull existence in the Mediterranean and Indian Ocean theatres, although some personnel experienced fighting in Crete, and became POWs.[38] John Stringer enlisted in the RM in 1941 and saw action with MNBDO 2 during the invasion of Sicily in July 1943: 'It was a pretty easy invasion as far as we were concerned ... we landed at Augusta harbour, and there did the job we were trained to do as MNBDO [i.e. mount a defence.] We had air raids to contend with [these were countered by the MNBDO's Bofors anti-aircraft guns] but no other fighting.'[39]

Later Stringer became an NCO with B Troop, 48 Commando RM, having successfully passed a short but intensive course at the Commando Training Centre at Achnacarry, Scotland, entitling him to wear the famous green beret:

It was very arduous training, we were in constant bivouacs, two to a bivouac, and the weather was wet and miserable. Every morning you were expected to turn out smart and clean on parade. And the moment you'd been inspected, you'd be sent through the mud bath to make you feel uncomfortable for the rest of the day, and you'd be wet through all day ... climbing mountains, abseiling down cliffs, some nights spending out on the mountains ...[40]

Stringer would go on to land on Juno Beach on D-Day, and saw combat during the campaign in north-west Europe, 1944–1945.

Officers and ratings were also employed in the various naval bases in Britain and overseas. While those such as Portsmouth, Plymouth, Scapa Flow and Singapore were well developed, the same could not be said of the limited Russian base organisation supporting the Arctic convoys. Moreover, the Russians generally proved an 'unappreciative ally' towards RN and Merchant Navy personnel, and relations were soured by their 'suspicions, prevarications and obstructions'.[41] Notably conditions in the hospitals at Polyarnoe, Murmansk and Archangel that dealt with wounded British seaman who had been carrying supplies to Russia were extremely primitive. Vice Admiral Sir Ian Campbell served as captain (D) of the 3rd Destroyer Flotilla, and recorded that patients' 'bedclothes [were] of dubious cleanliness', the wards packed, poorly ventilated and permanently blacked out, while 'the staff wore dirty overalls and scorned to make use of gloves'. Drugs were in short supply, and the 'dull monotonous food did nothing to comfort men lying in fear and pain, unable to make their simplest needs or symptoms known'.[42]

Welfare and Entertainment

An important aspect in facing the war was developing a suitable mental attitude as a form of coping strategy. One member of Coastal Forces noted how: 'Time was not important to us, we had all adopted this different way of life, and it seemed perfectly natural. We never talked of our lives before in "civvy street", and most of us never gave a thought as to what might be in store for us when the war eventually ended'.[43] Related to this was the close bond of comradeship that many felt with their crewmates, and which boosted their mental or psychological welfare. On joining the destroyer HMS *Tartar* as a young officer, Ludovic Kennedy encountered his fellow officers in the wardroom: 'the captain, ... small, dapper, almond-eyed, a brilliant ship handler and of much conscious charm', and the first lieutenant, a 'country gent and future admiral, ginger-haired and blue-eyed'. The No. 2 was a 'cheerful former Reserve officer' and the navigator 'Spider Wilson, a lean, hook-nosed sub-lieutenant RN who smoked cigarettes through a holder and had a habit of saying "Great Land!" when surprised'. There was also 'Tiny Archer-Shee, the ponderous 6 foot 6 inch RNVR lieutenant, a City man in peacetime'.

Their relationships were reinforced by their nicknames, and, as Kennedy wrote, 'my own nickname of Uckers was … inevitable, being the Navy's name for the popular messdeck game of Ludo'.[44]

Morale in the RN at sea depended largely on leave, which in turn was organised in relation to the nature of service and local operations. Essentially there were three types of leave: shore leave, granted by commanding officers for sailors dubbed Liberty Men for a short period of time such as an evening; home leave, which provided personnel with a longer break from their ship; and survivors' leave for those whose ship had been sunk or badly damaged, intended as a period of recuperation and to provide time for redrafting to occur. Additionally, emergency compassionate leave could be granted to sailors when necessary. The crew of MGB 320 discovered that they were sometimes granted shore leave in Felixstowe, where there were two dance halls. The one at the Cavendish Hotel proved popular, with its 'beautiful barmaids' and because it was within walking distance of their base, 'approximately 2 miles, not much when one was sober but much more after a few drinks'.[45] In contrast, Angela Mack experienced a few days' leave in New York while serving as a Wren cypher officer aboard the ocean-going liner RMS *Mauretania*, which had been pressed into service as a troopship bringing American personnel over to Britain ahead of D-Day: 'Everything I saw looked luxurious. Everything that people wore looked attractive, new and colourful. The sun shone; the windows of Saks were as elegant as I had imagined. There was Tiffany's … and there at last we were underneath the Empire State Building.[46]

A sailor aboard HMS *Intrepid* was granted a period of home leave in November 1939, after two and a half years away. This enabled him to have a 'joyful reunion' with his immediate family, and catch up on 'all the news of the rest of the family', plus bringing home gifts such as silk, 'four yards of shimmering pale blue material', for his mother (silk had become unobtainable in England), and 'a leather wallet for Dad from Port Said' and 'a necklace for sister Betty and a cuddly camel for her infant son'. However, he found it difficult to feel comfortable in his home village, which now seemed only to be inhabited by the elderly and very young, as those he'd grown up with had either married and moved away or left to join the Armed Forces. Soon he was 'looking forward to returning to what was my real home, *Intrepid*, and all my friends who thought and spoke my language'.[47]

Leave was also important in maintaining the morale of naval personnel posted ashore. HMS *Demetrius*, a camp near Wetherby, was where George Melly underwent some of his wartime training as a writer. For him, Leeds was a popular destination for 'shore leave' with 'enough tarts and drunkenness to earn itself one of those "revealing" articles in the *News of the World*', and by the time he visited the street lighting had improved as the threat of bombing receded, so that 'our reeling sorties from pub to dance-hall to pub to café to YMCA or Salvation Army hostel' were 'less hazardous'. There were also 'elegant glass-roofed arcades to explore' and as an art lover he found that 'you could take a tram out to a large Elizabethan manor house [Temple Newsam] on the outskirts ... where the Corporation housed many of its treasures', including, by contemporary standards, 'an adventurous modern collection'.[48]

Similarly, wartime London held its attractions for a 'run ashore'. One youthful FAA officer remembered spending a few days with a young widow whose husband had been killed flying with the RAF. This entailed 'dining and dancing at Quaglinos or the Berkley every evening and onto a night club afterwards ... we enjoyed going out together and made a good pair at the various parties ... it was what she needed to help her through a very bad period and it was good for me too.'[49]

Mail provided a vital link with home for sailors who were naturally concerned for the well-being of their families and loved ones facing the privations of wartime life at home. As Captain Whinney observed, during the early phases of the Battle of the Atlantic there was, 'not without good reason, much anxiety [among sailors] about air raids during blitzes and worry about the insufficiency of food [back home]'.[50] Letters could also bring great joy, such as when a bag of mail was hauled aboard the cruiser HMS *Hawkins* while on South Atlantic patrol, leading one sailor to record in his diary: 'I got thirteen letters, two lots of every body's and three Weekly Posts. Peace and quiet during forenoon watch, everybody happy and busy with mail.'[51] Similarly, on Christmas Day 1944 the crew of one landing craft in Falmouth received 'an unexpected delivery of mail [that] cheered us up no end'.[52]

Equally, however, letters could convey bad news, such as the death of a relative or the infidelity of a spouse. An officer with Combined Operations recounted that around a third of the crew of his landing craft were young married men, 'and consequently many family matters cropped up which often led to requests being made for compassionate leave'.[53] Family Welfare Centres operated at the main ports and naval bases in Britain, and were intended to tackle this type of challenge. 'Staffed by dedicated and professional social workers, these centres represented an extension of the responsibilities of the Admiralty' and worked with sailors' families and charities to deal with a host of domestic issues.[54]

Understandably, given its importance, the absence of mail could cause bitter resentment, and lead to a drop in morale, especially if there seemed to be no good reason for it. In 1942, for example, Anthony Eden, then Foreign

Secretary, had to be rushed to the Middle East to try to calm 'lower-deck representatives gathered in the beer garden of the Fleet Club in Alexandria', deeply angered by the failure of the authorities to provide mail from home for several weeks.[55]

Likewise, for personnel at home or in other shore establishments around the Empire, mail was equally welcomed. Not only did receiving a letter offer relief from the war, but writing letters provided a means for individuals to cope with their circumstances. As one former wartime Wren stressed, there were few telephones by modern standards, and these could seldom be used for personal calls anyway. So 'letters were the only way of communicating; we really did write and enjoy writing lots of letters to all our friends and relations, it was so important to keep in touch, and to receive a nice, long, newsy and gossipy letter was the greatest treat and one would re-read it a dozen times'.[56] However, as George Mack cautioned, for naval personnel replying to friends and family, they had to be aware of 'contravening the Official Secrets Act and making the censor officer use his blue pencil'.[57]

Sailors' welfare was a fundamental aspect of officer-man relations, and the King's Regulations and Admiralty Instructions urged officers to be mindful of the overall well-being of their men, plus to take responsibility for important subjects such as training. Henry Adlam's experience on returning from one leave provides a case in point. On alighting from a train at Edinburgh, he saw a large group of ratings from his squadron and went over to have a chat. 'I approached them, they all saluted me very properly. Had they not done so, that boot-faced Commander, who had been watching us, would doubtless have expressed to me in strong words the disapproval his face so clearly showed at my familiarity with the sailors. It must have been difficult ... for officers of his Dartmouth background to understand our FAA style,' whereby ratings who maintained aircraft felt equally responsible for their pilots.[58] Likewise, some ships ran lectures and discussion groups, the latter comprising 'organized group conversations under the supervision of an officer' in which sailors were free to 'explore political, social and cultural questions'.[59]

For many sailors, religion or faith helped them cope with active service. On larger ships there was normally a dedicated padre, with a compulsory Sunday service being a feature of life, whereas on smaller ships the situation could be more fluid, often with the captain taking prayer services. Most chaplains were Church of England, although other denominations were represented, and they were encouraged to remain below decks with the medical officer during action, where it was felt they could be of most support to sailors. Of course, as well as providing spiritual comfort, chaplains had an important role in offering pastoral care, and as they were 'outside of the normal officer hierarchy', this may have enabled troubled sailors to talk to them more freely than might otherwise have been the case.[60]

Reflecting on his wartime experience, C.B. Blackmore observed how: 'I always had a strong faith. But it was certainly never ... weakened at all in any way, not at all. I mean otherwise I would never have gone to theological college. [He decided to be ordained in 1957 and studied at theological college for two years.]'[61] Others found that their faith was tested or diluted by their war experience. George Henderson was a chapel lad from a staunch Methodist family in Gosforth, Newcastle-upon-Tyne, when he volunteered for the navy in 1942. He went on to see action on an LST in the Mediterranean and off Normandy, before serving on a submarine depot ship in the Far East and ending his war on a frigate. He recalled:

> I had my twenty-first birthday out in the Far East, and got pleasantly smashed, and you always had a drink of your mate's rum on your birthday. "Have a tot of that, Geordie – it'll take your head off!" Having said that, you were used to it. I am afraid my Methodist principles had disappeared to a large degree.[62]

Like chaplains, medical staff had a pastoral role to play at sea, as well as treating men for a variety of conditions and/or wounds. However, the numbers of doctors per men in the RN was small, there being only three per thousand men in 1945. For civilian doctors the navy presented an exciting opportunity 'with a reputation for excellence' and the prospect of playing 'a full role as part of a fighting ship', making it different from most other armed services where medics largely worked behind the lines.[63] As the war progressed, specialists such as dental officers became available, and the navy gave serious consideration to the role of psychiatry in countering the psychological effects of war. On the site of the present-day Kielder Reservoir in Northumberland, for example, stood an establishment where misfits from the navy were sent for evaluating and redrafting. This ensured that such sailors, who had proved unsuitable on active employment aboard ships, could still be found suitable work ashore.

The effects of war on mental health should not be underestimated. As one sailor on a destroyer, involved in sustained action in the Mediterranean, discovered, 'nervous, tense, unstable imaginations' could 'run riot' under pressure, leading a petrified crewmate to mistake a flock of seagulls for incoming enemy aircraft.[64] Similarly, combat stress was a significant concern for the FAA, as exemplified by Henry Adlam, who after three years in an operational squadron confessed: 'I had become nervy; the "twitch" we called it. There had been times when I had felt faint and shaky, not quite in my body, while walking across the deck to my aircraft. I had experienced a feeling of almost panic that I might lose control of myself ...'[65]

Material concerns were important too, including pay. An air mechanic with the FAA explained that 'we were paid fortnightly, in accordance with the correct amount stipulated in your Pay Documents', but when these failed to keep up with personnel, as could happen in wartime, 'you were given a "north-easter" – that is, the princely sum of ten shillings – to ensure you weren't overpaid'.[66] By contrast, a merchant seaman remembered being paid 'ten pounds a month plus ten pounds danger money – which was quite an excessive amount in those days for a youth of sixteen'.[67] Equally many Wrens valued their pay. When Angela Mack enlisted, she was informed that 'we would earn the handsome sum of £1.0s.11d per week, from which 5d (five pence) was deducted quarterly towards the cost of Health Insurance and Pensions'.[68] Often this was administered by antiquated-sounding pay parades, such as that described by Stephanie Batstone: 'You form fours with your toes on a chalk line, and when your number is called you step forward and say, "98765 sir" and put your Pay Book down inside a white square and they put a pound note and a soap coupon down on it.'[69]

Numerous other factors assisted sailors in coping with the demands of active service, particularly by relieving frustration, tension and boredom. A veteran of the Battle of the Atlantic recounted that there were 'Long periods of doing nothing. I even did a couple of tapestries during the war.'[70] Likewise, many valued the support of organisations such as the YMCA and British Sailors' Society in looking out for their welfare, especially by providing accommodation during hasty periods of shore leave. Notably, the voluntary provision of comforts to the forces was equally appreciated, and included groups of ladies knitting woollen garments for sailors. Brian Carter described how, in order to ward off the cold, his landing craft crew swapped their rig of the day for balaclava helmets and thick jumpers made by one such group – 'the colours of our sweaters were not uniform, so we looked like a lot of pirates, but we were warm and happy so nothing else mattered'.[71]

Keeping pets proved popular, despite complications in having an animal on a ship. The crew of the destroyer HMS *Aldenham* went through three dogs: a small one named Steakers, who lived in 'the chief and POs' mess, and soon learned to climb the ladder from the upper deck to the mess deck'; Whimpy, who sadly did not last long as he was terrified of the gunfire and disappeared over the stern; and Susie, with 'bluey-black hair and a very docile nature', who stayed with them a lot longer, and all the sailors enjoyed making a fuss of her, even 'fitting her with a collar with the ship's name inscribed'.[72] On HMS *Intrepid* for a time there was a mynah bird and, as George Mack recalled, 'we all liked his chatter'.[73] Monkeys were another favourite. One destroyer had a monkey named Jacko that a sailor had acquired in Freetown. He 'soon had the run of the ship' and 'loved to sit by a small hole in the bulkhead and pick up with delicate fingers the brown cockroaches as they came through'.[74]

Cinema/films offered another distraction when off duty, as shortly before the war RN ships had been able to apply for a film projector. One sailor recounted: 'As room on the mess decks was pretty restricted, the films were shown on the forecastle, and many is the time that we all had to scamper off the forecastle as a sharp shower soaked us all, and closed the show. Sometimes it took three or four sessions to completely see a film.' Another boon was that when ships were moored together, it was sometimes possible to 'stand on the quarterdeck of your ship and look at the back of the screen of the ship astern and see their film!'[75]

Music offered another avenue for recreation and relief from the realities of war. Sydney Greenwood, a stoker aboard a number of destroyers, noted how ownership of a melodeon had 'given me a taste of the pleasure of owning a portable piece to entertain with', and subsequently he usually kept a piano-accordion or guitar handy during his naval service.[76] Similarly, a crewman on MGB 320 appealed to the *Kentish Mercury*, his home newspaper, for a gramophone, and having obtained one it remained the boat's 'proud possession', even being used to play a Glenn Miller record over the outside broadcast system as they set out down the River Yare on one operation, although for security reasons this practice was not continued. Thereafter the gramophone remained a popular addition to their mess deck.[77] Ashore, music was popular too. At RNAS Machrihanish, Scotland, a bleak place at the best of times, a Wren who aspired to a post-war career as a singer, appreciated that one of the pilots 'was a really gifted pianist who often used to play for us on the old upright piano'. Sometimes they held 'impromptu concerts' when she 'used to sing through some of the popular arias and songs' accompanied by the pilot.[78]

Related pleasures were dance halls and theatrical pursuits, either as members of a production or as the audience. This could bring the opportunity to watch the stars of the day. One off-duty sailor in Malta remembered watching George Formby, whose 'raw humour was appreciated by the large Service audience', especially as many of them hailed from Lancashire. All his favourite songs were covered, including Mr Wu, the Air Raid Warden; Fanlight Fanny; and It's in the Air.[79] Many shows involving both famous and lesser known performers were put on by ENSA (Entertainments National Service Association), established by Basil Dean and Leslie Henson in 1939 to provide entertainments to the Armed Forces, and popularly dubbed Every

Night Something Awful. At one camp George Melly found that ENSA shows were well liked, although he admitted preferring the 'tatty hall in town ... where the comics were both blue and hopeless, the jugglers dropped their props' and 'performing dogs ran off stage'.[80] Equally, at sea raucous variety concerts put on by sailors to amuse their comrades were popular, and known as Sod's Operas. As historian Glyn Prysor outlines, naval life tended to incorporate degrees of intimacy between males that would have been 'unusual to most civilians at the time, and sailors were far from squeamish about appearing to flout traditional gender roles: from taking part in all-male dancing partnerships in the absence of women' to performing or watching 'male stripteases'.[81]

While serving in Hull, Angela Mack was delighted when the local Choral Society asked for Wrens to assist with a production of 'Merrie England', an appropriately uplifting show for wartime. The Society would be supporting professional singers from London, and for the Wrens 'it was an extremely welcome break in routine', plus 'the music was easy for beginners, very catchy tunes and stirringly patriotic'.[82] Likewise, John Davies, who served with Coastal Forces, fondly remembered 'Jolly Jack Nights' at Goodes Hotel in Great Yarmouth, where he was based for much of his war, especially as he worked as the MC: 'I was loving every minute of it all ... I was expected to dance with every girl that asked, and when the band struck up for a fresh dance I was expected to lead the floor. All this practice helped me to improve my dancing ...'[83]

Games and sports offered further relief from the war. When his ship moored in Manza Bay, Tanzania, in East Africa, Bernard Upton found that after months at sea on a 'stodgy diet of corned beef and dehydrated potatoes rounded off with soya bean imitation sausages', and with little exercise, the crew were desperate for a game of football. An informal 'kick-about' was started, soon joined by dozens of enthusiastic locals. Rapidly 'there was a seething mass of bodies with no sight of a ball' but eventually, despite the language barrier, it was arranged to have 'visitors v. village and football to exhaustion'.[84] Deck hockey was another popular sport, usually 'played with the utmost ferocity'.[85] As one Royal Marine described:

> Among the fleet, each ship 'fielded' a team for deck hockey. [Games] were played on *Warspite*'s quarter deck as it was the largest area. I never heard of any rules. It was played with a grummet (a circle of rope) and sticks like slightly bent walking sticks. The referee stood on top of 'Y' turret – it was the safest place! He blew his whistle to start and /or stop for an injury (broken leg or such like), or if anybody got tipped over the

side, or a goal being scored and to finish (only when the players got a bit thin on the deck!)[86]

Equally, official PT sessions were sometimes organised on larger ships, involving men exercising on or running around the decks.

As mentioned above, Uckers (Ludo) was universally popular. According to George Mack, 'the game was played on ships, had the majesty of a grand tournament, especially in the inter-mess finals when there would be witch doctors, heralds and grand masters to support their teams and charm the dice to fall the right way'.[87]

Another game often played on ships was Crown and Anchor, in which dice were thrown marked with a crown, anchor, heart, club, diamond and spade, which corresponded with markings on the board. The odds were stacked against the players, who would back a particular symbol; if a player backed diamonds, for example, and one showed on one of the dice, the operator would pay even money. Gambling was officially prohibited but clearly games such as Crown and Anchor lent themselves to it, as did the numerous card schools that flourished throughout the navy. Similarly, gambling was widespread in the Merchant Navy, and the large ships in the North Atlantic were notorious for it and this continued during the war.

Special occasions such as Christmas were cause for celebration, which broke up the routine and provided a source of comfort. A sailor aboard the carrier HMS *Formidable* noted that in December 1942: 'We attempted a Christmassy look to the mess, the decorations had been bought in Oran. The mess was festooned and paper hats, musical toys and similar nonsensities were in profusion ... and the Galley had excelled themselves.'[88] Ashore, celebrations would often take place as well. Wren officer Roxane Houston remembered Christmas that same year while stationed in Scotland:

> The kitchen staff had done us proud ... Later that evening the officers returned the compliment by helping to serve dinner to the naval and WRNS ratings, including the first draft of cooks and stewards who had been on duty at lunchtime. This became hilarious, as many of the officers, particularly the men, were anything but adept at offering food to everyone without spilling it ...[89]

Rations, Food and Drink

The quality of food could vary from one ship to another, especially on smaller ships, depending on those doing the cooking. On one minesweeper the cook was a particularly revolting and disagreeable individual. He spent much of his time in an 'alcoholic daze', and 'seemed to glory in filth, both in the galley and in his personal habits', seldom bathing, plus he was 'renowned for the extraordinary size of his penis of which he was extremely proud'. If he took umbrage at something it was not unheard of for him to leave a 'portion of old comb ... embedded in a wardroom apple pie' or to 'scatter a handful of cockroaches into the soup'.[90] Similarly, on the minesweeper HMS *Ross* the food was 'terrible', according to Sydney Hook, one of her crew: 'nuts and bolts we used to call it, stew with about an inch of fat on the top of it'. In contrast, on HMS *Chameleon*, another minesweeper on which he later served: 'We used to do all our own cooking, always had plenty of grub. Tie up alongside the NAAFI [Navy Army and Air Force Institutes] and have bacon and legs of pork, etc.'[91]

However, naval food was typically wholesome, if sometimes bland, although it could be enlivened by the use of exciting sounding slang, such as 'train smash' for tinned herring in tomato sauce.[92] George Amyes, an air mechanic with the FAA, vividly remembered that pound cake was common, whereby you would 'add a pound of everything with peeled potatoes on top and it came out as steamed pudding'. Alternatively, you would 'give it to the cooks without potatoes and it came out as cake, all the same mix'. The idea was that 'what doesn't fatten will fill'.[93] Often the scale of rations provided to sailors was more generous than that available to civilians, and depending on where a ship was operating, it would usually be possible to supplement supplies with items obtained locally. George Henderson and the crew of LST 8 saw extensive action in the Mediterranean, and:

> had meat, quite a lot of meat and stuff like that. We had a full-time cook, and one of the mess detailed off to help. I couldn't fault the grub, it wasn't first class cuisine but we were in the middle of a war, and we probably ate better than people at home. We could pick up stuff from ashore, and that gave us some variety, and we probably got things not possible for folk to get back home.[94]

Officers in their wardrooms tended to enjoy some filling if stodgy dishes as well. When Christian Lamb married Lieutenant John Lamb DSC, RN, the guest night dinner on his ship, HMS *Oribi*, included naval favourites, such as 'steak and kidney pie and plum duff for pudding, washed down with plenty of Pink Gins, White Ladies, Gimlets and Dry Martinis'.[95] Likewise, many sailors of all ranks probably appreciated a warm, sweet mug of kye, as cocoa was universally known, especially at sea in cold weather.

Three different types of messing existed for ratings. For general messing, 'the paymaster or his deputy would draw up a menu for all the lower deck, and each mess sent a duty "cook", chosen by roster, to collect the meals for the agreed number of men in the mess'.[96] Meals were then served on the mess deck, usually at wooden tables with men sitting on wooden stools or benches, and the space doubled up as sleeping accommodation. Alternatively, canteen messing was sometimes employed, where provisions were drawn from a ship's store, prepared by a duty 'cook' and taken to the galley to be cooked, with meals again being served in the same fashion as under general messing. Aboard the corvette HMS *Sweetbriar*:

> The stores people provided the meat and the rest of it you paid for out of the mess funds. So in a way you could prepare your own menus and when it was ready chef brought it to you. Surplus cash was shared round the mess if not used on food.[97]

On other ships, including escort carriers, there was cafeteria messing where 'eating and sleeping took place in different areas of the ship, and the ratings had their meals in a self-service cafeteria'.[98]

Eating at sea was not necessarily easy, particularly in bad weather, an issue often ignored during training. While serving aboard the destroyer HMS *Havelock*, Eric Denton discovered that in an Atlantic gale

> it was fatal to put the plate with the food on it down on the table – it would either land upside-down in our lap or in the lap of the sailor opposite. If the ship was rolling, it would slide along the table and end up on the floor. The technique was to hold it and the fork in the left hand, holding the plate on the table, and make a few quick cuts with the knife in the right hand; then, change hands and do some quick shovelling with the fork, or the fingers.[99]

An unfortunate upshot of this was that between courses sailors usually had to rush to the heads to be violently seasick. A related issue was the shortage of fresh water for laundry, shaving and bathing, especially on older ships. The carrier HMS *Furious*, a converted battlecruiser, for example, was 'never designed for the number of men aboard', so she soon ran out of fresh water. One remedy was to employ salt water for washing with a special soap that took time to lather.[100]

For merchant seamen food was often 'coarse' and on the average tramp steamer 'such frozen food as there might be was in an ice box, and when the ice had melted, salt meat in brine tubs and butter from tins provided much of the staple diet'. If the master of a ship was open to justifying the added expense to his employers, fresh produce might be taken on at ports of call.[101] On larger ships conditions could be better. As a cadet aboard the Union Castle refrigerator/food ship *Richmond Castle*, John Cutcliffe discovered, 'we lived exceedingly well, the *Richmond* had a wonderful old West Indian cook called Jim Marshall who used to feed everyone extremely well indeed. He was a great favourite ...'[102]

Ashore food was equally important. On joining the Wrens, Stephanie Batstone recounts how at one training establishment in the north west, they were ravenous, despite food parcels from home, perhaps as a result of taking up a more active lifestyle, and owing to 'the rather emasculated meals in camp'. On leave:

> In the Forces canteen at New Brighton ... we had fish cakes, potatoes, bread and butter, coffee, apple tart, and blancmange for 1s.2d. We went back to Liverpool and had corned beef and rice pudding for 6d. Then onto Warrington for pease pudding and toast at the YMCA. Then onto Lowton Church Canteen for pork pies and coffee, and back to camp for chocolate cake and fizzy lemonade.[103]

As indicated, in the RN the NAAFI provided additional treats to supplement a sailor's rations, both ashore and on larger ships, where NAAFI staff formed part of the ship's company, having been commissioned into the RNVR or enlisted in the RNR. Notably, on D-Day the NAAFI issued a special ration pack, many of which were given to landing craft crews. These 'contained cigarettes, tobacco, cigarette papers and matches; toothpaste, shaving soap, toilet soap and razor blades; cubes of meat extract, cocoa, milk tablets and chewing gum; letter cards and pencils'.[104] Smoking was popular, and in the 1940s people were less conscious about its health implications than today. Known as 'tickler' in the navy, the duty-free tobacco ration was typically generous, especially when compared to what was available to civilians. One sailor commented, 'we had a choice each month of buying tins of either cigarette or pipe tobacco, manufactured cigarettes, or the natural tobacco leaves'. With the latter it was common to add 'a little rum' and roll 'them tightly into the shape of a spindle; it was then tightly bound with tarred hemp, and stowed away to mature', thus providing a very strong form of pipe tobacco.[105]

Drinking was a distinct part of maritime and naval culture, despite the problems it could cause. According to the sociologist Tony Lane, hard drinking 'was more important in the culture of seafaring than "winning" women', and was not just confined to ordinary sailors. While these men enjoyed alcohol as a social liquidiser ashore and in public places, merchant navy officers 'had little public life', and were confined to sharing drinks in their cabins with fellow officers, in stark contrast to the collective life of the RN wardroom.[106]

In the RN alcohol was widely welcomed for its properties as a relaxant. One naval pilot reckoned that ideally the stress of completing a successful deck landing should be followed by 'a nice glass of pink gin in the ward-room'.[107] Similarly, as an officer with Combined Operations found, spirits were readily available, particularly for officers. 'One could get four bottles of whisky for a pound, and still have a bit of change, or four bottles of gin', although on his landing craft, for safety reasons, the spirits locker in the ward-room 'was never opened at sea', as with only three officers aboard they could not risk endangering the ship by one of them getting drunk.[108]

For ratings the daily rum ration (usually issued between 11am and noon) was a distinct boon, and bolstered their morale, particularly when under the pressure of operations. It was characterised by 'the careful procedure of draw-ing, in the presence of an officer, from the spirit room or store the measured issue of rum for the men on the ship's books entitled to an issue of undiluted spirit or grog. The careful observed blending of two parts of water with one of spirit for issue to those below the rank of petty officer was carried out even under enemy attack ...'[109] However, there were variations to this rule, includ-ing on smaller craft operated by Coastal Forces, where the daily tot was taken neat by all the crew, not just petty officers. This had the possibly unintended effect that 'after drinking it you were ready, willing and able to eat almost anything, however badly it was cooked, or whatever condition it was in'.[110]

The positive or medicinal benefits of rum were testified to by many sailors, including George Henderson, who explained that: 'There was nothing better when you came off watch at night, and it's raining and snowing and you've got to go on again in four hours. Just take your oilskins off, crash on your bunk, and feel the rum go right through you, lovely!'[111]

Another aspect of the rum ration was that it could be used as a currency to repay favours. As George Mack outlined: 'For a small favour you would give a "sippers", for something bigger it would be a "gulpers", and if someone saved your life or anything equally important it would be "drainers". Few things were more important to a sailor than his tot ...'[112]

Rum was also used for celebrations. When the crew of the carrier HMS *Formidable* heard that the Italian Fleet had surrendered on Sunday, 12 September 1943, the order was given to splice the mainbrace – i.e., issue a tot of rum. Similarly, it was an accepted custom, albeit not one officially encouraged, 'for any sailor who had a birthday to visit every mess claiming "sippers" until such time as he collapsed'.[113] However, the system was open to abuse, and could sometimes be manipulated by the crafty sailor. Once, George Melly and two comrades found they could draw their rum ration 'before going ashore, we would all give three tots to one of us in rotation, believing that the resultant intoxication would produce a feeling of un-inhibited fantasy that would take us all into absurd adventures. This it frequently did.'[114] Other sailors remembered how they were able to smuggle rum home via the post using stone jars once used for ginger beer, so 'we were not going without our rum while on leave'.[115]

Of course, drinking to excess raised the spectre of hangovers, albeit these might be more a feature of shore life than ship life. One FAA pilot had a novel approach to alleviating the problem 'by strong doses of neat oxygen as soon as I climbed into the cockpit'.[116] Drunkenness also posed a potential disci-plinary issue, although it seems to have been tolerated provided men did not cause a problem, or else was dealt with summarily. Captain Whinney narrates an episode that occurred on HMS *Duncan* after she had been damaged in a collision, blocking an outlet drain in the Ward Room, and two sailors volun-teered to help with the flooded compartment. Subsequently, he discovered them lying unconscious and rolling about:

> They had had the lot from the wardroom wine cupboard: beer, whisky, port, sherry, brandy – all of it. Hoisted onto the upper deck they recovered sufficiently to fight, until the torpedo coxwain, the senior rating on board a destroyer, rendered both harmless with a convenient wooden mallet and then had them lashed up in strait-jackets.[117]

Love, Romance and Sex

Prior to the Second World War the RN did not expect members of the lower deck to be eligible for marriage allowance until they were 25 years old. Many of these men had joined as boys, and were actively discouraged from marry-ing until that age, but the onset of war brought with it an influx of men who were already married and under 25. These men successfully obtained 'a con-cession in the form that the marriage allowance was to be available for ratings from the age of 21 subject to the proviso that the claimant had to make a minimum prescribed allotment to the wife from his daily pay'. However, the King's Regulations and Admiralty Instructions with their stipulations about marriage were not 'cancelled, merely suspended indefinitely'.[118] Likewise, there was scope for sailors to develop relationships with local women at the various places that their ship called at during its service. If these became more serious than a brief affair, 'legislation on servicemen's marriage meant that a letter from the commanding officer was often required for an officer or rating to wed, a safeguard which provided an opportunity for intervention'.[119]

Despite the above, many young men and women happily married during the war, including the 21-year-old air mechanic Robert Cosh, who on

17 November 1943 wed his sweetheart Ivy, also 21, and a serving Wren, at Holy Trinity Church, Fallowfield, Manchester. As he explained, it was rushed because they were both on leave and had limited time: 'A wartime romance, a wartime wedding and a wartime honeymoon, spent between Gloucester, Reading and Manchester, and would last for the next nine days – the honeymoon, that is – we couldn't plan ahead too far, only until the next leave.'[120]

Similarly, P. Bieber (née Furber) recounted how, although she later married a Canadian, as a young Wren serving in Britain she had

> become much enamoured of a gay (normal use of this adjective) Gordon Highlander who, to my astonishment, seemed quite taken with me. One day he announced that he was going overseas and had ten days' embarkation leave. He invited me to spend this leave with him at his home in Cheshire. I applied for leave and was told I could have 48 hours so we took off and I rang to say I was taking ten days and would accept the punishment on my return. We got engaged with his parents' blessing and we had a very happy time.[121]

When overseas, one sailor commented, at big naval bases such as Alexandria, there were usually relatively few Wrens, and those that were there were normally in the company of officers. So if a sailor 'was looking for female company, he would have to try his hand in one of the many bars that abounded ashore, and then about ... all it amounted to would be a dance, at the cost of an expensive drink'.[122] Others enjoyed more meaningful romantic relationships, including Sydney Greenwood, who served as a stoker on destroyers. During the war he carried on a correspondence with a girl he had first met in 1937, and found that their letters 'became the flotsam of hope on oceans of trials and tribulations that befell us both during those years'.[123]

Of course in Britain and at ports around the Empire there was frequently scope for sailors to embark on sexual relationships with willing local girls or older women or prostitutes. One FAA officer remarked that he was 'always surprised ... how many of our matelots were keen to dip their wicks in dark pools'.[124] As Sydney Greenwood found at Mediterranean ports in 1943, there tended to be no shortage of brothels 'for those that liked that sort of thing', especially as at that time there was no 'chance of normal romantic encounters with girls on our short visits'.[125] Equally, as author John Costello observed, 'the numbers of women who plied the ancient trade' both in London and around major military/naval bases and ports in Britain 'rose in direct proportion to the numbers of men conscripted'. As efforts to control prostitution were hampered by inadequate legislation, particularly against street walkers, this additionally 'encouraged the "amateur" whore and "goodtime girl" to take to blacked-out streets which encouraged opportunities for hurried intimacies'.[126]

In spite of the popular image of sailor Jack as a hard-drinking womaniser, as historian Glyn Prysor astutely comments, 'many sailors valued comfort, warmth, good food and a chance to rest' above all else when on leave, and such 'domesticity was a priceless luxury after the discomforts of the sea'.[127] Even so, illicit sex clearly posed a health risk, and the Admiralty sought to remedy this by issuing condoms to men going ashore. 'The ration was three for a night ashore and five for a long weekend', and any sailor 'who caught VD had a stoppage of pay unless they had worn a contraceptive'.[128] Sexually transmitted diseases were a significant concern for the Merchant Navy and with an increase in cases among seamen at Britain's major ports, 'a sinister Nazi plot to aid the U-boats in the Battle of the Atlantic was suspected'.[129] The issue of contraceptives could cause awkward situations, particularly for the less experienced. The young naval officer Brian Carter was asked by the coxswain of his landing craft whether the men had 'their sportsgear' ahead of going on leave. He racked his brain wondering what this could mean, 'thinking of football boots, tennis rackets, etc.' Then the coxswain discreetly whispered 'their French letters, sir' and he went down the line handing them out, his 'face as red as a beetroot'.[130]

A related issue was coping with matters of hygiene. The sanitary towel run was infamous at HMS *Cabbala*, a shore establishment where hundreds of Wren and male ratings were trained as wireless telegraphists, visual signallers and coders. Those Wrens tasked with it 'had to spread sheets of newspaper all over the lavatory floor and tip the contents of the bins on to it. There were a lot, with ninety-four Wrens in a block.' This then had to be made up into a parcel, 'hoping it wouldn't be too large and unwieldy' and carried through the Wren camp and sailors' camp to the boiler house, where it was handed to a scarlet-faced rating, often with sailors' voices on the air to add to the overall sense of mutual embarrassment.[131]

For women the danger of becoming pregnant was another significant issue revolving around matters of sex, especially as in the 1940s enormous stigma was attached to any unmarried woman who became pregnant. Regulations dictated that any unmarried Wren who became pregnant would be discharged, although they might be classed as '"Suitable for Re-entry" in appropriate cases where there were no additional disciplinary offences', although this was particularly hard 'on officers who, on re-entry, would have to start again in the ranks'.[132] However, many women who joined the WRNS were possibly aware that they had a certain exclusive reputation and appeal, and this was heightened by their smart blue uniform, the design of which, as Christian Lamb observed, tended to conceal 'deficiencies in one's figure', plus officers wore a much admired tricorn hat. By contrast, 'the ATS and WAAF were unlucky in that their less attractive khaki and air force blue jackets had wide waist bands which tended to exaggerate the hips – not a popular feature'.[133] As the war progressed, and Allied victory appeared possible, the question of the status of men and women also emerged. According to one Wren: 'There was a subtle difference of approach; some men [male officers] were beginning to appreciate the fact that we might soon have to be thought of as just women again and not someone of a lower rank to be issued with orders.'[134]

According to John Costello, 'deprivation homosexuality had long been recognised as a problem by navies', and the issue was encapsulated by a traditional RN saying that ran: 'Ashore it's wine, women and song, aboard it's rum, bum and concertina.'[135] More liberal-minded captains may have dealt with offenders in a way that least threatened the smooth running and combat efficiency of their ship, although the official line on homosexuality was tough, with a confidential fleet order of 1940 providing explicit advice to medical officers on how to identify whether an act was consensual or forced. Even so, many sailors would seem to have accepted homosexual behaviour, so long as it was between consenting adults, and did not hurt anyone else. The term 'winger', as George Melly outlined, denoted 'a young seaman who is taken under the wing of a rating or Petty Officer older and more experienced than himself to be shown the ropes'.[136] It could also imply a homosexual relationship, even on a relatively trivial or playful level, such as that he enjoyed with an older rating with whom he regularly shared kisses while barracked aboard HMS *Argus*. Shortly after the war Melly was serving on the cruiser HMS *Dido*, and noted how it was also accepted practice 'on my Mess Deck, that on Saturday make and mends (half days off) anyone who fancied some mutual masturbation would crash down in the coat locker', a cage-like structure.[137]

However, in other instances homosexual behaviour was a serious disciplinary issue. While serving on the cruiser HMS *Edinburgh*, Colin Kitching claimed he was not aware of any homosexuals aboard, but later the following situation came to light:

> The Chief Petty Officer of the boys' mess deck. Horrible, you know – blimey to think there were 16-year-old boys at sea, and a number, when the *Edinburgh* was [later] sunk – the number that died … Anyway it surfaced that he was a homosexual and had taken advantage of his position to corrupt a number of boys in the boys' mess deck. A dreadful business,

and he was court-martialled and sent to the naval prison down in Somerset, Shepton Mallet, but that is the only thing I ever came across of that sort. Only right at the end of my time. It all cropped up in a matter of days, because one of the boys eventually ... he broke down and he went to see his Divisional Officer or somebody, and then it all arose.[138]

Just as the RN brought sailors together in an all-male environment, especially at sea, the WRNS involved large numbers of women serving alongside each other. It would be naïve to think that lesbianism was not an issue under such conditions, although, as Angela Mack commented, 'there was never any behaviour of any sort in any of the establishments that I was in, packed full of women, organised and run by women, that gave me any suspicions'.[139] By contrast, when stationed at HQ Senior Officer Assault Ships and Craft (SOASC) at HMS *Warren*, Greenock, Scotland, Roxane Houston was deeply surprised to see a Wren sitting in another's lap as they were kissing, 'I mean really kissing!' As a result, by her own admission, she had to be instructed 'in some of the facts of life I'd never even heard of' by a more worldly-wise comrade.[140]

Survivors and POWs

The loss of a warship or merchantman was typically a dramatic and potentially terrifying event for those involved. However, most warships took time to sink, enabling damage control parties to secure the ship while the rest of the crew continued with their duties until ordered to do otherwise. When the destroyer HMS *Electra* was severely damaged during the Battle of the Java Sea (27–28 February 1942), one of her sailors recorded being blown into the water by a Japanese shell, as the order was given to abandon ship:

I saw them lowering the only boat that was left. I was left some 50 yards astern of the ship when they lowered it but I kept swimming away as at any minute I expected the flames of the now several fires to reach the magazine, and the ship to go up. It was bad enough to be in the water with shells bursting around me without being near a terrific explosion such as that would have been. There were times when I put my hand to my stomach to see if it had been torn from me or not.

When I got a good way from the ship, I had a look at the port side. It was a mass of twisted metal and wood. The boat was by this time full up and drifting astern. I saw a shell burst about 10 yards from it, after the splash had disappeared there was no boat. I learned after, that all but two had been killed. Many men were swimming about in the water and as the ship turned completely to port, there was the usual cheer of men saying 'good-bye' to their ship. She remained for about five minutes with just her stern showing, then sleepily sank.[141]

This sailor was lucky. With a handful of other survivors, he was picked up by an American submarine after enduring hours in the water, fearful of being attacked by sharks, electric eels and Japanese aircraft. Similarly, when the carrier HMS *Eagle* was torpedoed in the Mediterranean, some of the survivors, including Robert Cosh, were grateful to be rescued by the destroyer HMS *Keppel*. Eventually they made it back to Gibraltar, where arrangements were made for them to send telegrams to next of kin informing them that they were safe, plus they were 'given a casual payment, food and a shower and certain items of essential kit', making them feel 'ready for a run ashore'. What remained of Cosh's squadron (801 NAS) was then shipped back to Britain, the survivors 'deflated but not depressed', eventually to be processed at a naval air station near Warrington before being granted a spell of survivor's leave before being redrafted. Subsequently, at a depot in Liverpool, Cosh had to fill in a form to claim for personal possessions lost on *Eagle*. 'Well, as you can imagine, hard-up matelots in wartime could think of all kinds of personal things they had lost! Gold watches, silver discs, musical instruments, spectacles, cash, Parker pens and silk scarves, to mention just a few.'[142]

When SS *Auditor* was sunk by a U-boat in July 1941, her survivors embarked on an epic voyage in lifeboats to the Cape Verde Islands, which tested their seamanship, navigation, morale and discipline. One of the Merchant Navy officers involved explained that:

The instructions given by Naval Control at Oban were, if you are sunk DO NOT attempt any long lifeboat voyage. And we never quite understood the reason for this. [After waiting in the Atlantic for a few days, the officers decided that it might be possible to upsail and make for the Cape Verde Islands. Despite having no charts, the Master agreed, there being no sign of any rescue since *Auditor* sank]. Officers [would] have to allow for tide and wind drift and use compasses for the three lifeboats to follow. We worked on the requirement to travel 60 miles per day, [and] knew it was approximately 600 miles to the Cape Verde Islands from the position where we'd sunk.

There were various problems, such as we were running with quite a stiff breeze but we also had a very high swell some days and this did reduce our speed. Some days we took in water ... or took water over the bow which meant we had to continually bale. In fact we were baling water for the whole of the trip, although during some days we let the water rise up because the idea was that if we could sit on the thwarts of the boat with our feet in the water, this would ... enter our body through our feet and might stave off some of the thirst pains.[143]

Drinking water was in short supply, not helped by Lascar seamen having pilfered the supplies in No. 1 lifeboat. Consequently, tins of condensed milk proved a Godsend, and the survivors had a spoonful a day, but the lifeboat's biscuits were useless, being so dry that lots of water was needed to make them edible. Rainfall staved off 'one's thirst problem [as you'd] lick everything that had rain on it because each drop was a help to give you added sustenance'. At times physical intimidation was necessary to quell unrest among the crew. 'We had one man come aft. Fortunately I had a knife, so we just brought the knife out and this was sufficient ...' Another challenge was that they might easily miss any land as 'your visibility [from a lifeboat] is only perhaps 2–3 miles', but at least the Cape Verde Islands had the advantage of being around 9–10,000 feet high, plus the Master was familiar with them from a previous visit.[144]

Eventually they made landfall at Santo Antao during the night: 'we had no idea of the island's coastline and so we laid off until dawn and it was a very uninviting island but was very high'. Much to their relief, once it was daylight, Portuguese fisherman reached them with water.

> They took us in tow and we landed at their little port, which was only a concrete pier at Tarratao. All the officers walked ashore, except the Third Officer, who had been ill and tried to throw himself overboard ... But we managed to keep him in the bottom of the boat and we carried him ashore, and most of the natives [Lascars] had to be carried ashore.[145]

Alternatively, shipwrecked sailors and merchant seamen might be taken prisoner by the enemy. Such a fate befell the crew of the submarine HMS *Splendid* when she was caught by a German destroyer in the Tyrrhenian Sea, and subjected to a skilful depth-charge attack. Her captain remembered that as she went down:

> I told the chaps to get ready to abandon ship. Some of them had time to get lifebelts, but not many, I don't think, but clearly we were in a situation where the sooner we got out the better because the submarine was not going to stay afloat. And so when we hit the surface the chaps were ready to abandon her through the forward hatch, which was the gun tower hatch and through the conning tower ... the German destroyer opened up, ... and they started getting direct hits. And very sad to say that eighteen out of the crew altogether who emerged from the gun tower hatch either were killed or mortally wounded and drowned, and

that was the extent of our loss ... the First Lieutenant and I had made sure that the submarine was going to sink quickly, because we didn't want her to be captured. So we had to open the main vents ...

The boats were lowered [by the German destroyer] and my surviving members of the crew were picked up, including myself, taken on board the destroyer, which then proceeded into the Bay of Naples ...[146]

Subsequently, Captain McGeogh was made a POW in Italy, and separated from his and hospitalised owing to losing the sight in one eye. He then jumped train while being moved to an Italian POW camp, and successfully evaded capture, making it to Switzerland at about the same time as the Salerno landings. By contrast, J. Mariner was taken prisoner by the Japanese in December 1941 when HMS *Peterel*, a small vessel designed for patrol work on the great rivers of China, on which he was serving, was effectively blown to pieces after her captain refused to surrender his ship. Mariner endured years of captivity in a number of camps in the Far East, where conditions were frequently appalling: 'I shall never quite forget the many hardships, the hunger and thirst, the bitter cold, the intense heat, the ever present Japanese guards.' At one camp the

toilets consisted of open vats which we had to stoop over through holes in a raised platform, and running alive with maggots, the smell was inde-scribable. We were infested with rats, flies, mosquitoes, etc. Our camp consisted of seven dilapidated wooden sheds, surrounded by an electrified fence, with the toilets at the end of each shed. We were continuously suffering from dysentery, enteritis, malnutrition, scabies, malaria, lice, etc. Outside of this fence was a compound where the Japanese quarters were sited, next to which was the guard house, where offenders were punished, and where mental POWs were kept locked in cells.[147]

Others were incarcerated in Germany, where Marlag housed RN prisoners and Milag dealt with merchant seamen. The latter consisted of wooden huts with a high perimeter fence and guard towers armed with machine guns, surrounded by farmland and fir trees near the village of Westertimke. Food was in limited supply. The midday meal, for instance, usually comprised potatoes with either mashed swede or turnips or sauerkraut. Accordingly, prisoners welcomed Red Cross food parcels, such as that received by Arthur Bird in December 1941: 'After living for months on only stomach-inflating slops, it was a thrill hard to describe to see, and then enjoy, really good British foodstuffs; all labelled with familiar brand names too.' Many prisoners were expected to go on work parties, but not all guards were ardent Nazis, so that 'good relations were discreetly cultivated' with these individuals, which in some cases even led to prisoners bartering cigarettes for small items such as knives or hand tools. Likewise, an element of goading the guards occurred, as it did at other camps, especially as prisoners could play on their guards' fears of being sent to the Eastern Front. To maintain their spirits and relieve boredom, some prisoners made escape plans. Many also organised theatrical pursuits, a choir and educational activities. Despite their poor diet, for those who felt strong enough, sports offered 'a physical means of self-expression and personal fulfilment', with football, cricket, athletics, boxing, rugby, ice hockey and even tennis, baseball and table tennis proving popular, using equipment made in camp or from sources such as donations from ship owners.[148]

Chapter Seven

Demobilisation and Reflections

Many of those engaged in the war at sea developed a certain mind-set as a means of coping with the discomforts and dangers that they routinely faced. As one veteran of the Battle of the Atlantic stressed: 'We felt it was a job we had to do, after all the war was on. Houses had been bombed to pieces here, the merchantmen were being torpedoed without warning ... it was a "them or us" situation.'[1] Unsurprisingly, therefore, for those who survived and could manage it, there were riotous celebrations when the war ended. On VE-Day (8 May 1945) the German surrender was greeted at RNAS Crail in Scotland by ratings taking 'a load of furniture and other burnable objects from the mess halls and living quarters' to make a large bonfire 'in the middle of the parade ground', while 'others were setting off signal rockets and cartridges'. Robert Cosh, by then a petty officer, was riding his motorcycle with the OOW in his sidecar, 'pretending to keep some sort of order, but our hearts were not in it ... Who could deny them a celebration after nearly six years of blackout and misery?'[2] Others experienced more formal events, including a Wren serving in Cape Town, who attended the 'victory parade and the celebration in the City Hall'.[3]

Conversely, for many in Britain, the war in the Far East appeared distant and, as one trainee Wren signal officer noted, it did not occupy 'our daily thoughts in quite the same way as the European War had done'.[4] The crew of HMS *Formidable*, on operations in the Far East, learnt of the situation in Europe over the radio via a crackly American broadcast from Okinawa, and 'picked out that crowds were gathering in Piccadilly Circus'.[5] Although they celebrated this news, like other RN personnel in that theatre they were acutely aware that the war against Japan had still to be won. It was not until 15 August 1945 that news filtered through that Japan had officially surrendered, marking an end to the most destructive war in history. In the wake of the atomic bombs used against Hiroshima and Nagasaki, few probably realised the full implications of these new weapons, or the true extent of the horrors that had been unleashed. Understandably, servicemen and women stationed around the globe welcomed an end to the war, especially those serving in the Far East, for whom there was a palpable sense that they had been saved by the atomic bombs. The proposed invasion of Japan, had it gone ahead, would doubtless have led to heavy casualties. Similarly, in August 1945 Brian Carter was commanding an LCT engaged in preparations for landings on the Malayan coast: 'I shudder to think how we would have got on had the Japanese not surrendered ...'[6]

For Henry Adlam, a youthful naval pilot, the situation was initially bewildering. Throughout his adult life war was all that he had known. It was 'difficult to accept the fact of the war's end or to appreciate the enormity of what it meant ... my mind was attuned to think only in the short term'. His befuddlement was soon tempered by an overwhelming sense of relief at having survived, and the realisation that he would no longer have to risk his life flying combat operations against the Japanese, who had proved a 'barbaric and fanatical enemy'.[7] On completion of his war in the Pacific, the commander of 1833 NAS commented how:

> never again would we have to face the fearful flak over Ishigaki. Never again would our heads spin round at the cry of 'Rats!! Three o'clock up!' No more would the Corsairs screech to a stop as they pulled out the screaming arrestor wires. The basha huts of Trincomalee, the crocodiles in the estuary, the incredible green of the Sumatran jungle ... the limitless expanse of the great oceans – we had seen them all for the last time.[8]

In the aftermath of the war, numerous naval personnel found themselves engaged in activities to try to assist in dealing with the devastation that had been caused. During the summer of 1945, for example, Lieutenant Commander Ted Maughan (RNVR) and his minesweeping flotilla 'swept channels across the North Sea and we were working with the Post Office cable ships from Harwich to the Hook of Holland sweeping a channel through our minefields and the German minefields for the Post Office cable to be laid, to be hooked up on the telephone to Europe ...'[9]

Helping to repatriate recently liberated FEPOWs was another important issue. A Royal Marine officer witnessed horrendous scenes in this regard in the Tokyo Bay area shortly after VJ-Day:

> We actually went to the railhead where they were being brought in by train from prisoner of war camps all over the place, and the one thing I remember was that they looked like living skeletons. Some couldn't even walk, and the pathetic thing about it was that we were damned sure about 20 per cent of them would never live to see a few more days. We then went down to the beach, where again I saw a horrifying experience. American landing craft were coming in to take the prisoners of war off

and the prisoners of war were so delighted to see them coming they rushed down the beach. The first landing craft dropped its ramp right on top of two of the prisoners. Not that they would probably have lived anyway, but it was an experience which, you know, the sight of it really shook me ... it seemed so needless.[10]

Despite the horrors of war, and its immediate aftermath, for many HO naval personnel it looked as if it might be possible to start looking towards the future, or at least towards their demobilisation. As a newly qualified Wren signal officer, Angela Mack was posted to Commander in Chief Naval Forces, Minden, Germany, at the end of the war. She remembered that 'we worked quite hard in our piping hot factory office' but simultaneously life in post-war Germany for victorious Allied personnel held plenty of attractions in terms of 'the people, the parties, the excursions, the "swans" and the fun'.[11] This made for an interesting interlude prior to her demobilisation in the summer of 1946. Similarly, having served on a destroyer in the Mediterranean, Henry Hiley then retrained as a coder, encrypting and deciphering signals traffic, which was highly confidential work. He was returning from the Kola Peninsula in Russia when hostilities ended:

Finally, the war over, the Admiralty realised that there would be no risk in offering me a commission, but hedged its bets, making me a Temporary Acting Sub-Lieutenant, RNVR. It was as a naval officer that I spent my last six months in the Navy, interpreting for the naval branches of the occupying forces in Hamburg and NW Germany. [He was a fluent German speaker.] That was an interesting time but so sad, Hamburg being by now a heap of rubble. But as the train which carried me from Ostend reached the outskirts of Hamburg I could see on the slipways of the Blohm & Voss shipyard, no fewer than seven U-boats, apparently complete and ready to be launched.[12]

Another feature of the war at sea was the sheer diversity of experiences that young men and women had faced, either aboard ships or ashore. Many were thrust from civilian life into positions of danger and responsibility at a relatively young age. Eric Denton enlisted expecting to become a writer (clerk) but at age 21 he became an ordinary seaman in June 1940, and served on a depot ship at Scapa Flow prior to seeing service on a destroyer in the North Atlantic. Subsequently he was commissioned as a sub-lieutenant RNVR and spent three years at sea, mostly in the Mediterranean. 'I saw very many parts of the world which I would not otherwise have seen.'[13] By contrast, George Smith was too young to enlist at the start of the war, and spent a period with his local Home Guard unit on Tyneside, an experience that exposed him to basic military discipline. In February 1944 he enlisted in the RN and as an HO communications rating underwent basic training at HMS *Royal Arthur*, based on the former Butlins holiday camp near Skegness. From there he was drafted to HMS *Cabala* near Warrington for training as a coder. Having successfully passed this, he spent a further period of training in communications at HMS *Mercury* in Hampshire before being drafted to a number of French warships, as they were desperately short of coders. On VE-Day he was aboard the French heavy cruiser FS *Duquesne* and returned to Britain in late June 1945. After a couple of months he was drafted overseas to HMS *Golden Hind*, a shore establishment at Warwick Farm near Sydney, Australia, used to accommodate naval personnel on stand-by to join ships of the BPF. After working here for seven months, he left in March 1946 aboard HMS *Victorious*, then at Freemantle transferred to HMS *Indomitable* and took passage to Colombo in Ceylon (Sri Lanka), where he joined the shore establishment HMS *Gould*. He spent several weeks in the Far East before eventually joining the Algerine class minesweeper HMS *Serene* when she sailed for Britain, arriving on 11 October 1946. The remainder of his service was spent at HMS *Mercury*, before being demobbed the following December.[14]

At 18 George Trevett entered the FAA in late September 1940, trained at HMS *St Vincent*, a shore establishment at Gosport, and at RNAS Lee-on-Solent (HMS *Daedalus*), before notably undergoing further training at HMS *Goshawk*, an RNAS station in Trinidad. This led him to become an observer on the Supermarine Walrus aircraft, notably employed extensively by the RN in the spotter/reconnaissance role. He joined 700 NAS and from late 1941 until mid-1943 was employed first aboard the heavy cruiser HMS *Cumberland* and then the ill-fated battleship HMS *Prince of Wales*, followed by a spell ashore in Ceylon (Sri Lanka), before joining the light cruiser HMS *Mauritius*. This gave him a taste of war in the Far East, at a time when the tide had yet to turn against the Japanese. In early December 1942 he was promoted temporary sub-lieutenant, and was subsequently stationed with 701 NAS at HMS *Grebe*, the FAA shore station at Alexandria. By late 1943 he was back in Britain, and served with 826 NAS at HMS *Daedalus*, followed by secondment to HMS *Odyssey* (formerly HMS *Excellent II*) at Whale Island, Portsmouth, which coincided with D-Day (6 June 1944). He had now been promoted temporary lieutenant and did not leave HMS *Daedalus* until May 1945, as the war in Europe was ending. His remaining service took him to RNAS Raffray (HMS *Merganser*) in Aberdeenshire as an observer with 714 NAS then 717 NAS.[15]

Post-war service was not necessarily without its dangers for HO personnel seeing out their time until demobilisation. This was especially true for those undertaking potentially hazardous activities such as flying. At the end of June 1945 Gordon Wallace had returned from serving as an observer with the FAA in the Far East and received his final posting to 703 Squadron at the Naval Air Sea Warfare Development Unit based at RAF Thorney Island, Hampshire. He was fortunate not to be killed when the Barracuda in which he was flying crashed and 'cartwheeled through the water, shearing off both wings and the whole of the rear fuselage', followed by a 'rasping noise of tearing metal' and the suddenness of a 'too well remembered silence'. With water lapping around his neck, he somehow managed to escape from the wreckage and was soon picked up by a launch.[16]

For regular RN personnel the post-war period was a time of change as well. As one officer who had served on battleships and then transferred to submarines explained: 'I had seen the Navy was getting smaller and you know it felt it was contracting ... it was a 50/50 case but you had the option of leaving with a golden handshake which, to me, it was 51/49. I couldn't make my mind up which way it was but we factored it and I think that the biggest factor was that the Navy was in decline. Not in quality but in importance and numbers.'[17] Likewise, as Commander 'Mike' Crosley observed: 'Trying to discover peace after six years of war is a turbulent and insecure business', and for those who chose to remain in the RN 'there was much jostling for position'.[18] Having seen action as a naval pilot in the Atlantic during 1943–1945, John Shoebridge went on to become a test pilot during 1945–1948, before retiring as a staff officer with the FAA in 1959. Consequently, his naval career embraced the changeover from the Second World War to the onset of the Cold War, including a period as the flying officer aboard HMS *Ocean* during the Korean War, when the Cold War had effectively turned hot as the West confronted Communism in Asia.

For regular ratings, the reduced post-war navy potentially offered some enticing prospects. As Stanley Greenwood discovered, by the late 1940s the Admiralty 'were losing a lot of artificer tradesmen to civilian life' although 'they had hundreds of surplus senior ratings like myself who, but for the war, would not in such a short time have got so far up the ladder'.[19] Accordingly a two-year course was instituted to bring ex-stoker petty officers like Greenwood up to speed with the skills needed to be an engine room artificer (ERA). Rather than leave the navy at the end of his twelve-year engagement in 1947, he undertook this course and chose to re-enlist, having married in 1946 and started to raise a young family. The highlight of his post-war service comprised a series of cruises during 1951–1952 aboard the cruiser HMS *Sheffield*, which had undergone a refit and was based on the West Indies station at Bermuda. 'Floodlit in the harbours around the Americas, *Sheffield* was a joy to behold from the shore and citizens overflowed with praise, either through the press or in their personal kindness to the crew.'[20]

For others the end of the war did not necessarily bring about an end to their attachment to the RN because they had to fulfil some form of reserve liability. Brendan Maher, who spent much of the war on minesweepers, found that his discharge from active duty coincided with being appointed a lieutenant in the RNVR:

> From 1947 to 1950 I was an undergraduate at the University of Manchester. My duties to the RNVR required me to do a certain number of weekend drills in HMS *Eaglet* [the stone frigate that constituted Liverpool shore base]. As a student, I was excused from the requirement to spend two weeks at sea every summer. Upon graduation from the university in June 1950 my exemption terminated. I was assigned to HMS *Boxer* [a former tank landing ship converted to a fighter-control room] for two weeks in July as my summer sea-time requirement in the permanent RNVR.[21]

Like members of the other armed services, naval personnel and merchant seamen, depending on where they had served, were eligible for a range of campaign medals that could be worn with other awards for bravery and so on. Lieutenant Bernard Upton, for example, was awarded the 1939–45 Star; the Atlantic Star, with France and Germany clasp; the Africa Star, with North Africa 1942–43 clasp; the Italy Star; and the War Medal, 1939–45 with Bronze Oak Leaf (signifying a Mention in Despatches). Additionally, for his actions in helping survivors of the minesweeper HMS *Cromarty* when she was sunk (ironically by a mine) on 23 October 1943 in the Straits of Bonifacio, he was awarded the MBE.[22]

Regarding demobilisation, there were three main classes: Class A was based on an individual's length of service and age; Class B (National Reconstruction) incorporated all those deemed essential to helping the post-war economy recover; and Class C comprised those who could be released early on extreme compassionate grounds. As one Wren recalled, on 1 June 1946 she 'was discharged from service as a Class A release ... accordingly granted fifty-six days' resettlement leave, and it was stated that she could wear civilian clothing any time after the date of this Order, ceasing to wear uniform after the date of discharge. Fifty-six Clothing Coupons were issued – National Registration Identity No. S.A.K.W. 48-5.'[23] Another Wren released in March/April 1947 recounts how initially she spent her 'demob leave in

London, staying at a service hostel and buying some new civilian clothes with part of my gratuity'.[24]

Clothing was important for men as well, who after years in uniform were seeking to establish a civilian identity and find suitable employment. Ted Cook, who served with the Royal Marines for twelve years, including throughout the entire war, described a scene that became familiar to many leaving the navy during the immediate post-war period: 'I went to Portsmouth and got my discharge. We were allowed either a blue pin-striped suit with brown trilby or grey flannels and sports jacket with a flat cap plus accessories and a one-way ticket home!'[25] Similarly, Eric Denton found that his pale grey, pinstripe, double-breasted demob suit 'was quite marvellous ... a beautiful soft wool and I was wearing it for a long time as my number one suit'.[26] Another bonus that he discovered on demobilisation was that in addition to his capital sum and gratuity from the RN, he received prize money. As he explained, 'all the enemy ships captured during the war were valued and the proceeds were allocated to all the people serving in the Royal Navy according to their rank and length of service'.[27] In his case this amounted to around £300, which was a handy sum to have in the late 1940s to put towards a house.

However, for many, coping with peace was a tough proposition, albeit the end of hostilities was welcomed. One former petty officer claimed that many leaving 'The Andrew' (naval slang for the RN) were effectively 'being thrown up on the beach like unwanted jetsam, to begin a new life in civvy street. War-weary but totally untrained for peace.'[28] Yet for many, free vocational courses were offered. There was also the pressure, as one Wren officer stressed, that post-war 'we could, and must, put all our energies into the monumental task of ensuring the safety of the future that had been so bitterly fought for, and for which so many sacrifices had to be made'.[29] Arguably, the burden fell hardest on women leaving the WRNS, as it was highly unlikely they would stand a chance of employment in anything connected with their war service and many of the new skills they had mastered. Coupled with this was the question of equality. Angela Mack completed a secretarial course on demobilisation, and found that, whereas a good working rapport and relaxed attitude had existed between men and women in the wartime armed services, in civilian life men appeared 'weird, neolithic creatures whose attitudes were scandalously out of date'.[30]

Understandably, some who left the navy, including Brian Carter, found that 'they could not settle'. In his case, having re-entered the watch-making industry, 'it was heartbreaking having to break up magnificent watches which no one wanted' and which would be worth a fortune by present-day standards. This forced him into starting a day-hire business with punts and rowing boats.[31] Similarly, an able seaman who was demobbed in 1946:

> worked ashore for about two years as a trainee bricklayer under one of the government training schemes which was in force. Anyway, as after six months on a building site, the builder had to give you a rise so at the end of the six months they got rid of all the trainees and took on a fresh batch at the lower rate and this practice was common with all trades. We had two terrible winters in 1947 and 1948. I remember the snow was waist deep in 1947 in particular and as my blood had thinned down from years in hot climates I felt the cold terribly ... the sea called again ... So, being footloose and fancy free I decided to go back to sea in the Merchant Navy in September 1947 ... To my disgust I was told that all ex-Royal Navy had to join as Ordinary Seamen, and so my first trip to sea again had to be as an OS, the lowest form of life on board.[32]

When the war ended, the actor Alec Guinness, who had served as an officer on landing craft, feared that he would not get acting work again as the 'theatre seemed remote'. Then, shortly before his demobilisation, he was asked 'to play Herbert Pocket in a film to be made of Great Expectations', a step eagerly supported by his commanding officer, and so he 'embarked on a new career, in an unfamiliar world, but still wearing his Majesty's uniform'.[33] Others found that they could attend university, like Bernard Maher, or return to, or embark upon, a business career or one in a profession, such as becoming a solicitor or chartered surveyor. Lieutenant Commander John Wellham provides a case in point. A veteran of the famous raid on Taranto, and a professional regular officer in the FAA, he accepted a golden handshake post-war and went on the retired list owing to the cutbacks being made to the navy. Initially he became area manager for a wallpaper firm, then settled in Sunderland and worked as the national field manager for Vaux Breweries for several years, before becoming one of the founders of Albion Investment Management.[34]

Many veterans reflected fondly on their time in the RN, including wartime naval mine and bomb disposal officer C.B. Blackmore, who reckoned it had been: 'A great benefit. I wouldn't have missed it for anything quite honestly.'[35] Another officer, who in his early 20s was given command of 702 LCPL Flotilla, highlighted the distinctive bond that existed between officer and ratings on these small craft, and the effect of taking on such responsibility at a young age:

> you were huddled together in this tiny craft. You couldn't have a separate cabin or wardroom or anything like that. You ate exactly what they ate,

mainly in the form of sandwiches. Drank tea out of a huge Safari jar, as they called thermos flasks, and, if you were out on a big exercise or an operation and you were going to have a break, you just had to squat down in the cockpit where the driving seat was as they did ... And they always addressed me as 'Sir', although we knew each other tremendously well. It was a very interesting relationship from that point of view. They were very good men.

... the business of finding yourself in command at the age of 23 of twelve boats and sixty-six men. It's a corny old cliché, but by gum it certainly makes a man of you. You are either going to get through it successfully or you are going to make a complete muck of it, and well, that was an astonishing experience, and ... wonderful to get to know so many men. And I thought the calibre of them was immense, because with only, I think, two exceptions in the flotilla of over sixty people, including maintenance men, there were only two regulars ... the rest were like me – wartime only people ... [And they were involved in] this very long drawn out experience off Normandy. I don't think there were many ships, vessels of the Royal Navy that spent a total of ten weeks off those beaches.[36]

Ken Jump, son of a company secretary in the textile industry, served on a French warship and then the monitor HMS *Erebus*, and came away with a favourable view of life as a wartime rating:

I think being in the lower deck in the fo'c'sle was the best thing that could happen, because the wardroom is full of people of your own type. The fo'c'sle is full of every type, and in a Seaman's division you get various people who are quite different from what you would run into in normal life. And on the other hand, we had people who were university students and university-educated people of older years, and the mixture in my job was very, very useful. I found that I could make great use of knowing all the different types of people that you encounter in business as well as in wartime, and that was more than useful.[37]

Another man who enjoyed life on the lower deck was John Brown, who spent most of his war on the carrier HMS *Formidable*. 'I shall always remember the comradeship and the loyalty of those who serve in the Royal Navy. If I had to go again I hope that the Navy would accept me. It was my home.'[38] Similarly, looking back on her service, a former Wren, who had been drafted to Singapore, with all the travel that entailed, commented that:

During our service we were lucky in many ways. We saw so many beautiful parts of the world that we wouldn't normally have visited.

When we had leave we were given hospitality on rubber estates, tea plantations, game reserves in Kenya, etc. We were very healthy and had very little illness. We escaped injury though we had many brushes with enemy action, we made friendships that have lasted with great affection to the present day (twelve of us still meet at intervals) and we wouldn't have missed it for the world.

Our experiences gave us a great admiration for and loyalty to the Royal Navy and for all our lives we will feel a great affinity with that rightly named Senior Service. It was a great privilege to be part of it for the wartime years.[39]

For Stephanie Batstone, who endured many uncomfortable days working under primitive conditions at the War Signal Station at Ganavan in Scotland, her memories were more mixed. At the time there had been a sense of 'shared adversity' with her fellow Wrens, and a 'passionate pride in the job and the privilege of service in the Royal Navy'. However, as she grew older, she began to wonder if the sacrifices of her generation had been worthwhile, and even questioned the Wrens' contribution: 'Did we really help win the war, or were we just playing at sailors?'[40]

As a veteran who' saw active service in the Mediterranean, Europe and the Far East, George Henderson similarly worried about the futility of war and contemplated the losses it had caused. Yet simultaneously he was proud to have volunteered and played a role in countering fascism, and in 2015 he was among a handful of surviving Normandy veterans to be awarded the Legion d'Honneur by the French government at a special ceremony in Durham Cathedral.

People say, well did you regret being in the navy? I say, well, I didn't. As a young lad it was exciting, and people lose sight of the fact you were fighting for your existence. You weren't just swanning about. If Hitler had beaten us, the world would have been different ...

I went back to being a clerk, which was sublime to the ridiculous. But I was never troubled by nightmares. Some people had a rough time but I was never like that. You slotted back into civvy street. [Eventually he worked for many years for Fenwick's, the well-known family-run department store in Newcastle-upon-Tyne.] It must have been a great thing for parents to get their families back. We'd lost one [his brother Jack was killed in the army] and there were only two of us. I mean I would have had a brother who married, who had a family because he was a good-looking lad. And I would have had nieces and nephews and so on, which our generation was deprived of in lots of cases.

But no, I've no regrets. It's not something you want to pontificate about. It was not a choice, it was by the fact that you were fighting to survive. And when you consider Hitler had gobbled up most of Europe and [there was] one tiny little island [Great Britain], then of course America with her vast armaments ...

You wonder, well, what was it all about? It's not the common people who do it – it's the politicians or generals. I don't think anyone prior to the war was thinking we will fight Germany again, even though it was looking bad. It's greedy politicians wanting more land, and no one seems content with what they've got. We never seem to learn as people, do we? Necessity is a hard taskmaster, but it never put me off volunteering for the Royal Navy.[41]

Understandably, a rating who spent most of his war as a FEPOW had bitter memories that haunted him into old age. Writing in the 1980s, he explained how over his lifetime he had found some comfort in 'the comradeship forged in Japanese prison camps', but set against this was the brutal treatment he and his fellow prisoners endured at the hands of their captors. 'Today it seems ... difficult to bring home to a peace-loving folk that those ... at the mercy of the Japanese found them to be ruthless, wicked and cruel ... I view with gravest concern any effort to re-establish them as an important nation in world affairs, no matter from what motives.'[42]

Like their RN counterparts, members of the Merchant Navy during 1939–1945 similarly tended to experience moments of terror and high drama alongside gruelling, uncomfortable routine, plus lighter periods, especially when off duty and/or waiting for a position aboard a ship. A distinctive feature of their life was that the pre-war idea of owing loyalty to one particular shipping firm tended to dissolve under the pressure of necessity. As Neil Hulse, who served as an apprentice on the Ellerman Hall Line in 1937–1939 before becoming an officer, stated: 'The pool was formed. And this was where you'd report, say in Liverpool, to a reserve pool. There you were allocated a ship as it became available. So the tradition of serving with one company, that went in the war and you could be allocated to any vessel of any company.'[43]

In June 1940 George Monk was assigned to SS *Beaverbrae*, a 10,000-ton vessel of the Canadian Pacific Line, as her radio officer, and successfully completed a convoy with her to North America. In contrast, his next ship was the much smaller MV *Empire Confidence*, a motor vessel of about 5,000 tons, aboard which he experienced further convoys, both in the Atlantic and on the east coast of Britain. Subsequently, he was serving on SS *Auditor* when she was torpedoed, and was involved in the epic lifeboat voyage to the Cape Verde

Islands, which resulted in him losing the sight in one eye through exposure and the sun's glare. Later he joined the MV *La Paz* of the Pacific Steam Navigation Company of Liverpool, and in May 1942 she was torpedoed off Cape Canaveral, Florida. Although the crew were saved, she was a write-off. He went on to serve on SS *Lautaro*, an old ship with lots of defects and owned by the same company, before being medically downgraded and spending the remainder of his war solely on east coast convoys. His experiences gave Monk plenty of appreciation of the difficulties faced by merchant seamen. Notably, after the war he shared his impression of Distressed British Seaman/Subject (DBS) status.

> When a merchant seaman loses his ship through torpedoing or any other enemy action, the day that the ship sinks he is written off the articles and therefore doesn't get pay and is returned to the UK as DBS. And there were many incidents I understand where seamen had really bad treatment coming back. They're not paid, they don't get their War Bonus because they've signed off the ship, and they weren't treated very well when they should have been.[44]

Looking back on his war, another former seaman claimed:

> I think I was young enough and resilient enough at the time to, not to shrug it off but to accept it as being the sort of price that you paid for getting involved in bloody wars with Germans, and I was lucky, I felt that I got away with it. I was still alive at the end and I was still reasonably hale and hearty, and I hadn't been too damaged. I'd had some exciting times and some dreadful times but I think it made me very aware of the fact that fighting wars isn't fun, for anybody, either for us or the other side . . .[45]

Notes

Preface

1. Figures from Eric J. Grove, 'A Service vindicated, 1939–1946', in J.R. Hill (ed.), *The Oxford Illustrated History of the Royal Navy* (Oxford: OUP, 1995), p. 377.
2. Ibid.
3. Vera Laughton Mathews, *Blue Tapestry* (London: Hollis & Carter, 1948), pp. 146–8.
4. Tony Lane, *The Merchant Seamen's War* (Liverpool: Bluecoat Press, 1990), p. 12.
5. See, for example, Anon, *Merchantmen at War* (London: HMSO, 1944), pp. 130–5.

Chapter 1: Big Ships and Smaller Vessels

1. Captain S.W. Roskill, *The War at Sea, 1939–1945, Vol. I: The Defensive* (London: HMSO, 1954), p. 5.
2. Ibid., p. 3.
3. Ibid., p. 5.
4. George Mack, *HMS Intrepid: A Memoir* (London: William Kimber, 1980), pp. 9–10.
5. Douglas Bruce, *What Did You Do in the War Grandad? The Memoirs of Petty Officer Douglas Bruce Yeoman of Signals RNVR LD9/X5232* (Privately Published, 2014), p. 81.
6. Leslie Beavan, quoted in Edward Smithies with Colin John Bruce, *War at Sea, 1939–45* (London: Constable, 1992), p. 65.
7. IWM/DS 19571, Reel 1, Fetherston-Dilke, Capt. Charles.
8. Leslie Stevenson, quoted in G.G. Connell, *Jack's War: Lower Deck Recollections from World War II* (London: William Kimber, 1985), p. 78.
9. Anon, *The Navy and the Y Scheme* (London: HMSO, 1944), p. 12.
10. Dan Van Der Vat, *Standard of Power: The Royal Navy in the Twentieth Century* (London: Pimlico, 2001), esp. pp. 140, 147, 166.
11. Correlli Barnett, *Engage the Enemy More Closely: The Royal Navy in the Second World War* (London: Penguin, 2001), p. 40.
12. Brian Lavery, *Churchill's Navy: The Ships, Men and Organisation 1939–1945* (London: Conway, 2006), p. 161.
13. For more information on naval treaties *c.*1919–1939, see D.K. Brown, *Nelson to Vanguard: Warship Design and Development 1923–1945* (Barnsley: Seaforth Publishing, 2012), esp. pp. 12–17; H.T. Lenton and J.J. Colledge, *Warships of World War II* (London: Ian Allan, 1980), esp. pp. 13–15; Van Der Vat, *Standard of Power*, pp. 148–51.
14. See, for example, Lenton and Colledge, *Warships of World War II*, p. 21.
15. Eric Grove, Christopher Chant, David Lyon and Hugh Lyon, *The Hardware of World War II* (London: Gallery Press, 1984), p. 186.
16. Sir Stanley V. Goodall (Director of Naval Construction, 1936–1943), quoted in Brown, *Nelson to Vanguard*, p. 153.

17. Ralph Farrell, quoted in Smithies with Bruce, *War at Sea, 1939–45*, p. 30.
18. Second World War Experience Centre (SWWEC), Transcript of Tape 3057: Oral History Interview by Dr Peter Liddle with Commander R.A.C. Owen, September 2006, p. 8.
19. Cliff Smith, quoted in Connell, *Jack's War*, pp. 78–9.
20. SWWEC, Transcript of Tape 2509: Oral History Interview by Dr Peter Liddle with Sir John Harvey-Jones, May 2005, p. 5.
21. IWM/DS 19571, Reels 1–2, Captain Charles Fetherston-Dilke.
22. SWWEC, Transcript of Tape 3057: Oral History Interview with Commander R.A.C. Owen, p. 7.
23. Hugh Spensley, quoted in Smithies with Bruce, *War at Sea, 1939–45*, p. 134.
24. Arthur Rose, quoted in Smithies with Bruce, *War at Sea, 1939–45*, p. 21.
25. Ibid., pp. 23–4.
26. Barnett, *Engage the Enemy More Closely*, pp. 47–8.
27. IWM/DS 10206, Reel 2, Frederick James Hendy.
28. See, for example, Roskill, *The War at Sea, 1939–1945*, vol. I, pp. 73–4.
29. SWWEC, T/S Doc: Memories of HMS ROYAL OAK, by Stanley Ivan Cole, pp. 2–4.
30. T.J. Waldron and James Gleeson, *The Frogmen: The Story of the Wartime Underwater Operators* (London: Pan, 1955), pp. 13–14.
31. SWWEC, Transcript of Tape 445: Oral History Interview by Dr Peter Liddle with Commander Tom Dowling, February 2001, p. 3.
32. Brown, *Nelson to Vanguard*, p. 39.
33. For analysis of the Battle of Matapan see Martin Stephen (ed. Eric Grove), *Sea Battles in close-up: World War 2* (London: Ian Allan, 1996), pp. 48–69.
34. Anon, *East of Malta, West of Suez: The Admiralty Account of the Naval War in the Eastern Mediterranean, September 1939 to March 1941* (London: HMSO, 1943), p. 59.
35. Lieutenant Commander Peter Kemp, 'The Chase of the Bismarck' in *The History of the Second World War, Vol. 2 No. 5* (Paulton, nr Bristol: Purnell, 1967), pp. 573, 576.
36. Brian Lavery, *Hostilities Only: Training the Wartime Royal Navy* (London: National Maritime Museum, 2004), p. 221.
37. Ordinary Seaman Ronald Martin quoted in *Max Arthur, Lost Voices of the Royal Navy* (London: Hodder, 2005), p. 491.
38. Brown, *Nelson to Vanguard*, p. 81.
39. Angus Konstam, *British Heavy Cruisers 1939–45* (Oxford: Osprey, 2012), p. 5.
40. Ronnie Turner, quoted in Johnny Parker, *A Smack at the Boche: World War Two British Navy Diary of Leading Seaman Ronnie Turner* (Privately Published, 2016), p. 71.
41. IWM/DS 21191, Reel 1, Robert Henry Crick.
42. See, for example, Angus Konstam, *British Light Cruisers 1939–45* (Oxford: Osprey, 2012). For further details on RN Heavy and Light Cruisers also see Lenton and Colledge *Warships of World War II*, pp. 23–32, 49–53.
43. IWM/DS 18504, Reel 1, Eric Arthur Hills.
44. SWWEC, Transcript of Tape 3057: Oral History Interview with Commander R.A.C. Owen, p. 15.
45. Connell, *Jack's War*, p. 24.
46. IWM/DS 15450, Reel 1, Commander William Edward Grenfell.
47. SWWEC, Transcript of Tape 1537: Oral History Interview by Dr Peter Liddle with Mr Colin Kitching, July 2002, p. 5.
48. George Melly, *Rum, Bum and Concertina* (London: Futura, 1979), pp. 119–20.

49. Roy Bennett, quoted in Smithies with Bruce, *War at Sea 1939–45*, p. 40.
50. John Keller, quoted in Smithies with Bruce, *War at Sea 1939–45*, pp. 40–1.
51. SWWEC, Transcript of Tape 3057: Oral History Interview with Commander R.A.C. Owen, pp. 11–12.
52. SWWEC, Transcript of Tape 1537: Oral History Interview with Mr Colin Kitching, p. 8.
53. SWWEC, Transcript of Tape 743: Oral History Interview by Dr Peter Liddle with Gen. Sir Peter Whiteley, July 2001, p. 2.
54. Ibid., pp. 4–5.
55. Major General Julian Thompson, *Royal Marines: From Sea Soldiers to a Special Force* (London: Pan, 2001), pp. 253–4.
56. IWM/DS 10798, Reels 1–2, William Harold Bradshaw.
57. See, for example, Stephen Roskill, *The Navy at War, 1939–1945* (Ware, Herts: Wordsworth Editions, 1998), pp. 320–4.
58. IWM/DS 25217, Reel 3, George Burridge.
59. Ibid.
60. Anon, *The Navy and the Y Scheme*, p. 14.
61. Sydney Greenwood, *Stoker Greenwood's Navy* (Tunbridge Wells: Midas Books, 1983), p. 43.
62. F.A. Mason, *The Last Destroyer: HMS Aldenham, 1942–44* (London: Robert Hale, 1988), p. 69.
63. Eric Denton, *My Six Wartime Years in the Royal Navy* (London: Minerva Press, 1999), p. 55.
64. SWWEC, Transcript of Tape 3244: Oral History Interview by Trevor Mumford with Rev. C.B. Blackmore, April 2006, pp. 10–11.
65. For details of British destroyer development *c.*1917–1945 see, for example, Lenton and Colledge, *Warships of World War II*, esp. pp. 71–80 and 97–126.
66. IWM/DS 27308, Reel 6, Ronald Walsh.
67. Denton, *My Six Wartime Years in the Royal Navy*, p. 45.
68. Mack, *HMS Intrepid*, p. 16.
69. IWM/DS 17394, Reel 1, Rear Admiral Edward Findlay Gueritz.
70. Ludovic Kennedy, *On My Way to the Club: An Autobiography* (London: Collins, 1989), p. 104.
71. Mason, *The Last Destroyer*, pp. 17–19.
72. SWWEC, Transcript of Tape 445: Oral History Interview with Commander Dowling, p. 5.
73. Greenwood, *Stoker Greenwood's Navy*, p. 77.
74. IMM/DS 19391, Reel 3, Thomas Henry Jones.
75. Denton, *My Six Wartime Years in the Royal Navy*, pp. 39–40.
76. Ibid., pp. 50–2.
77. Greenwood, *Stoker Greenwood's Navy*, pp. 78, 84.
78. Mack, *HMS Intrepid*, p. 64.
79. For an overview of Rev. C.B. Blackmore's wartime RN service, see James Goulty, *Second World War Lives* (Barnsley: Pen & Sword, 2012), pp. 41–52.
80. SWWEC, Transcript of Tape 3244: Oral History Interview with Rev. C.B. Blackmore, p. 8.
81. SWWEC, Lieutenant Commander C.H. Knollys Papers: Extracts from his Memoirs, 'Anecdotage' 1940–1944, pp. 141–4.
82. Lenton and Colledge *Warships of World War II*, p. 173.
83. Lavery, *Churchill's Navy*, p. 228.

84. See, for example, App. II Escort Vessels, in Alan Burn, *The Fighting Captain: The Story of Frederic Walker RN CB DSO and The Battle of the Atlantic* (Barnsley: Pen & Sword, 2006), pp. 182–4.

85. IWM/DS 10772, Reel 1, Denis Charles Logan.

86. J.B. Lamb, quoted in David K. Brown, 'Atlantic Escorts 1939–45', in Stephen Howarth and Derek Law (eds), *The Battle of the Atlantic 1939–1945: 50th Anniversary Naval Conference* (London: Greenhill Books, 1994), p. 467.

87. IWM/DS 20277, Reel 1, Jack Leonard Cole.

88. IWM/DS 25182, Reel 3, Sir Robert Atkinson.

89. Lieutenant James Reeve (RNVR) quoted in Paul Lund and Harry Ludlam, *Trawlers Go To War* (London: NEL, 1972), p. 113.

90. Anon, *The Navy and the Y Scheme*, p. 21.

91. Anonymous naval officer quoted in Paul Lund and Harry Ludlam, *Out Sweeps! The Exploits of the Minesweepers in World War II* (London: NEL, 1979), p. 64.

92. IWM/DS 18547, Reel 1, Sydney Charles Hook.

93. Lund and Ludlam, *Out Sweeps!*, p. 115.

94. For further details, see Lenton and Colledge, *Warships of World War II*, esp. pp. 173–6 and 199–215; Bernard Upton, *On the Road to Normandy and a little beyond: A Sailor's Life Story* (Privately Published, 2017), pp. 121–8.

95. See, for example, Lund and Ludlam, *Out Sweeps!*, pp. 169–78.

96. Ibid., p. 197.

97. Brendan A. Maher, *Passage to Sword Beach: Minesweeping in the Royal Navy* (Annapolis, Maryland: Naval Institute Press, 1996), p. 46.

98. Ibid., p. 44.

99. SWWEC, Transcript of Tape 2731: Oral History Interview by David Talbot with Lieutenant Commander T. Maughan RNVR, 22 November 2005, pp. 11–12.

100. Ibid., p. 8.

101. IWM/DS 29430, Reel 1, John Trelawney Curnock.

102. SWWEC, Transcript of Tape 2731: Oral History Interview with Lieutenant Commander Maughan, p. 12.

103. Maher, *Passage to Sword Beach*, pp. 42–3.

104. See, for example, Lund and Ludlam, *Trawlers Go To War*, and Lavery, *Churchill's Navy*, pp. 253–6.

105. Commander D.A. Rayner, *Escort: The Battle of the Atlantic* (London: William Kimber, 1955), p. 39.

106. Lund and Ludlam, *Trawlers Go To War*, p. 121.

107. Ibid., pp. 123–8.

108. IWM/DS 8984, Reel 5, Commander Christopher William Stuart Dreyer.

109. Lenton and Colledge, *Warships of World War II*, pp. 543–5.

110. SWWEC, Transcript of Tape 446: Oral History Interview by Dr Peter Liddle with Lieutenant Commander Charles Coles, February 2001, p. 9.

111. John W. Davies, *Jack – The Sailor with the Navy Blue Eyes* (Durham: Pentland Press, 1995), pp. 26–7.

112. Maher, *Passage to Sword Beach*, p. 101.

113. SWWEC, Transcript of Tape 446: Oral History Interview with Lieutenant Commander Coles, p. 4.

114. Davies, *Jack – The Sailor with the Navy Blue Eyes*, p. 51.

115. Ibid., pp. 42–3.
116. SWWEC, Transcript of Tape 446: Oral History Interview with Lieutenant Commander Coles, p. 6.
117. Lavery, *Churchill's Navy*, p. 245.
118. IWM/DS 8984, Reel 2, Commander Christopher William Stuart Dreyer.
119. IWM/DS 12400, Reel 3, John Rayner Bone.
120. SWWEC, Transcript of Tape 446: Oral History Interview with Lieutenant Commander Coles, p. 9.
121. IWM/DS 8984, Reel 4, Commander Christopher William Stuart Dreyer.

Chapter 2: Naval Aviation and Aircraft Carriers

1. Roger Chesneau, *Aircraft Carriers of the World, 1914 to the Present: An Illustrated Encyclopedia* (London: Arms & Armour Press, 1992), p. 11.
2. Ibid., p. 90.
3. George Melly, *Rum, Bum and Concertina* (London: Futura, 1979), p. 64.
4. Imperial War Museum, Department of Documents (IWM/DS) 21587, Reel 1, Stanley Reynolds.
5. Stephen Roskill, *The Navy at War, 1939–1945* (Ware, Herts: Wordsworth Editions, 1998), pp. 27–9.
6. J.H.B. Chapman (Royal Corps of Naval Constructors), quoted in David K. Brown, *Nelson to Vanguard: Warship Design and Development 1923–1945* (Barnsley: Seaforth Publishing, 2012), p. 40.
7. Brian Lavery, *Churchill's Navy: The Ships, Men and Organisation 1939–1945* (London: Conway, 2006), p. 188.
8. Henry 'Hank' Adlam, *On and Off the Flight Deck: Reflections of a Naval Fighter Pilot in World War II* (Barnsley: Pen & Sword, 2009), p. 37.
9. Norman Hanson, *Carrier Pilot* (London: Silvertail Books, 2016), p. 128.
10. IWM/DS 16355, Reel 2, George Alfred Amyes.
11. Ibid.
12. See, for example, Chesneau, *Aircraft Carriers of the World*, pp. 95–6.
13. Robert Cosh, *Inside and Out: My Experiences in the Royal Navy and HM Prison Service in War and Peace* (Bognor Regis: Woodfield Publishing, 2005), p. 22.
14. Commander R. 'Mike' Crosley, DSC, RN, *They Gave Me a Seafire* (Shrewsbury: Airlife, 1986), p. 55.
15. Brown, *Nelson to Vanguard*, p. 43.
16. Crosley, *They Gave Me a Seafire*, p. 132.
17. Brown, *Nelson to Vanguard*, pp. 50–1.
18. John L. Brown, *Diary of a Matelot 1942–1945* (Worcester: Square One Publications, 1991), p. 20.
19. Gordon Wallace, *Carrier Observer* (Shrewsbury: Airlife, 1993), p. 28.
20. Adlam, *On and Off the Flight Deck*, p. 140.
21. Wallace, *Carrier Observer*, p. 59.
22. Crosley, *They Gave Me a Seafire*, pp. 139–40.
23. IWM/DS 18458, Reel 2, Charles Wilfred Hawthorn.
24. Brown, *Diary of a Matelot 1942–1945*, p. 61.
25. IWM/DS 20967, Reel 1, Tony Clarke.
26. Lavery, *Churchill's Navy*, p. 187.

27. Cosh, *Inside and Out*, p. 46.
28. IWM/DS 20967, Reel 1, Tony Clarke.
29. Captain Eric 'Winkle' Brown CBE, DSC, AFC ,RN, *Wings on my Sleeve* (London: Phoenix, 2007), p. 17.
30. Chesneau, *Aircraft Carriers of the World, 1914 to the Present*, p. 108.
31. Brown, *Wings on my Sleeve*, p. 18.
32. Second World War Experience Centre (SWWEC), Transcript of oral history interview by John Larder with Lieutenant Commander John Wellham about his experiences with the FAA in the Second World War, Sunderland, 29 April 1999, p. 14.
33. Ibid., p. 15.
34. See, for example, Brown, *Nelson to Vanguard*, p. 66.
35. IWM/DS 31408, Reel 5, John Shoebridge.
36. Ibid.
37. Captain S.W. Roskill, *The War at Sea, 1939–1945, Vol. I: The Defensive* (London: HMSO, 1954), p. 477.
38. IWM/DS 20978, Reel 2, Henry Norman Gostelow.
39. Ibid.
40. See, for example, Kenneth Munson, *Helicopters and other Rotorcraft since 1907* (London: Blandford Press, 1975), esp. pp. 30 and 116–17.
41. Lavery, *Churchill's Navy*, p. 200; David Mondey, *British Aircraft of World War II* (London: Chancellor Press, 1995), pp. 194–5.
42. Appendix 11 Seafire – some of the problems (h) Decklanding trials of the Seafire in Crosley, *They Gave Me a Seafire*, p. 241.
43. SWWEC, Transcript of oral history interview with Lieutenant Commander John Wellham, p. 5.
44. Ibid., p. 3.
45. IWM/DS 11720, Reel 1, Vice Admiral Sir Hugh Richard Benest Janvrin.
46. Wallace, *Carrier Observer*, pp. 34–5.
47. Mondey, *British Aircraft of World War II*, p. 104.
48. Wallace, *Carrier Observer*, p. 174.
49. IWM/DS 28497, Reel 4, Owen Charles Bert Smith.
50. Ibid.
51. IWM/DS 27756, Reel 2, William Fenwick Smith.
52. IWM/DS 15533, Reel 2, Douglas Granger Parker.
53. Crosley, *They Gave Me a Seafire*, p. 56.
54. Mondey, *British Aircraft of World War II*, p. 210.
55. Appendix 5: Some Reasons for the Seafire's Poor Showing at Salerno in 1943 in Crosley, *They Gave Me a Seafire*, pp. 217–18.
56. Brown, *Wings on my Sleeve*, p. 10.
57. Hanson, *Carrier Pilot*, p. 171.
58. Ibid., pp. 103–4.
59. Ibid., p. 123.
60. IWM/DS 28937, Reel 6, Geoffrey Hyde.
61. IWM/DS 16355, Reel 1, George Alfred Amyes.
62. Lavery, *Churchill's Navy*, p. 194.
63. Wallace, *Carrier Observer*, pp. 22–3.
64. Brown, *Wings on my Sleeve*, p. 8.

65. Adlam, *On and Off the Flight Deck*, p. 6.

66. SWWEC, Transcript of oral history interview with Lieutenant Commander John Wellham, pp. 2–3.

67. Crosley, *They Gave Me a Seafire*, esp. pp. 32, 36, 42, 52.

68. Adlam, *On and Off the Flight Deck*, p. 16.

69. Ibid., p. 5.

70. Hanson, *Carrier Pilot*, esp. pp. 18, 19, 21–2, 27.

71. Ibid., p. 41.

72. IWM/DS 28497, Reel 2, Owen Charles Bert Smith.

73. Hanson, *Carrier Pilot*, p. 43.

74. Wallace, *Carrier Observer*, p. 43.

75. Adlam, *On and Off the Flight Deck*, p. 33.

76. IWM/DS 31408, Reel 3, John Shoebridge.

77. Brown, *Wings on my Sleeve*, p. 15.

78. IWM/DS 27756, Reel 3, William Fenwick Smith.

79. IWM/DS 15533, Reel 1, Douglas Granger Parker.

80. IWM/DS 11720, Reel 1, Vice Admiral Sir Hugh Richard Benest Janvrin.

81. Lieutenant Commander John Moffat, quoted in Mike Rossiter, *Ark Royal: The Life, Death and Rediscovery of the Legendary Second World War Aircraft Carrier* (London: Corgi, 2007), p. 293.

82. IWM/DS 11720, Reel 2, Vice Admiral Sir Hugh Richard Benest Janvrin.

83. Lieutenant A.W.F. Sutton, quoted in Ray Sturtivant, *The Swordfish Story* (London: Arms & Armour Press, 1993), p. 58.

84. Martin Stephen (ed. Eric Grove), *Sea Battles in close-up: World War 2* (London: Ian Allan, 1996), p. 40.

85. IWM/DS 11720, Reel 2, Vice Admiral Sir Hugh Richard Benest Janvrin.

86. SWWEC, Transcript of oral history interview with Lieutenant Commander John Wellham, pp. 10–11.

87. IWM/DS 31408, Reel 4, John Shoebridge.

88. IWM/DS 11088, Reel 1, Stephen Andrew Mearns.

89. Brown, *Diary of a Matelot 1942–1945*, p. 135.

90. IWM/DS 28497, Reel 4, Owen Charles Bert Smith.

91. Hanson, *Carrier Pilot*, p. 217.

92. See, for example, John Winton, *The Forgotten Fleet: The Story of the British Pacific Fleet 1944–45* (Wadhurst, E. Sussex: Douglas-Boyd Books, 1991), pp. 77–101.

93. IWM/DS 27756, Reel 3, William Fenwick Smith.

Chapter 3: Underwater Warfare and Anti-Submarine Warfare

1. Anon, *The Navy and the Y Scheme* (London; HMSO, 1944), p. 21.

2. Dan Van Der Vat, *Standard of Power: The Royal Navy in the Twentieth Century* (London: Pimlico, 2001), p. 316.

3. Anon, *The Navy and the Y Scheme*, p. 40.

4. John Winton, *The Forgotten War: The Story of the British Pacific Fleet 1944–45* (Wadhurst, E. Sussex: Douglas-Boyd, 1991), p. 264.

5. For good coverage of Royal Navy wartime submarine experience see Peter Padfield, *War Beneath the Sea: Submarine Conflict 1939–1945* (London: Pimlico, 1997) and for the Far East see Winton, *The Forgotten War*, pp. 236–68.

6. Imperial War Museum, Department of Sound, (IWM/DS) 9153, Reel 1, Captain Mervyn Robert George Wingfield.
7. IWM/DS 28531, Reel 1, Des Radwell.
8. Second World War Experience Centre (SWWEC), T/S of Tape 2509: Oral History Interview with Sir John Harvey-Jones by Dr Peter Liddle, May 2005, p. 8.
9. IWM/DS 26588, Reel 4, Alec Wingrave.
10. IWM/DS 21644, Reel 1, William Harris Douglass.
11. SWWEC, T/S of Tape 2509: Interview with Sir John Harvey-Jones, p. 5.
12. SWWEC, Chris West: A British Submariner in the Far East, T/S 6 p Account, p. 3.
13. IWM/DS 9153, Reel 1, Captain Mervyn Robert George Wingfield.
14. SWWEC, T/S of Tape 2080, Oral History Interview with Mr A. Sumption DSC by David Talbot, 27 February 2004, p. 12.
15. IWM/DS 10188, Reel 1, John Henry Bromage.
16. SWWEC, T/S of Tape 1556, Oral History Interview with Vice Admiral Sir Ian McGeogh KCB, DSO, DSC by David Talbot, 26 February 2003, p. 2.
17. IWM/DS 28531, Reel 1, Des Radwell.
18. IWM/DS 21644, Reel 1, William Harris Douglass.
19. IWM/DS 28531, Reel 2, Des Radwell.
20. IWM/DS 26588, Reel 5, Alec Wingrave.
21. SWWEC, Chris West: Life on board HMS/M *Sleuth*, 1p T/S Note/Memoir.
22. IWM/DS 26588, Reel 4, Alec Wingrave.
23. IWM/DS 9167, Reel 1, William John Pook.
24. IWM/DS 10188, Reel 1, John Henry Bromage.
25. Ibid., Reel 3.
26. IWM/DS 9167, Reel 1, William John Pook.
27. IWM/DS 10188, Reel 3, John Henry Bromage.
28. For details of British submarine development *c.*1930–1945, see David K. Brown, *Nelson to Vanguard: Warship Design and Development 1923–1945* (Barnsley: Seaforth, 2012), esp. pp. 108–20; and H.T. Lenton and J.J. Colledge, *Warships of World War II* (London: Ian Allan, 1980), pp. 147–67.
29. IWM/DS 9167, Reel 1, William John Pook.
30. IWM/DS 9137, Reel 1, Admiral Christopher Haynes Hutchinson.
31. SWWEC, West: A British Submariner in the Far East, p. 3.
32. SWWEC, T/S of Tape 2509: Interview with Sir John Harvey-Jones, p. 6.
33. SWWEC, West: A British Submariner in the Far East, p. 4.
34. IWM/DS 28417, Reel 2, Sir John Henry Harvey-Jones.
35. IWM/DS 28531, Reel 3, Des Radwell.
36. IWM/DS 9167, Reel 2, William John Pook.
37. IWM/DS 26588, Reel 4, Alec Wingrave.
38. IWM/DS 28531, Reel 2, Des Radwell.
39. IWM/DS 9167, Reel 2, William John Pook.
40. IWM/DS 21644, Reel 1, William Harris Douglass.
41. IWM/DS 10188, Reel 1, John Henry Bromage.
42. SWWEC, T/S of Tape 2509: Interview with Sir John Harvey-Jones, p. 6.
43. IWM/DS 9153, Reel 1, Captain Mervyn Robert George Wingfield.
44. IWM/DS 9858, Reel 5, Vice Admiral Sir Ian Lachlan MacKay McGeogh.
45. Ibid., Reel 4.

46. IWM/DS 9137, Reel 2, Admiral Christopher Haynes Hutchinson.
47. Ibid.
48. SWWEC, West: A British Submariner in the Far East, p. 4.
49. SWWEC, T/S of Tape 1556, Vice Admiral McGeogh, p. 10.
50. See, for example, T.J. Waldron and James Gleeson, *The Frogman: The Story of the Wartime Underwater Operators* (London: Pan, 1955), esp. pp. 92–115.
51. Ibid., p. 62.
52. IMW/DS 11769, Reel 1, Conrad Leonard Berey.
53. Waldron and Gleeson, *The Frogman*, p. 72.
54. Captain S.W. Roskill, *The War at Sea, 1939–1945, Vol. II: The Period of Balance* (London: HMSO, 1956), pp. 342–3.
55. IMW/DS 11769, Reel 2, Conrad Leonard Berey.
56. IWW/DS 9822, Reel 2, Ian Edward Fraser.
57. Waldron and Gleeson, *The Frogman*, p. 83.
58. See, for example, Ibid., pp. 84–7.
59. IWW/DS 9822, Reel 2, Ian Edward Fraser.
60. Ibid.
61. Sir Samuel Hoare, quoted in Peter Padfield, *War Beneath the Sea*, p. 23.
62. Bob Whinney, *The U-Boat Peril: A Fight For Survival* (London: Cassell, 1986), p. 43.
63. IWM/DS 27308, Reel 4, Ronald Walsh.
64. IWM/DS 19571, Reel 4, Captain Charles Fetherston-Dilke.
65. Whinney, *The U-Boat Peril*, p. 43.
66. Alan Burn, *The Fighting Captain: The Story of Frederic Walker RN CB DSO and The Battle of the Atlantic. Appendix Five: The Asdic System* (Barnsley: Pen & Sword, 2006), pp. 185–7.
67. IWM/DS 25182, Reel 2, Sir Robert Atkinson.
68. Ibid.
69. IWM/DS 19571, Reel 4, Captain Charles Fetherston-Dilke.
70. Lieutenant Commander Peter Kemp, 'The Warships' in *History of the Second World War, Vol. 7 No. 9* (Paulton, Nr Bristol: Purnell, 1968), p. 2,914.
71. IWM/DS 19571, Reel 4, Captain Charles Fetherston-Dilke.
72. IWM/DS 10772, Reel 1, Denis Charles Logan.
73. IWM/DS 19571, Reel 4, Captain Charles Fetherston-Dilke.
74. Kemp, 'The Warships,' p. 2,916.
75. Ibid., p. 2,917.
76. IWM/DS 24629, Reel 3, Christopher Patrick Ridsdale Collis.
77. IWM/DS 10772, Reel 1, Denis Charles Logan.
78. IWM/DS 25182, Reel 3, Sir Robert Atkinson.
79. IWM/DS 19571, Reel 4, Captain Charles Fetherston-Dilke.
80. IWM/DS 24629, Reel 3, Christopher Patrick Ridsdale Collis.
81. IWW/DS 12023, Reel 2, Commander David Edward Balme.
82. Kemp, 'The Warships,' p. 2,914.
83. IWM/DS 19571, Reel 4, Captain Charles Fetherston-Dilke.
84. IWM/DS 24629, Reel 3, Christopher Patrick Ridsdale Collis.
85. IWM/DS 25182, Reel 4, Sir Robert Atkinson.
86. SWWEC: Transcript of Tape 1185, Dr Peter Liddle Oral History Interview with Mr R. Crang regarding his wartime service in the RN, July 2002, pp. 6–7.

87. IWM/DS 21587, Reel 2, Stanley Reynolds.
88. SWWEC: Transcript of Tape 1185, Interview with Mr R. Crang, July 2002, p. 8.
89. Ibid., pp. 9–10.
90. IWM/DS 21587, Reel 3, Stanley Reynolds.
91. Ibid.
92. IWM/DS 25921, Reel 2, John Druce Sayer (Pilot, 811 Squadron FAA, HMS *Biter*, Atlantic, 1942–1943).
93. IWM/DS 19105, Reel 2, Cmdr Maurice William Henley (Pilot, 813 Squadron FAA, HMS *Campania*, Arctic, 1944–1945).
94. Ibid.

Chapter 4: The Experience of Convoy Work

1. Richard Woodman, *The Real Cruel Sea: The Merchant Navy in the Battle of the Atlantic, 1939–1943* (London: John Murray, 2005), p. 28.
2. Peter Elphick, *Life Line: The Merchant Navy at War 1939–1945* (London: Chatham Publishing, 1999), p. 19.
3. Imperial War Museum/Department of Sound (IWM/DS) 21191, Reel 1, Robert Henry Crick.
4. IWM/DS 21645, Reel 2, John Arthur Carteret Maule.
5. Albert Johns, *Theatre of Life: The Memoirs of Albert Edward Johns: From Merchant Navy Gunner to Pantomime Dame* (Privately Published, 2019), p. 24.
6. Captain Stephen Roskill, *The Navy at War, 1939–1945* (Ware, Herts: Wordsworth Editions, 1998), p. 315.
7. IWM/DS 15332, Reel 1, Neil Sydney Hulse.
8. Alan Burn, *The Fighting Captain: The Story of Frederic Walker RN, CB, DSO and The Battle of the Atlantic* (Barnsley: Pen & Sword, 2006), App. II: The Escort Vessels, pp. 182–3.
9. IWM/DS 25182, Reel 2, Sir Robert Atkinson.
10. Lieutenant Commander Peter K. Kemp, 'Struggle for the Sealanes' in *History of the Second World War, Vol. 1 No. 14* (Paulton, nr Bristol: Purnell, 1967), p. 378.
11. Rear Admiral Sir Kenelm Creighton, *Convoy Commodore* (London: William Kimber, 1956), p. 23.
12. Tony Lane, *The Merchant Seaman's War* (Liverpool: Bluecoat Press, 1990), p. 14.
13. Elphick, *Life Line*, p. 20.
14. Lane, *The Merchant Seaman's War*, p. 16.
15. Woodman, *The Real Cruel Sea*, pp. 39–40.
16. IWM/DS 11509, Reel 1, Henry Cedric Fellingham.
17. IWM/DS 11441, Reel 5, George Victor Monk.
18. Ibid., Reel 1.
19. Creighton, *Convoy Commodore*, pp. 44–5.
20. IWM/DS 11509, Reel 1, Henry Cedric Fellingham.
21. IWM/DS 19105, Reels 2–3, Maurice William Henley.
22. IWM/DS 18504, Reel 1, Eric Arthur Hills.
23. Alan Burn, *The Fighting Commodores: Convoy Commanders in the Second World War* (Barnsley: Leo Cooper, 1999), p. 51.
24. IWM/DS 11441, Reel 5, George Victor Monk.
25. IWM/DS 20978, Reel 2, Henry Norman Gostelow.
26. Richard Woodman, *The Arctic Convoys 1941–1945* (London: John Murray, 1995), p. 22.

27. For further details, see Vice Admiral B.B. Schofield, *The Russian Convoys* (London: Pan Books, 1984), Appendix I: Analysis of the Russian Convoys and Appendix II: War Equipment Shipped to Russia, pp. 223–5.

28. Burn, *The Fighting Commodores*, p. 32.

29. Ibid., p. 27.

30. Creighton, *Convoy Commodore*, pp. 24–5.

31. Woodman, *The Arctic Convoys*, p. 23.

32. Creighton, *Convoy Commodore*, p. 83.

33. D.A. Rayner, *Escort: The Battle of the Atlantic* (London: William Kimber, 1955), p. 127.

34. IWM/DS 27211, Reel 1, Ida Stedman.

35. IWM/DS 13126, Reel 2, Audrey Sylvia Roche.

36. IWM/DS 11441, Reel 1, George Victor Monk.

37. IWM/DS 15332, Reel 1, Neil Sydney Hulse.

38. Anon, *Merchantmen at War: The Official Story of the Merchant Navy 1939–1944* (London: HMSO, 1944), p. 90.

39. Creighton, *Convoy Commodore*, p. 43.

40. IWM/DS 15332, Reel 1, Neil Sydney Hulse.

41. IWM/DS 11441, Reel 5, George Victor Monk.

42. Ibid., Reel 1.

43. IWM/DS 11509, Reel 1, Henry Cedric Fellingham.

44. IWM/DS 10936, Reel 2, Alexander Lavey Downing.

45. Ibid.

46. IWM/DS 11509, Reel 1, Henry Cedric Fellingham.

47. Ibid.

48. David W. Bone, *Merchantman Rearmed* (London: Chatto & Windus, 1949), p. 139.

49. Creighton, *Convoy Commodore*, p. 78.

50. Bone, *Merchantman Rearmed*, p. 50.

51. IWM/DS 11441, Reel 2, George Victor Monk.

52. IWM/DS 25182, Reel 2, Sir Robert Atkinson.

53. G. Drake, 'Without Incident' in J. Lennox Kerr (ed.), *Touching the Adventures ... of Merchantmen in the Second World War* (London: George G. Harrap & Co. Ltd, 1953), p. 217.

54. Ibid.

55. IWM/DS 27308, Reel 6, Ronald Walsh.

56. IWM/DS 11509, Reel 1, Henry Cedric Fellingham.

57. Drake, 'Without Incident', p. 217.

58. IWM/DS 11509, Reel 1, Henry Cedric Fellingham.

59. IMW/DS 20284, Reel 4, Robert Craddock.

60. IWM/DS 19532, Reel 1, Sidney William Taylor.

61. IWM/DS 25217, Reels 2–3, George Burridge.

62. IWM/DS 11509, Reel 4, Henry Cedric Fellingham.

63. Ibid.

64. Captain Jack Broome, *Convoy is to Scatter* (London: William Kimber, 1972), pp. 33–4.

65. IMW/DS 20284, Reel 4, Robert Craddock.

66. IWM/DS 16355, Reel 2, George Alfred Amyes.

67. IWM/DS 11509, Reel 2, Henry Cedric Fellingham.

68. Captain S.W. Roskill, *The War at Sea, 1939–1945, Vol. I: The Defensive* (London: HMSO, 1954), pp. 288–9.
69. IWM/DS 19391, Reel 2, Thomas Henry Jones.
70. IWM/DS 11441, Reel 2, George Victor Monk.
71. IWM/DS 16355, Reel 3, George Alfred Amyes.
72. IWM/DS 20612, Reel 2, Robert Frank Collins.
73. IWM/DS 15332, Reel 2, Neil Sydney Hulse.
74. IWM/DS 15450, Reel 2, William Edward Grenfell.
75. Broome, *Convoy is to Scatter*, p. 35.
76. See, for example, Richard Woodman, *Malta Convoys 1940–1943* (London: John Murray, 2003).
77. F.A. Mason, *The Last Destroyer: HMS Aldenham, 1942–44* (London: Robert Hale, 1988), p. 40.
78. Broome, *Convoy is to Scatter*, p. 85.
79. IWM/DS 12023, Reel 1, David Edward Balme.
80. Burn, *The Fighting Captain*, App. III Close Escort For Convoys, pp. 184–5.
81. For detailed coverage of the ill-fated Convoy PQ17, see, for example, Broome, *Convoy is to Scatter*; Schofield, *The Russian Convoys*; Paul Lund and Harry Ludlam, *I Was There: On Convoy PQ17. The Convoy to Hell: Through the Icy Russian Waters of World War II* (London: Foulsham, 2010); Captain S.W. Roskill, *The War at Sea, 1939–1945, Vol. II: The Period of Balance* (London: HMSO, 1956), pp. 134–46.
82. Schofield, *The Russian Convoys*, p. 82.
83. IWM/DS 20817, Reel 2, Percy Thomas Price.
84. IWM/DS 18461, Reel 1, Alfred George Webster.
85. Rayner, *Escort*, pp. 137–8.
86. Ibid., p. 138.
87. Burn, *The Fighting Captain*, p. 39.
88. Ibid., p. 38.
89. IWM/DS 19105, Reels 2–3, Maurice William Henley.

Chapter 5: Amphibious Warfare

1. Anon, *Combined Operations 1940–1942* (London: HMSO, 1943), p. 7.
2. Brian Lavery, *Hostilities Only: Training the Wartime Royal Navy* (London: National Maritime Museum, 2004), p. 207.
3. H.T. Lenton and J.J. Colledge, *Warships of World War II* (London: Ian Allan, 1980), p. 599.
4. Brendan A. Maher, *A Passage to Sword Beach: Minesweeping in the Royal Navy* (Annapolis, Maryland: Naval Institute Press, 1996), p. 125.
5. Imperial War Museum Department of Sound (IWM/DS) 28767, Reel 3, John Thomas Tarbit.
6. Sub-Lieutenant John Hilton (RNVR) quoted in Paul Lund and Harry Ludlam, *The War of the Landing Craft* (London: NEL, 1976), p. 63.
7. Alec Guinness, *Blessings in Disguise* (New York: Knopf, 1986), pp. 107–8.
8. Major General J.I.H. Owen, quoted in Major General Julian Thompson, *The Royal Marines: From Sea Soldiers To A Special Force* (London: Pan, 2001), p. 324.
9. Lenton and Colledge, *Warships of World War II*, p. 627.
10. Ibid., p. 630.
11. W. Brian Carter, *Saved by the Bomb* (Lewes, E. Sussex: Book Guild, 2001), p. 82.

12. Ibid., pp. 82–3.

13. Ibid., p. 54.

14. IWM/DS 27071, Reel 2, Dennis Till.

15. IWM/DS 21656, Reel 2, Victor Henry Edward Longhurst.

16. IWM/DS 9956, Reels 4–5, Hugh Michael Irwin.

17. Sub-Lieutenant Braithet Harper (RNVR), quoted in Lund and Ludlam, *The War of the Landing Craft*, p. 143.

18. IWM/DS 9956, Reel 5, Hugh Michael Irwin. On D-Day Irwin was OC 591st LCA (HR) Flotilla.

19. IWM/DS 18567, Reel 1, Howard Geoffrey Dowell.

20. Sir David W. Bone CBE, 'Landing-Ship, Infantry' in J. Lennox Kerr (ed.), *Touching the Adventures of Merchantmen in the Second World War* (London: George G. Harrap & Co. Ltd, 1953), p. 149.

21. See, for example, Lenton and Colledge, *Warships of World War II*, esp. pp. 607–10, 615–18.

22. Lund and Ludlam, *The War of the Landing Craft*, p. 65.

23. IWM/DS 18547, Reel 2, Sydney Charles Hook.

24. See, for example, Lenton and Colledge, *Warships of World War II*, esp. pp. 611–15; James Goulty, 'Landing Ship Tanks' in *Everyone's War: The Journal of the Second World War Experience Centre*, No. 41, 2020, pp. 36–42; Brian Macdermott, *Ships without Names: The Story of the Royal Navy's Tank Landing Ships of World War Two* (London: Arms & Armour, 1992); Gordon L. Rottman, *Landing Ship, Tank (LST) 1942–2002* (Oxford: Osprey, 2013).

25. Brian Lavery, *In Which They Served: The Royal Navy Officer Experience in the Second World War* (London: Conway, 2008), p. 243.

26. IWM/DS 21656, Reel 1, Victor Henry Edward Longhurst.

27. Lavery, *In Which They Served*, p. 235.

28. For more details see, for example, Lavery, *Hostilities Only*, esp. pp. 210–14.

29. Lund and Ludlam, *The War of the Landing Craft*, p. 82.

30. IWM 14217, Reel 1, Thomas Arthur Sutton.

31. Ibid.

32. Carter, *Saved by the Bomb*, p. 45.

33. Ludovic Kennedy, *On My Way to the Club: An Autobiography* (London: Collins, 1989), p. 123.

34. Anon, *Combined Operations 1940–1942*, p. 35.

35. Kennedy, *On My Way to the Club*, p. 124.

36. IWM/DS 15450, Reel 1, Commander William Edward Grenfell. Commander Grenfell joined HMS *Edinburgh* in 1940 at North Shields as a young seaman specialising in radar, and left her 18 months later at South Shields as a leading seaman, having experienced much action, notably in the Mediterranean and on Arctic convoys.

37. Lord Mountbatten, quoted in James Ladd, *Commandos and Rangers of World War II* (London: Book Club Associates, 1978), p. 33.

38. Anon, *Combined Operations 1940–1942*, p. 52.

39. See, for example, Ladd, *Commandos and Rangers of World War II*, pp. 32–8.

40. RN officer, quoted in Anon, *Combined Operations 1940–1942*, p. 55.

41. Ibid., pp. 55–6.

42. Anon, *Combined Operations 1940–1942*, p. 72.

43. For further detail on Operation Chariot, and the gallantry of many involved, see Roskill, *The War at Sea, 1939–1945*, vol. II, pp. 168–73; T.N. Williams, 'Operation Chariot: The

Raid on St Nazaire', in *History of the Second World War Vol. 3 No. 2* (London: Purnell, 1967), pp. 925–31; Ken Ford, *St Nazaire 1942: The Great Commando Raid* (Botley, Oxford: Osprey, 2008).

44. Second World War Experience Centre (SWWEC), Colin Kitching Papers: T/S Memoir entitled: Paper 3 Excursion to Dieppe, 1942, p. 1. For more details on Colin Kitching's RN war service, see James Goulty, *Second World War Lives* (Barnsley: Pen & Sword, 2012), pp. 141–54.

45. Roskill, *The War at Sea, 1939–1945*, vol. II, p. 241.

46. Ibid., pp. 250–1.

47. Thompson, *The Royal Marines*, p. 268.

48. SWWEC, Excursion to Dieppe, 1942, p. 1.

49. Ibid., pp. 3–5.

50. Letter from Evelyn Waugh to his wife Laura, November 1940, in Mark Amory (ed.), *The Letters of Evelyn Waugh*, p. 147.

51. Captain S.W. Roskill, *The War at Sea, 1939–1945, Vol. I: The Defensive* (London: HMSO, 1954), p. 308.

52. Ibid., p. 319. For a good overview, see also Commander M.G. Saunders, 'Operation Menace: The Move To Take Dakar' in *History of the Second World War*, Vol. 1 No. 11 (London: Purnell, 1966), pp. 296–9.

53. Captain S.W. Roskill, *The War at Sea, 1939–1945, Vol. II: The Period of Balance* (London: HMSO, 1956), p. 185.

54. SWWEC, Lieutenant Commander C.H. Knollys Papers: Extracts from his T/S Memoir/ 'Anecdotage' 1940–1944, pp. 109–10.

55. Vincent Jones, *Operation Torch: Anglo-American Invasion of North Africa* (London: Pan/ Ballantine, 1972), p. 42.

56. SWWEC T/S Transcript of Tape 1556: Oral History Interview by David Talbot with Vice Admiral Sir I. McGeogh, KCB, DSO, DSC, on 26 February 2003, p. 5.

57. Jones, *Operation Torch*, p. 117.

58. SWWEC, Commander J.E. Lewis RN, Papers: Wartime Account of Operation Torch, p. 1.

59. Eric Denton, *My Six Wartime Years in the Royal Navy* (London: Minerva Press, 1999), p. 104.

60. F.A. Mason, *The Last Destroyer: HMS Aldenham, 1942–44* (London: Robert Hale, 1988), p. 123.

61. SWWEC, T/S Transcript: Interview by John Critchley with John Derrick Cutcliffe about his wartime experiences in the MN, 10 February 2005, pp. 11–12.

62. Carlo D'Este, *Bitter Victory: The Battle for Sicily 1943* (London: Fontana, 1988), pp. 157–8.

63. Ibid., p. 153.

64. IMW/DS 12590, Reel 3, Vice Admiral Patrick Uniack Bayly.

65. Author's Interview: Mr George Henderson re: his wartime service with the RN, 19 November 2015.

66. Author's Interview: Mr George Henderson re: his wartime service with the RN, 19 October 2015.

67. Author's Interview: George Henderson, 19 November 2015.

68. Guinness, *Blessings in Disguise*, p. 126.

69. Ibid., p. 127.

70. SWWEC, A.H. Lee, Extract from untitled memoir regarding Operation Husky, p. 14.

71. Denton, *My Six Wartime Years in the Royal Navy*, pp. 136–7.

72. SWWEC, J. Bayley Papers: Midshipman's Log, HMS *Eggesford*, Operation Husky, pp. 5–7.

73. Mason, *The Last Destroyer*, p. 125.

74. SWWEC, T/S Transcript of Interview by David Talbot with Ken Jump about his wartime RN service, 23 January 2003, p. 18.

75. Author's Interview: George Henderson, 19 November 2015.

76. IMW/DS 12590, Reel 3, Vice Admiral Patrick Uniack Bayly.

77. See, for example, David Mason, *Salerno: Foothold in Europe* (London: Pan/Ballantine, 1972).

78. IWM/DS 24944, Reel 1, Steve Pooley.

79. John Lyson, quoted in George Mack, *HMS Intrepid: A Memoir* (London: William Kimber, 1980), p. 174.

80. Author's Interview: George Henderson, 19 October 2015.

81. IWM/DS 15533, Reel 2, Douglas Granger Parker.

82. David Wragg, *Royal Navy Handbook 1939–1945* (Stroud, Gloucs: Sutton Publishing, 2005), p. 78.

83. See, for example, Captain S.W. Roskill, *The War at Sea, 1939–1945, Vol. III, Part I: The Offensive, 1st June 1943–31st May 1944* (London: HMSO, 1960), pp. 298–322.

84. Author's Interview: George Henderson, 19 October 2015.

85. Author's Interview: George Henderson, 19 November 2015.

86. Figures from Eric J. Grove, 'A Service Vindicated, 1939–1946' in J.R. Hill (ed.), *The Oxford Illustrated History of the Royal Navy* (Oxford: OUP, 1995), p. 375.

87. Eric Grove, 'Operation Neptune' in *Sea Battles in Close Up, World War 2: Vol. Two* (Shepperton, Surrey: Ian Allan, 1992), p. 141.

88. IWM/DS 30095, Reel 2, Lucian Ingram 'Tod' Raven-Hill.

89. IWM/DS 17394, Reel 4, Rear Admiral Edward Findlay Gueritz.

90. IWM/DS 19672, Reel 2, Warwick Nield-Siddall (41 Commando RM).

91. Grove, 'A Service Vindicated, 1939–1946,' p. 375.

92. For more detail see Correlli Barnett, *Engage the Enemy More Closely: The Royal Navy in the Second World War* (London: Penguin, 2001), pp. 781–97.

93. IWM/DS 9709, Reel 1, George Butler Honour.

94. IWM/DS 17394, Reel 4, Rear Admiral Edward Findlay Gueritz.

95. IWM/DS 18468, Reel 2, John Clegg.

96. Carter, *Saved by the Bomb*, p. 62.

97. IWM/DS 21656, Reel 2, Victor Henry Edward Longhurst.

98. IWM/DS 28767, Reel 3, John Thomas Tarbit.

99. IWM/DS 17839, Reel 2, Henry Charles Sivelle.

100. IWM/DS 20485, Reel 2, John Clive 'Joe' Stringer.

101. IWM/DS 18468, Reel 3, John Clegg.

102. IWM/DS 30095, Reel 2, Lucian Ingram 'Tod' Raven-Hill.

103. SWWEC, Colin Kitching Papers: T/S Memoir entitled: Paper 4 D-Day 1944: A Personal Memoir, pp. 1–2.

104. Author's Interview: George Henderson, 19 October 2015.

105. Denton, *My Six Wartime Years in the Royal Navy*, p. 178.

106. Mason, *The Last Destroyer*, pp. 174–6.

107. Stephen Roskill, *The Navy at War, 1939–1945* (Ware, Herts: Wordsworth Editions, 1998), pp. 385–7.
108. IWM/DS 20485, Reel 3, John Clive 'Joe' Stringer.
109. Roskill, *The Navy at War, 1939–1945*, pp. 395–6.
110. IWM/DS 27071, Reel 4, Dennis Till.
111. IWM/DS 18567, Reel 2, Howard Geoffrey Dowell.
112. IWM/DS 19672, Reel 3, Warwick Nield-Siddall.
113. Major General J.I.H. Owen, quoted in Thompson, *The Royal Marines*, p. 404.
114. IWM/DS 18555, Reel 2, Robert Arthur West.
115. Ibid.
116. Ibid.
117. Thompson, *The Royal Marines*, p. 406.
118. IWM/DS 18555, Reel 2, Robert Arthur West.

Chapter 6: Discipline and Morale

1. Glyn Prysor, *Citizen Sailors: The Royal Navy in the Second World War* (London: Viking, 2011), p. 109.
2. Bernard Upton MBE, *On the Road to Normandy and a little beyond: A Sailor's Life Story* (Privately Published, 2017), p. 1.
3. Douglas Bruce, *What Did You Do in the War Grandad? The Memoirs of Petty Officer Douglas Bruce Yeoman of Signals RNVR, LD9/X5232* (Birkenhead: Appin Press, 2014), p. 8.
4. Robert Cosh, *Inside and Out: My Experiences in the Royal Navy and HM Prison Service in War and Peace* (Bognor Regis, W. Sussex: Woodfield Publishing, 2005), p. 14.
5. Lilian Pickering, *The War Years by 'One Small Wren'* (London: Athena Press, 2006), pp. 8–10.
6. Second World War Experience Centre (SWWEC), Oral History Interview Transcript: John Derrick Cutcliffe interviewed by John Critchley re his wartime service in the Merchant Navy, 10 February 2005, p. 1.
7. SWWEC, Tape No. 3925, Oral History Interview Transcript: Joe Lafferty interviewed by Pat Oliver, 4 May 2009, p. 3.
8. Norman Hanson, *Carrier Pilot* (London: Silvertail Books, 2016), p. 55.
9. Prysor, *Citizen Sailors*, p. 407.
10. Bruce, *What Did You Do in the War Grandad?*, p. 16.
11. SWWEC, Oral History Interview Transcript: John Derrick Cutcliffe, p. 1.
12. *Webster's Seventh New College Dictionary* (Springfield, Massachusetts: G. & G. Merriam, 1967), p. 550.
13. Imperial War Museum, Department of Sound (IWM/DS) 17935, Reel 1, Rear Admiral Edward Findlay Gueritz.
14. Captain Stephen Roskill, *The Navy at War, 1939–1945* (Ware, Herts: Wordsworth Editions, 1998), p. 213.
15. SWWEC, Tape 445, Oral History Interview Transcript: Commander Tom Dowling interviewed by Dr Peter Liddle, February 2001, pp. 5–6.
16. For more details on this tragic incident, see David Wragg, *Royal Navy Handbook, 1939–1945* (Stroud: Sutton Publishing, 2005), pp. 83–5.
17. Gordon Wallace, *Carrier Observer* (Shrewsbury: Airlife, 1993), pp. 15–19.

18. See, for example, James Goldrick, Ch. 12 'Work-up' in Stephen Howarth and Derek Law (eds), *The Battle of the Atlantic, 1939–1945: The 50ᵗʰ Anniversary Naval Conference* (London: Greenhill Books, 1994), pp. 221–5.

19. Richard Baker, *The Terror of Tobermory: Vice Admiral Sir Gilbert Stephenson KBE, CB, CMG* (London, W.H. Allen, 1972), p. 121.

20. Ibid., p. 144.

21. Paul Lund and Harry Ludlam, *Trawlers Go to War* (London: NEL, 1972), p. 103.

22. Commander D.A. Rayner, *Escort: The Battle of the Atlantic* (London: William Kimber, 1955), p. 107.

23. Bob Whinney, *The U-Boat Peril: A Fight for Survival* (London: Cassell, 2000), p. 56.

24. SWWEC Tape 743/2, Oral History Interview Transcript: General Sir Peter Whiteley interviewed by Dr Peter Liddle, July 2001, pp. 4–5.

25. IWM/DS 31408, Reel 5, John Shoebridge.

26. John L. Brown, *Diary of a Matelot, 1942–1945* (Worcester: Square One Publications, 1991), p. 121.

27. Anne Partridge, quoted in Edward Smithies with Colin John Bruce, *The War at Sea, 1939–45* (London: Constable, 1992), pp. 184–5.

28. Ursula Stuart Mason, *The Wrens, 1917–77: a history of the Women's Royal Naval Service* (Reading: Educational Explorers, 1977), p. 117.

29. SWWEC, P. Bieber Papers: T/S memoir entitled: Twitterings of a Very Ancient Wren (1940–1944), p. 1.

30. SWWEC, Barbara Hadden-Scott Papers: Notes Entitled: Lime Grove Eastcote Station X Enigma, Nov 1943–May 1945.

31. SWWEC, Mrs J. Dinwoodie Papers: Untitled T/S 5 page Memoir, 1988, p. 3.

32. Roxane Houston, *Changing Course: The Wartime Experiences of a Member of the Women's Royal Naval Service, 1939–1945* (London: Grub Street, 2005), p. 35.

33. Christian Lamb, *I Only Joined for the Hat* (London: Bene Factum, 2007), p. 22.

34. Lund and Ludlam, *Trawlers Go to War*, p. 134.

35. Pickering, *The War Years by 'One Small Wren'*, pp. 30–1.

36. Les Roberts, quoted in Smithies with Bruce, *The War at Sea, 1939–45*, pp. 88–93.

37. SWWEC, Tape 3244, Oral History Interview Transcript: Rev C.B. Blackmore interviewed by Trevor Mumford, April 2006, p. 17.

38. Major General Julian Thompson, *The Royal Marines: From Sea Soldiers To A Special Force* (London: Pan, 2001), p. 4.

39. IWM/DS 20485, Reel 1, John Clive 'Joe' Stringer.

40. Ibid.

41. Richard Woodman, *Arctic Convoys* (London: John Murray, 1994), p. 109.

42. Vice Admiral Sir Ian Campbell, quoted in Vice Admiral B.B. Schofield, *The Russian Convoys* (London: Pan, 1984), pp. 103–4.

43. John W. Davies, *Jack: The Sailor with Navy Blue Eyes* (Durham: Pentland Press, 1995), p. 129.

44. Ludovic Kennedy, *On My Way to the Club: An Autobiography* (London: Collins, 1989), p. 107.

45. Davies, *Jack: The Sailor with Navy Blue Eyes*, p. 87.

46. Angela Mack, *Dancing on the Waves: A Wartime Wren at Sea* (Andover: Benchmark Press, 2000), p. 81.

47. George Mack, *HMS Intrepid: A Memoir* (London: William Kimber, 1980), pp. 90–1.

48. George Melly, *Rum, Bum and Concertina* (London: Futura, 1978), p. 37.
49. Henry 'Hank' Adlam, *On and Off the Flight Deck: Reflections of a Naval Fighter Pilot in World War II* (Barnsley: Pen & Sword, 2009), p. 63.
50. Whinney, *The U-Boat Peril*, p. 17.
51. Johnny Parker, *A Smack at the Boche: World War Two British Navy Diary of Leading Seaman Ronnie Turner* (Privately Published, 2016), p. 48.
52. W. Brian Carter, *Saved By The Bomb* (Lewes, E. Sussex: Book Guild, 2001), p. 101.
53. Ibid., p. 94.
54. Prysor, *Citizen Sailors*, p. 391.
55. G.G. Connell, *Jack's War: Lower-Deck Recollections from World War II* (London: William Kimber, 1985), p. 148.
56. Lamb, *I Only Joined for the Hat*, p. 49.
57. Mack, *HMS Intrepid*, p. 179.
58. Adlam, *On and Off the Flight Deck*, p. 65.
59. Prysor, *Citizen Sailors*, p. 421.
60. Ibid., p. 394.
61. SWWEC, Tape 3244, Oral History Interview Transcript: Rev C.B. Blackmore, p. 31.
62. Author's Interview with Mr George Henderson re his wartime RN service, 19 November 2015.
63. Prysor, *Citizen Sailors*, p. 394.
64. F.A. Mason, *The Last Destroyer: HMS Aldenham, 1942–44* (London: Robert Hale, 1988), p. 62.
65. Adlam, *On and Off the Flight Deck*, p. 147.
66. Cosh, *Inside and Out*, p. 36.
67. SWWEC, Tape No. 3925, Oral History Interview Transcript: Joe Lafferty, p. 4.
68. Mack, *Dancing on the Waves*, p. 16.
69. Stephanie Batstone, *Wren's Eye View: Adventures of a Visual Signaller* (Tunbridge Wells: Parapress, 2001), p. 27.
70. IWM/DS 2518, Reel 3, Sir Robert Atkinson.
71. Carter, *Saved By The Bomb*, p. 96.
72. Mason, *The Last Destroyer*, pp. 117–19.
73. Mack, *HMS Intrepid*, p. 75.
74. Sydney Greenwood, *Stoker Greenwood's Navy* (Tunbridge Wells: Midas Books, 1983), p. 49.
75. Mack, *HMS Intrepid*, pp. 142, 144.
76. Greenwood, *Stoker Greenwood's Navy*, p. 40.
77. Davies, *Jack: The Sailor with Navy Blue Eyes*, pp. 110–13.
78. Houston, *Changing Course*, p. 117.
79. Brown, *Diary of a Matelot*, p. 53.
80. Melly, *Rum, Bum and Concertina*, p. 22.
81. Prysor, *Citizen Sailors*, p. 137.
82. Mack, *Dancing on the Waves*, pp. 39–40.
83. Davies, *Jack: The Sailor with Navy Blue Eyes*, p. 100.
84. Upton, *On the Road to Normandy and a little beyond*, p. 20.
85. Adlam, *On and Off the Flight Deck*, p. 109.
86. SWWEC, E. Cook T/S Unpublished Memoir: Adventures of a Sea Cossack, p. 5.
87. Mack, *HMS Intrepid*, p. 179.
88. Brown, *Diary of a Matelot*, p. 28.

89. Houston, *Changing Course*, p. 139.

90. Paul Lund and Harry Ludlam, *Out Sweeps! The Exploits of the Minesweepers in World War II* (London: NEL, 1979), p. 213.

91. IWM/DS 18547, Reel 1, Sydney Charles Hook.

92. Wragg, *Royal Navy Handbook, 1939–1945*, p. 137.

93. IWM/DS 16355, Reel 2, George Alfred Amyes.

94. Author's Interview with Mr George Henderson re his wartime RN service, 19 October 2015.

95. Lamb, *I Only Joined for the Hat*, p. 68.

96. Wragg, *Royal Navy Handbook, 1939–1945*, p. 135.

97. IWM/DS 20277, Reel 1, Jack Leonard Cole.

98. Wragg, *Royal Navy Handbook, 1939–1945*, p. 136.

99. Eric Denton, *My Six Years in the Royal Navy* (London: Minerva Press, 1999), pp. 52–3.

100. Wragg, *Royal Navy Handbook, 1939–1945*, p. 137.

101. Lane, *The Merchant Seamen's War*, p. 30.

102. SWWEC, Oral History Interview Transcript: John Derrick Cutcliffe, p. 4.

103. Batstone, *Wren's Eye View*, pp. 32–3.

104. Harry Miller, *Service to the Services: The Story of the Naafi* (London: Newman Neame, 1971), p. 71.

105. Davies, *Jack: The Sailor with Navy Blue Eyes*, p. 154.

106. Lane, *The Merchant Seamen's War*, pp. 148–9.

107. Adlam, *On and Off the Flight Deck*, p. 123.

108. Carter, *Saved By The Bomb*, p. 147.

109. Connell, *Jack's War*, pp. 62–3.

110. Davies, *Jack: The Sailor with Navy Blue Eyes*, p. 53.

111. Author's Interview with Mr George Henderson re his wartime RN service, 19 October 2015.

112. Mack, *HMS Intrepid*, p. 138.

113. Melly, *Rum, Bum and Concertina*, p. 191.

114. Ibid., p. 132.

115. Davies, *Jack: The Sailor with Navy Blue Eyes*, pp. 53–4.

116. Adlam, *On and Off the Flight Deck*, p. 143.

117. Whinney, *The U-Boat Peril*, p. 56

118. Connell, *Jack's War*, pp. 13–14.

119. Prysor, *Citizen Sailors*, p. 390.

120. Cosh, *Inside and Out*, p. 45.

121. SWWEC, P. Bieber Papers: T/S memoir entitled: Twitterings of a Very Ancient Wren (1940–1944), p. 5.

122. Mason, *The Last Destroyer*, p. 110.

123. Greenwood, *Stoker Greenwood's Navy*, p. 114.

124. Wallace, *Carrier Observer*, p. 48.

125. Greenwood, *Stoker Greenwood's Navy*, p. 94.

126. John Costello, *Love, Sex and War, 1939–1945* (London: Pan, 1986), p. 127.

127. Prysor, *Citizen Sailors*, p. 391.

128. Carter, *Saved By The Bomb*, p. 45.

129. Costello, *Love, Sex and War, 1939–1945*, p. 127.

130. Carter, *Saved By The Bomb*, p. 44.

131. Batstone, *Wren's Eye View*, pp. 15–16.
132. Vera Laughton Mathews, *Blue Tapestry* (London: Hollis & Carter, 1948), pp. 121–2.
133. Lamb, *I Only Joined for the Hat*, p. 9.
134. Mack, *Dancing on the Waves*, p. 103.
135. Costello, *Love, Sex and War, 1939–1945*, p. 156.
136. Melly, *Rum, Bum and Concertina*, p. 64.
137. Ibid., p. 175.
138. SWWEC, T/S Tape 1537 Oral History Interview Transcript: Colin Kitching interviewed by Dr Peter Liddle, July 2002, pp. 6–7.
139. Mack, *Dancing on the Waves*, p. 13.
140. Houston, *Changing Course*, p. 175.
141. SWWEC, Anonymous Sailor (Range Finder on HMS *Electra*), T/S Reminiscences re Battle of the Java Sea; Entitled: 'I Was There,' p. 2.
142. See Cosh, *Inside and Out*, pp. 22–30.
143. IWM/DS 11441, Reels 2–3, George Victor Monk.
144. Ibid., Reel 3.
145. Ibid.
146. SWWEC, Tape 1556, Oral History Interview Transcript: Vice Admiral Sir Ian McGeogh interviewed by David Talbot, February 2003, pp. 10–12.
147. SWWEC, LEEWW/2003-2124, J. Mariner Papers: T/S 6 p Memoir re: HMS *Peterel* and the Shanghai Incident and his FEPOW Experience, esp. p. 5.
148. See, for example, Arthur H. Bird MBE, *Farewell to Milag* (Privately Published, 1995).

Chapter 7:

1. Imperial War Museum, Department of Sound (IWM/DS) 10772, Reel 1, Denis Charles Logan. Logan was an HO signaller aboard HMS *Starling*, with the 2nd Support Group, North Atlantic and Arctic, 1943–1945).
2. Robert Cosh, *Inside and Out: My Experiences in the Royal Navy and HM Prison Service in War and Peace* (Bognor Regis: Woodfield, 2005), p. 58.
3. Lilian Pickering, *The War Years by 'One Small Wren'* (London: Athena Press, 2006), p. 37.
4. Angela Mack, *Dancing on the Waves: A Wartime Wren at Sea* (Andover: Benchmark Press, 2000), p. 139.
5. John L. Brown, *Diary of a Matelot 1942–1945* (Worcester: Square One Publications, 1991), p. 134.
6. W. Brian Carter, *Saved by the Bomb* (Lewes: Book Guild, 2001), p. 145.
7. Henry 'Hank' Adlam, *On and Off the Flight Deck: Reflections of a Naval Fighter Pilot in World War II* (Barnsley: Pen & Sword, 2009), pp. 200–1.
8. Norman Hanson, *Carrier Pilot* (London: Silvertail Books, 2016), p. 282.
9. Second World War Experience Centre (SWWEC), Tape 2731, Oral History Interview Transcript: Lieutenant Commander T. Maughan RNVR, interviewed by David Talbot, November 2005, p. 15.
10. SWWEC, Tape 743/2 Oral History Interview Transcript: General Sir Peter Whiteley interviewed by Dr Peter Liddle, July 2001, pp. 5–6.
11. Mack, *Dancing on the Waves*, p. 176.
12. SWWEC, Notes Re: RN War service of Henry Hiley, compiled by Henry Hiley, January 2003.

13. Eric Denton, *My Six Years in the Wartime Royal Navy* (London: Minerva Press, 1999), p. 247.
14. Based on: Notes on the Wartime RN Service of Coder George Smith JX678420 (kindly supplied by his son David Smith).
15. Based on: RN Service Record George Albert Trevett. (His granddaughter Jess Trevett kindly allowed me access to these documents.)
16. Gordon Wallace, *Carrier Observer* (Shrewsbury: Airlife, 1993), p. 205.
17. SWWEC, Tape 445 Oral History Interview Transcript: Commander Tom Dowling interviewed by Dr Peter Liddle, February 2001, p. 12.
18. R. 'Mike' Crosley, *They Gave Me a Seafire* (Shrewsbury: Airlife, 2001), p. 196.
19. Stanley Greenwood, *Stoker Greenwood's Navy* (Tunbridge Wells: Midas Books, 1983), p. 134.
20. Ibid., p. 139.
21. Brendan A. Maher, *A Passage to Sword Beach: Minesweeping in the Royal Navy* (Annapolis, Maryland: Naval Institute Press, 1996), pp. 212–13.
22. Bernard Upton, *On the Road to Normandy and a little beyond: A Sailor's Life Story* (Privately Published, 2017), pp. 97–8.
23. Louisa M. Jenkins, *Bellbottoms and Blackouts: Memories of a Wren* (New York: iUniverse, 2004), p. 113.
24. Pickering, *The War Years by 'One Small Wren'*, p. 40.
25. SWWEC, E. Cook Papers, T/S Unpublished Memoir entitled: 'Adventures of a Sea Cossack', p. 26.
26. Denton, *My Six Years in the Wartime Royal Navy*, pp. 231–2.
27. Ibid., p. 245.
28. Douglas Bruce, *What did You Do in the War Grandad? The Memoirs of Petty Officer Douglas Bruce Yeoman of Signals RNVR LD9/X5232* (Birkenhead: Appin Press, 2014), p. 125.
29. Roxane Houston, *Changing Course: The Wartime Experiences of a member of the Women's Royal Naval Service, 1939–1945* (London: Grub Street, 2005), p. 268.
30. Mack, *Dancing on the Waves*, p. 185.
31. Carter, *Saved by the Bomb*, pp. 176–7.
32. SWWEC, E.J. Hayes Papers, T/S Unpublished Memoir entitled: 'A Touch of Sea Fever', p. 16.
33. Alec Guinness, *Blessings in Disguise* (New York: Alfred A. Knopf, 1986), p. 142.
34. See, for example, SWWEC, Transcript of Oral History Interview: Lieutenant Commander J.W.G. Wellham DSC, RN (Retd) interviewed by John Larder, April 1999, pp. 17–18.
35. SWWEC, Tape 3244, Oral History Interview Transcript: Rev C.B. Blackmore interviewed by Trevor Mumford, April 2006, p. 31.
36. SWWEC, Tape 1538, Oral History Interview Transcript: Colin Kitching interviewed by Dr Peter Liddle, July 2002, p. 5.
37. SWWEC, Tape 1508, Oral History Interview Transcript: Ken Jump interviewed by David Talbot, January 2003, p. 27.
38. Brown, *Diary of a Matelot 1942–1945*, p. 172.
39. SWWEC, Mrs J. Dinwoodie Papers: Untitled T/S 5 page Memoir, 1988, p. 5.
40. Stephanie Batstone, *Wren's Eye View: Adventures of a Visual Signaller* (Tunbridge Wells: Parapress, 2001), p. 180.
41. Author's Interview with Mr George Henderson re: his wartime RN service, 19 November 2015.

42. SWWEC, LEEWW/2003-2124, J. Mariner Papers: T/S 6 p Memoir re: HMS *Peterel* and the Shanghai Incident and his FEPOW Experience, esp. pp. 5–6.
43. IWM/DS 15332, Reel 1, Neil Sydney Hulse.
44. IWM/DS 11441, Reel 4, George Victor Monk.
45. SWWEC, Oral History Interview Transcript: John Derrick Cutcliffe interviewed by John Critchley, February 2005, p. 14.

Bibliography

Imperial War Museum (Department of Sound), London

The following oral history interviews were consulted:

16355: Amyes, George Alfred
25182: Atkinson, Sir Robert
12023: Balme, Commander David Edward
12590: Bayly, Vice Admiral Sir Patrick Uniack
11769: Berey, Conrad Leonard
20617: Bigland, Walter George
12400: Bone, John Rayner
10798: Bradshaw, William Harold
12926: Branscombe, Alfred Frank
10188: Bromage, John Henry
25217: Burridge, George
25052: Butler, Brian
30008: Capon, John
16304: Cheshire, Charles William
20967: Clarke, Tony
18468: Clegg, John
20277: Cole, Jack Leonard
20216: Collins, Robert Frank
24629: Collis, Christopher Patrick Ridsdale
10177: Cosgrove, Henry Frank
20284: Craddock, Robert
10673: Crawford, Vice Admiral William Godfrey
21191: Crick, Robert Henry
29430: Curnock, John Trelawney
21644: Douglass, William Harris
18576: Dowell, Howard Geoffrey
10936: Downing, Alexander Lavey
 8984: Dreyer, Commander Christopher William Stuart
11509: Fellingham, Henry Cedric
27756: Fenwick Smith, William
19571: Fetherston-Dilke, Captain Charles
 9822: Fraser, Ian Edward
20978: Gostelow, Henry Norman

15450: Grenfell, Commander William Edward
17394: Gueritz, Rear Admiral Edward Findlay
19103: Hammond, Ernest
13268: Harris, Raymond Vincent
28417: Harvey-Jones, Sir John
18458: Hawthorn, Charles Wilfred
10206: Hendy, Frederick James
19105: Henley, Maurice William
18504: Hills, Eric Arthur
 9709: Honour, George Butler
18547: Hook, Sydney Charles
15332: Hulse, Neil Sydney
 9137: Hutchinson, Rear Admiral Christopher Haynes
28937: Hyde, Geoffrey
 9956: Irwin, Hugh Michael
11720: Janvrin, Vice Admiral Hugh Richard Benest
19391: Jones, Thomas Henry
10772: Logan, Denis Charles
21656: Longhurst, Victor Henry Edward
 9858: McGeogh, Vice Admiral Sir Ian Lachlan MacKay
21645: Maule, John Arthur Carteret
18200: Maxted, Denis John
11088: Mearns, Stephen Andrew
11441: Monk, George Victor
25270: Muller, Henry Norman
19672: Nield-Siddall, Warwick
10764: Nye, George Thomas
15533: Parker, Douglas Granger
14218: Pavey, Francis William
 9167: Pook, William John
24944, Pooley, Steve
20817: Price, Percy Thomas

28531: Radwell, Des
30095: Raven-Hill, Lucian Ingram 'Tod'
21587: Reynolds, Stanley
13126: Roche, Audrey Sylvia
25921: Sayer, John Druce
28642: Shean, Maxwell Henry
31480: Shoebridge, John
17838: Sivelle, Henry Charles
28497: Smith, Owen Charles Bert
27211: Stedman, Ida
20485: Stringer, John Clive 'Joe'

14217: Sutton, Thomas Arthur
28767: Tarbit, John Thomas
19532: Taylor, Sidney William
27071: Till, Dennis
18462: Walker, Reginald
27308: Walsh, Ronald
18461: Webster, Alfred George
18555: West, Robert Arthur
 9153: Wingfield, Captain Mervyn Robert
        George
26588: Wingrave, Alec

Second World War Experience Centre, Otley

Material relating to the following individuals was consulted:

Bayley, J.
Bieber, P.
Blackmore, Rev. C.B.
Coles, Lieutenant Commander C.
Conlon, L.
Cook, E. 'Ted'
Crang, Reg
Crawford, Captain Michael
Cutcliffe, John Derrick
Dinwoodie, J.
Dowling, Commander Tom
Drayton, G.R.
Gadsden, Jean
Harvey-Jones, Sir John
Haynes, E.J.
Henderson, George
Higham, M.S.
Hiley, Henry
Howes, G.D.

Hutchcroft, B.
Jump, Ken
Kitching, Colin
Knollys, Lieutenant Commander C.H.
Lafferty, Joe
Lee, A.H.
Lewis, Commander J.E.
McGeogh, Vice Admiral Sir Ian
Mariner, J.
Maughan, Lieutenant Commander Ted
Maxwell, Robert G.I.
Moore, Captain John
Owen, Commander R.A.C.
Sumption, A.
Washbourne, R.E.
West, Chris
Whiteley, General Sir Peter
Yates, E.F.

Author's Collection

George Henderson was interviewed during January–November 2015 about his wartime experiences in the Royal Navy

George Henderson, Draft to LST 8, Private Log of Places Visited in (America) and the Mediterranean Area, Wed, 17 February 1943–Saturday, 22 April 1944

Papers and Photographs re RN service of George Smith

Papers regarding RN service of Alexander Robert Talarowski, July 1941–January 1945

Papers and Photographs re RN service of George Albert Trevett

Secondary Sources

Note: below are listed those publications that have proved most useful. Readers will find details on the sources consulted in the various chapter notes as well.

Adlam, Henry 'Hank', *On and Off the Flight Deck: Reflections of a Naval Fighter Pilot in World War II* (Barnsley: Pen & Sword, 2009)

Anon, *Combined Operations 1940–1942* (London: HMSO, 1943)

Anon, *East of Malta West of Suez* (London: HMSO, 1943)

Anon, *Merchantmen at War* (London: HMSO, 1944)

Anon, *The Mediterranean Fleet: Greece to Tripoli* (London: HMSO, 1944)

Anon, *The Navy and the Y Scheme* (London: HMSO, 1944)

Anon, *The Battle of the Atlantic* (London: HMSO, 1946)

Arthur, Max, *Lost Voices of the Royal Navy* (London: Hodder, 2005)

Bacon, Admiral Sir Reginald H.S., *Britain's Glorious Navy* (London: Odhams Press Ltd, undated)

Baker, Richard, *The Terror of Tobermory: Vice Admiral Sir Gilbert Stephenson* (London: W.H. Allen, 1972)

Barnett, Correlli, *Engage the Enemy More Closely: The Royal Navy in the Second World War* (London: Penguin, 2001)

Batstone, Stephanie, *Wren's Eye View: Adventures of a Visual Signaller* (Tunbridge Wells: Parapress, 2001)

Bigland, Eileen, *The Story of the W.R.N.S.* (London: Nicholson & Watson, 1946)

Bird, Arthur H., *Farewell to Milag* (Privately Published, 1995)

Bone, David W., *Merchantman Rearmed* (London: Chatto & Windus, 1949)

Broome, Captain Jack, *Convoy is to Scatter* (London: William Kimber, 1972)

Brown, David K., *Nelson to Vanguard: Warship Design and Development 1923–1945* (Barnsley: Seaforth Publishing, 2012)

Brown, Captain Eric 'Winkle', *Wings on My Sleeve* (London: Phoenix, 2007)

Brown, John L., *Diary of a Matelot 1942–1945* (Worcester: Square One Publications, 1991)

Bruce, Colin John, *Invaders: British and American Experience of Seaborne Landings 1939–1945* (London: Caxton Editions, 2003)

Bruce, Petty Officer Douglas, *What Did You Do In The War Grandad?* (Birkenhead: Appin Press, 2014)

Burn, Alan, *The Fighting Commodores: Convoy Commanders in the Second World War* (Barnsley: Pen & Sword, 1999)

—, *The Fighting Captain: The Story of Frederic Walker RN CB DSO and the Battle of the Atlantic* (Barnsley: Pen & Sword, 2006)

Carter, Brian W., *Saved by the Bomb* (Lewes, East Sussex: Book Guild, 2001)

Connell, G.G., *Jack's War: Lower Deck Reflections from World War II* (London: William Kimber, 1985)

Cosh, Robert, *Inside and Out: My Experiences in the Royal Navy and HM Prison Service in War and Peace* (Bognor Regis: Woodfield, 2005)

Creighton, Rear Admiral Sir Kenelm, *Convoy Commodore* (London: William Kimber, 1956)

Crosley, Commander R. 'Mike', *They Gave me a Seafire* (Shrewsbury: Airlife, 2001)

Davies, John W., *Jack: The Sailor with the Navy Blue Eyes* (Durham: Pentland Press, 1995)

Denton, Eric, *My Six Wartime Years in the Royal Navy* (London: Minerva Press, 1999)

Edwards, Bernard, *The Quiet Heroes: British Merchant Seamen at War 1939–1945* (Barnsley: Pen & Sword, 2017)

Elphick, Peter, *Life Line: The Merchant Navy at War 1939–1945* (London: Chatham Publishing, 1999)

Falconer, Jonathan, *D-Day Operations Manual* (Yeovil, Somerset: Haynes, 2017)

Gannon, Michael, *Black May: The Epic Story of the Allies' Defeat of the German U-boats in May 1943* (London: Aurum Press, 1998)

Greenwood, Sydney, *Stoker Greenwood's Navy* (Tunbridge Wells, Midas Books, 1983)

Grove, Eric, *Sea Battles in Close Up World War Two Vol. Two* (Shepperton, Surrey: Ian Allan, 1993)

Grove, Philip D., Grove, Mark J. and Finlan, Alastair, *The Second World War (3): The War at Sea* (Oxford: Osprey, 2002)

Guinness, Alec, *Blessings in Disguise* (New York: Alfred A. Knopf, 1986)

Hanson, Norman, *Carrier Pilot* (London: Silvertail Books, 2016)

Haskell, W.A., *Shadows on the Horizon: The Battle of Convoy HX-233* (London: Caxton Editions, 2003)

Hill, J.R. (ed.), *The Oxford History of the Royal Navy* (Oxford: OUP, 1995)

Houston, Roxane, *Changing Course* (London: Grub Street, 2005)

Howarth, Stephen and Law, Derek (eds), *The Battle of the Atlantic 1939–1945: 50th Anniversary Naval Conference* (London: Greenhill Books, 1994)

Jenkins, Louisa M., *Bellbottoms and Blackouts* (New York: iUniverse, Inc., 2004)

Johns, Albert, *Theatre of Life: The Memoirs of Albert Edward Johns: From Merchant Navy Gunner to Pantomime Dame* (Privately Published, 2019)

Kemp, Paul, *Convoy! Drama in Arctic Waters* (London: Brockhampton Press, 1999)

Kennedy, Ludovic, *On My Way to the Club: An Autobiography* (London: Collins, 1989)

Lamb, Christian, *I Only Joined for the Hat* (London: Bene Factum Publishing, 2007)

Lane, Tony, *The Merchant Seaman's War* (Liverpool, The Bluecoat Press, 1990)

Laughton Mathews, Vera, *Blue Tapestry* (London: Hollis & Carter, 1948)

Lavery, Brian, *Hostilities Only. Training the Wartime Navy* (London: National Maritime Museum, 2004)

—, *Churchill's Navy: The Ships, Men and Organisation 1939–1945* (London: Conway, 2008)

—, *In Which They Served: The Royal Navy Officer Experience in the Second World War* (London: Conway, 2008)

Lennox Kerr, J. (ed.), *Touching the Adventures of Merchantmen in the Second World War* (London: George G. Harrap & Co. Ltd, 1953)

Lenton, H.T. and Colledge, J.J. *Warships of World War II* (London: Ian Allan Ltd, 1980)

Lund, Paul and Ludlam, Harry, *Trawlers Go To War* (London: NEL, 1972)

—, *The War of the Landing Craft* (London: NEL, 1976)

—, *Out Sweeps! The Exploits of the Minesweepers in World War II* (London: NEL, 1979)

—, *I Was There: On Convoy PQ17 The Convoy to Hell: Through the Icy Russian Waters of World War II* (London: Foulsham, 2010)

Macdermott, Brian, *Ships without Names: The Story of the Royal Navy's Tank Landing Ships of World War Two* (London: Arms & Armour, 1992)

Mack, Angela, *Dancing on the Waves: A Wartime Wren at Sea* (Andover: Benchmark Press, 2000)

Mack, George, *HMS Intrepid: A Memoir* (London: William Kimber, 1980)

Maher, Brendan A., *A Passage to Sword Beach: Minesweeping in the Royal Navy* (Annapolis, Maryland: Naval Institute Press, 1996)

Mason, F.A., *The Last Destroyer: HMS Aldenham, 1942–44* (London: Robert Hale, 1988)

Mason, Ursula Stuart, *The Wrens 1917–77: A History of the Women's Royal Naval Service* (Reading: Educational Explorers, 1977)

Melly, George, *Rum, Bum and Concertina* (London: Futura, 1979)

Middlebrook, Martin, *Convoy: The Battle for Convoys SC 122 and HX 229* (London: Penguin, 1978)

Padfield, Peter, *War Beneath the Sea: Submarine Conflict 1939–1945* (London: Pimlico, 1995)

Parker, Johnny, *A Smack at the Boche: World War Two British Navy Diary of Leading Seaman Ronnie Turner* (Privately Published, 2016)

Pickering, Lilian, *The War Years 'by One Small Wren'* (London: Athena Press, 2006)

Prysor, Glyn, *Citizen Sailors: The Royal Navy in the Second World War* (London: Viking, 2011)

Rayner, Commander D.A., *Escort: The Battle of the Atlantic* (London: William Kimber, 1955)

Roskill, Captain S.W., *The War at Sea, 1939–1945, Vol. I: The Defensive* (London: HMSO, 1954)

—, *The War at Sea, 1939–1945, Vol II: The Period of Balance* (London: HMSO, 1956)

—, *The War at Sea, 1939–1945, Vol. III Part I: The Offensive, 1st June 1943–31st May 1944* (London: HMSO, 1960)

—, *The War at Sea, 1939–1945, Vol. III Part II: The Offensive, 1st June 1944–14th August 1945* (London: HMSO, 1961)

—, *The Navy at War, 1939–1945* (Ware, Herts: Wordsworth Editions, 1998)

Schofield, Vice Admiral B.B., *The Russian Convoys* (London: Pan Books, 1984)

Smith, Peter C., *Pedestal: The Malta Convoy of August 1942* (Crécy Books, 1994)

Smithies, Edward, with Bruce, Colin John, *War at Sea 1939–45* (London: Constable, 1992)

Stephen, Martin (ed. Eric Grove), *Sea Battles in Close-Up World War Two* (London: Ian Allan, 1996)

Thompson, Major General Julian, *The Royal Marines: From Sea Soldiers to a Special Force* (London: Pan, 2000)

Upton, Bernard, *On the Road to Normandy and a Little Beyond: A Sailor's Life Story* (Privately Published, 2017)

Van der Vat, Dan, *Standard of Power: The Royal Navy in the Twentieth Century* (London: Pimlico, 2001)

Waldron, T. and Gleeson, J., *The Frogmen: The Story of the Wartime Underwater Operations* (London: Pan, 1955)

Wallace, Gordon, *Carrier Observer: A Back Seat Aviator's Story* (Shrewsbury: Airlife, 1993)

Whinney, Captain Bob, *The U-boat Peril: A Fight for Survival* (London: Cassell, 1998)

Winton, John, *The Forgotten Fleet: The Story of the British Pacific Fleet 1944–1945* (Wadhurst, E. Sussex: Douglas-Boyd Books, 1991)

Woodman, Richard, *The Arctic Convoys, 1941–1945* (London: John Murray, 1995)

—, *Malta Convoys, 1940–1943* (London: John Murray, 2003)

—, *The Real Cruel Sea: The Merchant Navy in the Battle of the Atlantic, 1939–1943* (London: John Murray, 2005)

Index